DISTORTING DEFENSE

DISTORTING DEFENSE

Network News and National Security

STEPHEN P. AUBIN

 PRAEGER

Westport, Connecticut
London

Library of Congress Cataloging-in-Publication Data

Aubin, Stephen P.
   Distorting defense : network news and national security / Stephen
P. Aubin.
      p.   cm.
   Includes bibliographical references and index.
   ISBN 0–275–96303–9 (alk. paper)
   1. Television broadcasting of news—United States.   2. National
security—United States.   I. Title.
PN4888.T4A93   1998
070.1'95—dc21   98–25228

British Library Cataloguing in Publication Data is available.

Library of Congress Catalog Card Number: 98–25228
ISBN: 0–275–96303–9

First published in 1998

Praeger Publishers, 88 Post Road West, Westport, CT 06881
An imprint of Greenwood Publishing Group, Inc.

Printed in the United States of America

The paper used in this book complies with the
Permanent Paper Standard issued by the National
Information Standards Organization (Z39.48–1984).

10 9 8 7 6 5 4 3 2

Copyright Acknowledgments

The author and the publisher gratefully acknowledge permission for use of the following material:

The Society of Professional Journalists' "Code of Ethics," *Quill*, November 1993. Excerpts used
with permission from the publisher.

To my wife, Cheryl,
whose love and support were always present
To my son, Charles,
whose birth inspired me to finish this book
And to my parents,
who taught me how to believe in myself

Contents

Illustrations

FIGURES

Acknowledgments

I wish to thank Dr. Harry Gelber, David Anable, and Dr. Loren Thompson, whose criticism and advice helped me enormously throughout the process of writing and researching this book. I also wish to thank John Correll for patiently reviewing my manuscript on two different occasions, and Gen. Monroe W. Hatch, Jr., USAF (Ret.), and Gen. John A. Shaud, USAF (Ret.), who, as my bosses, encouraged me and provided me with the work flexibility I needed to complete this book.

I am grateful to many people who influenced me in the fields of national security and media analysis. Harry Zubkoff, who served as the chief of the Pentagon's newsclipping and analysis service for 36 years, first encouraged me as a budding writer/editor and has been a mentor and friend for many years. F. Clifton Berry, Jr., has also been a mentor and friend who gave me valuable counsel, professional advice, and several opportunities to work beside him on editorial projects. I will always be grateful to Dr. H. Joachim Maitre for giving me the opportunity to do research and work at the Center for Defense Journalism at Boston University. And I am indebted to John Corry, who, as an adjunct professor at Boston University and long-time media critic, first piqued my interest in television news analysis and criticism.

Finally, I would like to thank Dr. Heather Ruland Staines, military editor of the Greenwood Publishing Group, Linda Ellis, my production editor, and the production and marketing staffs at Greenwood who worked with me to make this book a reality.

While many people have helped me with this manuscript, any errors or shortcomings in this book are my own.

DISTORTING DEFENSE

Introduction

Targeting the Content of Network News

In the 1980s, the United States undertook the largest peacetime military buildup in its history. This buildup was a natural and newsworthy target of the media. Like their print counterparts, the television network news divisions gave this story more than passing coverage.

In fact, millions of Americans who regularly tuned into one of the three evening newscasts—ABC's World News Tonight, CBS's Evening News, or NBC's Nightly News—were treated to images of weapons that did not work as advertised, corrupt contractors, and outrageously high defense budgets. There were tales of hard-liners threatening the peace of the world by not being more flexible during arms control negotiations with the Soviet Union. And there were reports of US foreign policy run amok in Central America.

But just how accurate was this picture of national defense and foreign policy painted by the networks? Were these important issues framed in the proper context or did the networks distort the facts and sacrifice their own journalistic standards? And what about coverage in the 1990s?

This book tries to shed some light on these questions by zeroing in on the content of the evening newscasts of ABC, CBS, and NBC during representative periods in the 1980s and 1990s. The issue here is not whether on occasion a network news report falls short. There will always be individual examples of a correspondent inserting his own views or conveniently ignoring a particular side of an issue. Even journalists make mistakes.

Most of those mistakes, however, get swallowed up in the larger impressions created over time. But what if a series of such mistakes, compounded by repetition, added up to a pattern that created false impressions among a public with no real firsthand experience or base of knowledge to draw upon? Certainly, support for particular policies might be affected.

Conveying the substance of national security certainly poses challenges for the media as a whole, not to mention the evening newscasts with their 22-minute format. How do you capture in 30 seconds, for instance, the context of a 10 to 12 year development cycle when framing a failed weapons test? And how do you describe technology conceived but not yet proven?

STRATEGIC DEFENSE INITIATIVE AND THE NETWORK EVENING NEWSCASTS

Take the case of the Strategic Defense Initiative (SDI). During a nationally televised speech on March 23, 1983, President Ronald Reagan startled both the American public and a fair number of his own top policy-makers by outlining a revolutionary concept he called SDI. It was revolutionary because it turned upside down the conventional wisdom of the nuclear age, namely that if each superpower possessed enough offensive nuclear weaponry to survive a first strike and still be able to retaliate, neither superpower would dare initiate a potentially devastating nuclear war. This theory was aptly named Mutual Assured Destruction (MAD).

At the time, the president hoped to capture the imagination of the American people by presenting a vision of a world without nuclear ballistic missiles. "What if free people," he said, "could live secure in the knowledge that their security did not rest upon the threat of instant US retaliation to deter Soviet attack, that we could intercept and destroy strategic ballistic missiles before they reached our own soil or that of our allies." The president also posed another poignant question: "Wouldn't it be better to save lives than to avenge them?"

In the speech, Reagan challenged the scientific community to solve the technological problems and help build a strategic defense system that would protect both the United States and US allies. This technological challenge was comparable in scope to previous US scientific endeavors, including developing the atomic bomb and the first Intercontinental Ballistic Missiles (ICBMs) and placing a man on the moon.

The next day, ABC World News Tonight quoted Senator Ted Kennedy (D-MA), who referred to the proposal as "Star Wars." Anchor Peter Jennings cited overseas reaction to Reagan's "ray gun," reporting that such a development might divide the United States from Europe. CBS Evening News framed the initiative in terms of "science fiction" and then focused on reaction in the Soviet Union, where officials were saying that SDI could launch a new arms race. And NBC Nightly News framed the issue in terms of whether the United States wanted to break out of the 1972 Anti-Ballistic Missile (ABM) Treaty because the Soviets had an advantage in this area. NBC also suggested the technology would not be available until the twenty-first century.

Based on a content analysis of network evening newscasts, which reviewed similar periods in 1983, 1985, 1990, 1991, and 1994, it is clear that these early themes lived on and dominated coverage of SDI. In fact, SDI was most often covered as an impediment to obtaining a strategic arms control agreement with the Soviet Union. Questions about the feasibility of SDI were also a dominant feature of the coverage.

What was regularly missing was a presentation of SDI in terms of nuclear deterrence and the strategic shift represented by a renewed emphasis on defensive measures against nuclear missile attack. This was a highly complex strategic issue, but it went to the heart of the debate over whether SDI should have been pursued.

One side contended that strategic defense would upset the delicate balance of nuclear arms and the treaties that underpin it, that the technology would cost too much, and that it likely would not be feasible to defend the United States against a full-scale Soviet attack.

The other side contended that the strategic deterrence equation should be shifted to a balance between offense and defense, that the ABM Treaty should be reconsidered in the broader strategic context, and that the technology would be feasible and worth the investment of resources, especially if defensive measures on the part of the United States complicated the strategic calculus of Soviet military planners.

Did both of these arguments come across on network newscasts? The answer is no. The content analysis revealed that the first set of arguments dominated coverage, at least in the periods reviewed.

THE MEDIA: ONE REASON FOR PUBLIC CONFUSION

Does it matter that network news coverage of SDI fell short? The answer is yes, because the media play a number of important roles within the dynamic relationship between policy-maker and the public, from watchdog, to conveyor of information, to public interpreter of government policies.

In the periods surveyed during the 1980s, and to some extent the 1990s, in a number of key areas of national security, the evening newscasts failed to live up to their own existing journalistic standards of fairness, accuracy, and objectivity, standards well established by the earliest television reporters, most of whom had come from print journalism.[1] Too often, especially in the 1980s, the network newscasts simply failed to explain adequately the different sides of complex defense and foreign policy issues.

Not surprisingly, in the case of SDI, public ignorance and general confusion over its relationship to arms control were evident during the 1980s and beyond. In November 1985, for example, over 70 percent of those surveyed believed that an arms reduction agreement was more important than building space weapons, yet a majority also opposed stopping the development of SDI in order to obtain an agreement.[2]

In another poll in February 1985, 90 percent responded yes to the question, "Do you want the United States to defend Americans against Soviet missiles?" But to another question, 83 percent said no when asked, "Did you know that the United States has a treaty with the Soviet Union not to protect Americans from a Soviet missile attack."[3]

In June 1987, 64 percent of those polled thought that the United States had a system to defend against nuclear missile attack.[4] Again in March 1988, over 50 percent of those polled opposed building an SDI defense system if it meant no more progress in US-Soviet nuclear arms talks.[5]

And well over a decade after Reagan first announced SDI, another poll found that 58 percent of the American public still thought that the US military could destroy a ballistic missile launched against the United States. Only 29 percent knew that the United States had no such capability.[6] Was network news coverage of SDI the reason? Not entirely, but it certainly contributed to the American public's basic lack of understanding of US military capabilities.

Richard R. Burt, who served in a number of national security positions during the two Reagan administrations, including ambassador to the Strategic Arms Reduction Talks, director of the Bureau of Politico-Military Affairs in the State Department, and as an assistant secretary of state, has maintained that "the media have failed to keep pace in explaining defense and arms control issues to a confused American public. Indeed, the performance of the press and broadcast journalism in reporting and analyzing these issues is one reason why the national security debate in the United States (and the West more broadly) has become increasingly chaotic, simplistic and ill informed."[7]

Burt was careful to say that the performance of the media *was one reason* why the debate was ill informed. It is important to state up front that the media are not the only responsible parties when it comes to creating an informed American electorate. For one thing, the US educational system is partly to blame and has drawn some well-deserved criticism, as a spate of studies during the 1980s made clear.[8]

For another, policy-makers have a role to play when it comes to informing the public and engendering support for their policies. In the case of SDI, they often fell short. There were continuing battles within the Reagan administration's highest national security policy-making circles, with the Defense Department pushing for funding and the earliest possible deployment of a missile defense system and the State Department showing less enthusiasm and sometimes outright hostility to SDI in light of sensitive arms negotiations and the implications of SDI with respect to the ABM Treaty. This made the media's job of scrutinizing and explaining government policies to the American public difficult, but it did not excuse the media from doing their job and adhering to their own journalistic standards.

The other part of the equation of policy-maker, media, and public concerns the responsibility of individual members of the public to make an effort to keep up with complex policy issues so that they might make informed decisions when voting or expressing their views to their elected representatives. But where does most of the public's information on complex topics like national security come from? Outside of the routine of daily life, to a rather large degree, the public depends on the media for such information, and the evening newscasts are one of the principal sources of news.

HOW THE NETWORKS PERFORMED IN THE 1980s
AND EARLY 1990s

SDI was not the only case of a complex issue that was inadequately covered during the 1980s and early 1990s. It was one part of a pattern of reporting on the evening newscasts that presented Americans with distorted information in key areas of national security, including arms control, the defense budget, defense industry, procurement, weapons, and some facets of foreign policy.

Taken as a whole, this pattern of reporting was notable for its lack of balance and context, which often violated the basic journalistic standards of fairness, accuracy, and objectivity. It was by these very standards—set forth by journalists themselves—that the network newscasts were judged. Fortunately, the same pattern was not reflected in other areas, from military operations and personnel issues to general foreign policy coverage, including coverage of the Soviet Union and, later, Russia.

What is clear is that the themes and general points running through the network coverage analyzed did not reflect the full range of competing viewpoints when it came to complex national security issues. In fact, they most often reflected views that were generally hostile to the Reagan defense buildup of the 1980s, as well as to the "hard-line" arms control policies advocated by Pentagon policymakers during the Reagan years.

Coverage of weapons and defense procurement persistently reflected the view that weapons did not work as advertised, that the defense industry was corrupt, and that the Pentagon system for buying weapons was full of waste. Likewise, and contrary to other foreign policy coverage, coverage of Reagan administration policy toward Central America was heavily skewed toward critics of the administration.

Interestingly, the pattern was driven by particular issues, not particular administrations. For example, the hostility toward defense spending was evident also in the period sampled during the Bush administration but disappeared during the Clinton administration sample period when the administration was cutting the defense budget. Similarly, as the tougher Reagan-era approach toward arms control negotiations disappeared in both the Bush and Clinton administrations, so, too, did the previous pattern of coverage. In the areas of weapons and industry, which involve relatively constant issues from administration to administration, the network stereotypes persisted through all four administrations.

In dissecting national security coverage, my goal was simply to analyze the content. It was not to render any judgments on the particular policies of particular administrations; rather, it was to determine if there was adequate coverage of the key aspects of these highly complex—and often controversial—policies and issues.

To the extent coverage was inadequate or distorted, the reasons were fairly obvious:

▸   The networks often allowed the attitudes of producers, correspondents, and anchors to surface in "news" reports, creating problems in the areas of balance and context.

When such attitudes were spotted, they were usually anti–defense spending, pro–arms control, negative toward new weapons technology, and anti–industry.

▸ Decisions taken in the area of news selection and presentation too often reflected these prevalent points of view.

▸ The large number of anchor-only reports (or anchor "tells") devoted to national security coverage often made it difficult, if not impossible, to present context when reporting on highly complex and oftentimes controversial areas of national security.

▸ And beat correspondents and producers with the most expertise in national security—the Pentagon, the State Department, and foreign beats—tended to report on national security less frequently as a group than did White House correspondents, anchors and general assignment and other Washington beat correspondents.

THE HISTORICAL CONTEXT

That certain attitudes reflecting hostility to higher defense spending (and associated policies) were present in the 1980s is not terribly surprising. Americans have a long tradition of resistance to high military expenditures and to the reliance on a professional military.

From colonial days onward, Americans have preferred the less expensive militia approach to national defense. Indeed, there was an American fear of a standing army and only a reluctant acceptance of the need for a navy to protect trade routes in the early period of the republic. Although George Washington counseled that "to be prepared for war is one of the most effectual means of preserving peace," the United States has made it a habit of being stingy with military spending until confronted with immediate threats to its security or interests.[9]

For example, when inaugurated as president in 1801 with no immediate security threats on the horizon, Thomas Jefferson began a dramatic series of cuts in military expenditures. Even the war with Tripoli shortly after his inauguration only slowed some planned cuts to the small US Navy. After Jefferson's two terms of reduced military spending, James Madison found the United States' military ill prepared for the War of 1812. As one writer put it, "America declared war against the mistress of the seas with a military and naval establishment whose puniness startled even the British. A paper Army, a dispersed Navy, and mediocre leadership in the former, was the extent of the military might that could be thrown against England in June 1812."[10]

Typically, the United States has had to depend on its abundant resources to surge its military capability in the face of war. This was true throughout the nineteenth century and once again manifested itself in the two world wars of the twentieth century. True to form, massive cuts in the military followed both of these wars. The same cycle of quick buildup and rapid demobilization was evident also in the cases of both the Korean and Vietnam wars.

For its part, the Reagan buildup, which actually began toward the end of the Carter administration, was yet another typical American response to what appeared to be an imminent threat from a Soviet Union that had steadily improved and increased its military might. Moreover, as in other times, this buildup followed a period of post-Vietnam military cuts and foreign policy withdrawal.

Among other developments in the late 1970s, like the debate over Carter administration arms control policies, the Soviet invasion of Afghanistan in 1979 prompted the Carter administration to reassess Soviet military intentions. It also helped crystallize a public consensus for higher defense spending, which had been steadily emerging in the face of the Soviet threat.

Yet even with the presence of the Soviet military threat, higher defense spending in a nonwar period was remarkable, given the American tendency not to spend on the military unless absolutely necessary. On the other hand, it also could be argued that at the height of the Cold War, with its bellicose rhetoric and the threat of instant nuclear annihilation, the distinction between "cold" (or nonwar) and "hot" wars was not terribly important to a worried American public. Before the consensus for increased defense spending crumbled in 1985, the Reagan administration had secured substantial increases in defense expenditures for four consecutive years.

But when the Cold War came to a symbolic end in November 1989, with the fall of the Berlin Wall, and the Soviet Union collapsed at the end of 1990, the American response was predictable: the Bush administration proposed a 25 percent cut in the US military; and the Clinton administration took those cuts even further.

One of the more interesting dimensions of the American allergy toward defense spending is that it transcends parties and administrations. Republican Thomas Jefferson cut defense, while fellow Republican James Madison had to increase it. In more recent times, Democrats engineered the World War II buildup *and* the dramatic cuts that followed the war. Republican Dwight Eisenhower went after defense on the cheap with his emphasis on nuclear weapons instead of more expensive conventional forces, while Democrat John Kennedy increased defense spending to build up conventional forces, which his administration saw as more useful in combating smaller brush wars. Moreover, what Reagan administration Secretary of Defense Caspar Weinberger called the "decade of neglect" in the 1970s spanned two Republican and one Democratic administration.

What is at issue in this book is not what appears to be a strong undercurrent of public resistance to defense spending and associated policies or the recurring historical cycle of increased defense spending in the face of an external threat, followed by dramatic cuts in periods of relative peace. Such tendencies and patterns of national behavior are well established. Instead, the focus here is on how well national security policies, including decisions about defense spending, were covered by the networks during the 1980s and early 1990s.

In the early years of the Reagan buildup, there was a public consensus *in favor of* defense spending. Yet, any viewer of the evening newscasts probably received just the opposite impression. From all indications, it appears that only certain aspects of important national security issues were covered adequately during these periods. In fact, a number of significant arguments and viewpoints were either downplayed, dismissed, or ignored entirely.

To the extent such coverage diminishes public understanding of defense and other national security issues, it should be of great concern to all Americans. After all, in recent years defense alone has consumed 18 to 25 percent of the federal budget. And, as Jefferson found out when the US military initially had trouble fending off the Barbary pirates,[11] US military capability matters when it comes to defending the nation's vital and other interests, from protecting American citizens abroad to deterring nuclear war.

Whether it is a period of military buildup, as in the 1980s, or a period of military cuts, as in the 1990s, the American public deserves adequate coverage of national security issues. Indeed, in many respects, the public depends on adequate coverage.

The framers of the US Constitution saw fit to make providing for the common defense one of the fundamental responsibilities of the government. Unfortunately, network coverage of how the government carried out this responsibility during the periods reviewed leaves much to be desired.

Chapter 1

National Security and Network News

For most Americans, "national security" is a rather abstract term. But mention the Gulf War, the deployment of US troops abroad for "peacekeeping" duties, or a terrorist bombing where US citizens are killed, and the abstract quickly becomes concrete.

If news interest surveys are any indication, Americans do pay attention to news about wars and crises when they hit home. Wars and crises rank right up there on the public attentiveness scale alongside disasters, like the explosion of the space shuttle Challenger in January 1986, the San Francisco earthquake of 1989, and the destruction caused by hurricane Andrew in August 1992.[12]

Aside from war and crises, on most days Americans also are fed a steady diet of more mundane national security information through the media, from stories about the defense budget, weapons purchases, and arms control to recent developments among allies and potential foes. While such stories may not be as remarkable as war, in many respects they are every bit as important.

The government, after all, depends on public support of its policies. It also depends on the media to convey information about its policies to the public.

This complex interaction among the public, policy-makers, and the media has real consequences. For example, the annual level of defense budgets has a direct effect on the number and quality of military personnel, the type of weapons purchased, the kind of training conducted, and the overall ability of the armed forces to respond to threats to US security interests around the world.

In the area of foreign policy, the day-to-day relationships with countries like Russia, China, and regional powers around the world can have a profound influence on global security. And international economic policies, from trade agreements to trade sanctions, can have a substantial impact on US business, from the balance of trade to prices at the local supermarket. Taken as a whole, these "mundane" subjects of national security have a direct effect on the livelihood of every

American. In discussing the role of the media in terms of national security, former Secretary of Defense William J. Perry stated: "I start off with the belief that communication—communicating a policy, a program, or action we're going to take—is a very important part of my job. If we cannot get public support—congressional support—for it, we won't be able to carry it out, or won't be able to carry it out effectively, or will have barriers put in the way of carrying it out. It just goes with running a military in a democracy."[13]

One of the longest serving secretaries of defense, Caspar W. Weinberger, also placed a great deal of emphasis on public support. He explained that the Reagan administration's effort to increase military spending was going to be "difficult to sustain for more than a few months or a year. And, therefore, public opinion, and what the public was seeing or what the public was hearing was a matter of extreme importance."[14]

Weinberger's concern about the unpopularity of defense spending reflected both the post–Korean War defense budget trends[15] and the historical reluctance of Americans to spend large sums on national defense or to encourage the establishment of a professional military.[16]

A FEW WAYS TO LOOK AT "NATIONAL SECURITY"

By its traditional and official uses, the term "national security" encompasses the nation's foreign, economic, and defense policies. The National Security Act of 1947 established the Department of Defense, in essence subordinating the military services to a secretary of defense; it also created the National Security Council, chaired by the president with the secretaries of defense and state among its principal members, to coordinate domestic, military, and foreign policy; and it replaced the Central Intelligence Group with the Central Intelligence Agency (CIA). While some critics worried that the 1947 act might "militarize" foreign policy, it mainly served as a means to integrate policies affecting the nation's security and to bring to the forefront the government's constant responsibility to provide for the common defense.[17]

In recent years, the Goldwater-Nichols Defense Department Reorganization Act of 1986 began requiring the president to issue a document each year called "The National Security Strategy of the United States." Though different in emphasis and tone, each report since President Ronald Reagan's first in 1987 has addressed these three principal areas: foreign policy, economic policy, and defense policy. In Reagan's 1987 report, economic policy was subsumed under the section on foreign policy, as was an item called "political and informational elements of national power," which had a lot to do with fighting the war of ideas with the Soviet Union. President George Bush divided his 1990 report into political, economic, and defense "agendas," with foreign policy subsumed under the political agenda. And President Bill Clinton organized his 1994 report under the rubrics "enhancing security," "promoting prosperity at home," and "promoting democracy." While Clinton's report was different in style, emphasis, and organization, the key foreign, economic, and defense components were all there.

National security news reflects these same three components in varying de-grees. Foreign policy news, for example, is fairly self-explanatory in the narrow diplomatic sense, as the media cover US officials making state visits, the executive branch and Congress debating policies toward particular countries, and the president signing treaties. Defense news, too, in the narrow sense of conducting military interventions, training at home and abroad, recruiting personnel for the armed forces, and the buying of weapons, is fairly obvious. But there is also a great deal of overlap between defense and foreign policy news, from the president making an actual decision to intervene abroad, weighing both military and diplomatic considerations, to negotiating a major arms control treaty, affecting both the status of the nation's military posture and relations with major foreign powers. In actuality, many national security topics, like arms control or relations with the Soviet Union and, later, Russia, cut across the foreign policy and defense spheres.

For its part, the economic dimension of national security does not draw nearly as much media attention as defense and foreign policy do. In this economic area of national security strategy, the Reagan administrations and the Bush administration focused on free trade, with a clear emphasis on export controls of sensitive technologies. Secure energy supplies represented another focus of both the Reagan and Bush administrations. Clinton's economic security policy, however, took a far more expansive view of national security, including an emphasis on reducing the federal deficit and promoting economic growth as a means of increasing US global competitiveness, promoting trade agreements without the Cold War dimension of technology transfer, and even focusing on environmental and population issues.

For my purposes here, the news items analyzed were drawn from transcripts of national security news obtained from the Pentagon's Current News Analysis and Research Service archives. For years, the Pentagon has contracted with an outside service that transcribes items of interest to the Department of Defense from each of the network newscasts. These transcripts are also distributed to the State Department, the White House, Congress, the National Security Council, and the CIA.

The Pentagon's news clipping and analysis service has been geared toward capturing the broadest range of national security news since its inception after World War II. This service will be discussed more extensively in chapter 13.

THE REACH OF NETWORK NEWS

Except for the small number of specialists in the field of national security, most Americans must rely on the media for national security information.

Based on what Americans have been telling the Roper Organization in its annual polls, the actual number of people who say they get their news from television has been steadily increasing even as the networks' audience share has been shrinking.[18] In recent years, 44 to 50 percent of respondents said they get their news only from television, 14 to 22 percent only from newspapers, and 13 to 23 percent from both. The rest turned to other media or a combination of newspapers and other media or television and other media.[19] Other research suggests that these survey results do not tell the real story and that, in fact, anywhere from 50 to 66 percent of the public get some news from both television and newspapers.[20]

Even with its declining audience share, television news still provides information to a sizeable audience. For the 1994–1995 ratings season, the evening newscasts of ABC, CBS, and NBC were routinely viewed in 26.4 million out of 95.4 million television households. Twenty-five years earlier, in the 1970–1971 ratings season, the network newscasts were viewed in 24.2 million out of 60.1 million households. At their peak, in the 1979–1980 season, 32.5 million out of 76.3 million households tuned in to the evening newscasts.[21]

Where the networks have lost substantial ground is in the area of audience share, or what percentage of the total television audience watching at any given time is tuned in to the newscasts. The network newscasts reached 75 percent of the actual viewing audience in the 1970–1971 season and were as high as 77 percent in the 1979–1980 season, but they have been gradually declining ever since, dipping to 54 percent of the audience in the 1994–1995 season.

But while the audience share has shown a marked decline, the continually expanding universe of television households has enabled the three newscasts to steadily reach between 24 and 32.5 million households for more than 25 years. Moreover, the number of viewers per household is normally greater than one.[22] Though Nielsen Media Research shares the demographics and audience multiples of given shows only with its clients, estimates of 50 million viewers of the evening newscasts during the networks' heyday were common. More recently, estimates have been in the 35 to 40 million range.[23]

Americans also buy about 60 million newspapers each day, and the Newspaper Association of America estimates readership at over 130 million.[24] Still, the largest national newspapers have a considerably smaller reach than the network evening newscasts. The daily circulation of the *New York Times*, for example, was 1.06 million in 1995; *USA Today*'s was 1.42 million in 1995, and the *Wall Street Journal*'s was 1.85 million in 1995.[25]

Even if the criticisms of the ratings system for television are taken into account, including the point that reaching an audience may not be the same thing as having an audience pay attention, the numbers are significant.[26] Newspaper circulation, too, is open to such criticism. How many people, for instance, have a newspaper delivered but never read it, or how many skip over hard news to find the sports scores or to clip supermarket coupons?

The point, here, is not to quibble too much about which is more influential, television or newspapers; rather, it is to suggest that the public relies on both for information not encountered in the routine of daily life. It is also to suggest that the evening newscasts are one of the public's principal sources of information about national security and that the presentation of national security information by the networks can help shape public views on these issues.

TELEVISION'S "EFFECTS"

There would be no point in undertaking a study of the national security content of network news if one did not believe that network news does indeed have some influence on public opinion. While communications research may never prove with scientific certainty that there is a link between what the public sees and hears on network newscasts and public opinion, there is a fair amount of past and recent evidence that suggests some influence and a correlation.

In the area of media effects research, scholarship over the past few decades has greatly expanded and challenged the earliest conclusions that television's effects were minimal.[27] Nevertheless, there is still plenty of room for debate. Over the past two decades, scholarly opinion has ranged from the outright dismissal of the power of television news[28] to the assertion that it shapes public opinion in pervasive ways.[29] In speaking of the influence of media, one scholar addressed the inability to conclusively prove such influence in this way: "Even if one takes a totally negative position, arguing that the media are nothing but a conduit of information over which they have no control, one cannot deny that people throughout the world of politics consider the media to be powerful and behave accordingly. This importance, which is an effect of media coverage, is reflected in efforts by governments everywhere, in authoritarian as well as democratic societies, to control the flow of information produced by the media lest it subvert the prevailing political system."[30]

Over the years, research on media and politics has certainly improved, moving from the narrowly focused election research of the 1940s[31] to the multidimensional approaches of the 1990s, involving learning experiments, survey data, depth interviews, and content analysis, along with a greater focus on the practical dimensions of political communications theory.[32]

In the area of national security, there have been growing questions about television's influence on the conduct of defense and foreign policy, including the so-called "CNN effect" on foreign policy and military operations. Here, the research is not very extensive, but recent studies[33] suggest that while television news plays an increasing role during crises, its effect on the policy process is not nearly as powerful as anecdotal information reported in the media would suggest.[34]

Taken as a whole, media effects research is still not able to answer conclusively those who ascribe little or no influence to television; nevertheless, there is enough evidence over the past few decades to comfortably assert that television news does exert some influence on the public and the policy-maker, from setting the political agenda from time to time, to framing issues, to providing selective information to a rather substantial audience.[35]

NETWORK NEWS: FROM PUBLIC TRUST TO PROFIT CENTER?

In the 1980s, the emergence of cable changed the television landscape, offering viewers many choices for the first time, including news 24 hours a day from CNN and what was then CNN2, soon to be "Headline News." The 1980s also saw all three broadcast networks taken over by corporations, ABC by Capital Cities Communications, Inc., NBC by General Electric Co., and CBS by Laurence Tisch of Loews Corp.

By the early 1990s, after steady declines in the three networks' ratings and audience share, not to mention sometimes dramatic cutbacks in staffing forced by the new corporate owners, many began writing the networks' obituaries. The catalyst for much of the speculation about the networks' demise was a 1991 book by Ken Auletta, titled *Three Blind Mice: How the TV Networks Lost Their Way*. The *Wall Street Journal* reviewed Auletta's book under the headline, "The Twilight of the Networks."[36] The *Washington Post*'s review carried the headline, "Changing TV's Golden Age into Lead,"[37] and the *New York Times* simply settled for "Zapped!"[38]

Auletta's thesis was built around a number of trends. Over a 15-year period, the networks, which had claimed nine out of ten viewers, lost a third of their audience—nearly 10 million viewers. Channels had proliferated from seven in 1976 to around thirty-three when Auletta was writing. The VCR was present in 70 percent of homes. And cumulative network profits sank from $800 million in 1984 to $400 million in 1998, with projections suggesting they might fall to zero by 1991.[39]

Indeed, in the summer of 1991, the *New York Times* reported that the networks were in a "crisis," and that there was "talk of sweeping changes." Even some of the network executives cited were unsure whether all the networks would survive.[40]

As for the news divisions, a piece in the *Columbia Journalism Review* the following spring suggested that broadcast journalism had been "knocked off its pins." The article added that the worst was not over and that "new technological Godzillas will be stirring," diverting viewers from news to other activities. Among these beastly threats were local cable news, video games, pay-per-view offerings, C-SPAN, the Baby Bells, and television newsmagazines less oriented toward hard news.[41]

But despite such dire predictions, within just a few years, ABC, CBS, and NBC seemed to have met many of the challenges and survived. "Major TV Networks, Dinosaurs No More, Tune In to New Deals," was the headline in the *Wall Street Journal* in early 1994.[42] The article spoke about how the networks proved they could hold on to a mass audience and the attendant slice of the advertising pie. Deals with producers and studios were also going to benefit the networks once they were freed to enter the US syndication market, the reporter wrote.

By that point, the networks' stock prices had been rising and there were predictions of more mergers. Two of these mergers came about within a day of each other in August 1995. First, Walt Disney Co. announced its $19 billion deal to merge with Capital Cities/ABC, and next Westinghouse Electric Corp. said it would acquire CBS in a $5.4 billion merger.[43] These mergers prompted speculation about NBC's future, with analysts suggesting that GE was well positioned to form a strategic alliance of its own at some point.[44]

While such mergers might have been good for the bottom line, they raised another set of concerns related to network news. The notion that the three news divisions are in essence public trusts seemed more and more remote as megacorporations looked to squeeze more profits from all operations and to turn their focus toward the lucrative entertainment market.

News of the ABC merger sent shock waves through its news division,[45] especially when the jokes about news anchor Peter Jennings wearing Mickey Mouse hats began. Most network correspondents also had lingering memories of the cutbacks that followed the first set of acquisitions in the mid-1980s and were none too excited about another round.

On a less parochial note, Bill Kovach of Harvard University's Nieman Foundation worried that "for the past decade, journalism has been slowly squeezed into a smaller and smaller corner of the expanding corporations that make up the communications industry. The values and norms of journalism have been steadily eroded as corporate managers order news divisions to produce more 'infotainment' programs."[46]

Part of what Kovach was referring to was the mushrooming of television newsmagazines, like ABC's "PrimeTime Live," NBC's "Dateline NBC," and CBS's "48 Hours," among others. These shows are cheaper to produce than an hour of entertainment, by about $500,000 to $1.4 million, and they are very profitable.[47] But content is quite another thing, ranging from Diane Sawyer's "Turning Point" interview with Charles Manson to the "Eye to Eye with Connie Chung" interview with Tonya Harding.[48]

One of the problems with the appearance of a family of newsmagazines, as the *American Journalism Review* has pointed out, is that "the evening newscasts now routinely carry reports that essentially plug features on that night's news-magazines. . . . All three networks routinely do such cross-plugging."[49]

With all the soft features and titillation swirling around them on the networks' own newsmagazines, the evening newscasts themselves have experimented with longer segments, like ABC's "American Agenda," NBC's "Daily Difference," and CBS's "Focus," among other recent spinoffs. In actuality, with some of these segments running up to four minutes, there is a great opportunity to delve more deeply into hard news, but that is not always what happens.[50]

In a scathing criticism of the general trend away from hard news, CBS Evening News anchor Dan Rather urged his colleagues to choose "quality and substance" over "sleaze and glitz." He added, "We've all gone Hollywood—we've all succumbed to the Hollywoodization of the news—because we were afraid not to. We trivialize important subjects. We put videotape through a Cuisinart trying to come up with high-speed, MTV-style cross-cuts. And just to cover our asses, we give the best slots to gossip and prurience."[51]

While the first set of corporate takeovers spawned a lot of tinkering with the evening newscasts, there are considerable limitations. ABC World News Tonight anchor Peter Jennings has said, "I have been listening to people talk about the changing format of the evening news since God was a boy. There are not many ways you can change a 22-minute format and still pretend to tell any of the news of the day."[52]

According to one analysis of network news operations, the 22-minute format has "reached its mature stage." Moreover, "efforts to shake up the structure mainly push at the edges, eliminating some elements, rearranging others, and rummaging among a finite range of already tested options."[53]

What's clear is that the news divisions will continue to be more tightly managed than they were in the past because they are under huge ratings and profits pressures. That means they also will continue to have fewer resources to use in gathering news than they did in the past.[54]

But despite these trends, the networks can still deliver the largest concentrated audience of any medium, and their evening newscasts are still a principal source of news and information for a large number of Americans.

Chapter 2

National Security: The New York–Washington Axis

"The system is the system, because it works," said one senior network news producer based in New York.[55] He was referring to a system of domestic beats around the country and foreign beats around the globe, all of which interact continuously with the central hub in New York. These beats give meaning to the word *network*, for they are the eyes and ears of the New York gatekeepers and the tentacles through which New York can reach out for confirmation, background or investigation.

As Edward Jay Epstein pointed out in his seminal 1973 book, *News from Nowhere*, within the overall organization of network news, there is also a set of "operational rules." Though these rules "may not predetermine any particular stories, they do define more general characteristics of network news, such as the length of film reports . . . , the amount of time and money available for individual film reports (which, in turn, may define the 'depth' of news coverage), the areas which are most heavily covered (which might be said to delineate the geography of news), the models for dealing with controversy (whether it is a 'dialectical' model, in which two sides are presented along with a synthesis, or the 'thesis' model, which tries to prove one side is correct), the ratio of 'prepared' or delayed news to immediate news . . . , and the general categories which are given preference by producers."[56]

Such basic operating rules, technology advances aside, still help define the daily routine of determining what is important enough to make the cut and be slotted in the 22-minute evening news hole on the network newscasts.

As was already suggested, what the networks determine to be national security "news" matters because the evening newscasts are one of the principal sources of news for most Americans. In terms of the *what*, the networks have certain strengths, particularly in the areas of war, crisis coverage, and general foreign policy coverage, and some clear weaknesses, particularly in certain areas of defense coverage, like weapons and the industry that produces them.

The *how* and *why* of network coverage of national security, for obvious reasons of space and scope, are not the main focus of this study, but they do, nevertheless, demand some attention. While it is not the intention here to revisit the institutional and organizational issues brought up in Epstein's work, or to try to map the networks' decision-making process in as comprehensive a fashion as Herbert Gans did in his 1979 book covering the CBS Evening News and NBC Nightly News,[57] there is room for a few observations on the New York–Washington axis and how it relates to producing national security news.

The following observations are based on a series of interviews[58] with New York network producers and Washington producers and correspondents, as well as a general review of the literature.

THE DAILY LINE-UP

Before taking their battle stations in front of computer screens and telephone lines, top producers and anchors in New York have already perused the major newspapers and read the wires. The same can be said for the Washington producers and correspondents. The sense one gets from direct conversations and from reviewing what others have written about network journalists is that these "news junkies" thrive on the creative and sometimes heated exchanges among themselves and with the beat producers and correspondents.[59]

Unlike Epstein's play on words, news does not come from "nowhere." The major breaking stories are obvious from the day's newspaper headlines, wire reports, and often from what Washington beat reporters are learning from their sources, since Washington is frequently a source of major stories. Other stories are proposed by correspondents around the country and by producers, who may have come across a story or may have been "pitched" by a source or interest group, and still others result from scoops or from assignments made in advance for the long-form, or feature, stories.

What finally makes the cut is the result of a complex process of interaction between the beats and New York, with all the various inputs, external and internal, and the give-and-take of the news process. Structure and time impose one set of limits; and what is happening in the United States and overseas imposes another challenge—namely, the art of selection—for there is always too much to pick from.

At the top of the decision-making ladder is, in theory, the executive producer in New York, who has overall responsibility for the evening broadcast. In practice, the anchors work hand-in-hand with the executive producers. Both Dan Rather at CBS and Tom Brokaw at NBC have the title of "managing editor" as well as anchor.[60] This puts them both in a position to overrule, or at least heavily influence, the executive producers. For his part, Peter Jennings of ABC has the title of "senior editor," but he still wields tremendous influence over the broadcast.

At the next rung down are the two senior broadcast producers. Each network has a senior producer in charge of domestic stories and one in charge of foreign stories. One oversees all the news being pitched by the domestic beats, and one oversees the news being pitched from overseas.

A host of producers, writers, editors, researchers, and technicians helps them prepare the stories that might be included in the evening's broadcast. To borrow a military analogy, the anchor and executive producer view and manage the broadcast from the strategic level; the two senior producers manage it from the operational level, where key decisions are being made about what to select and where to focus the resources required to get stories prepared; and the rest form the tactical level, where the key decisions are executed and supported.

At the top echelons, the executive producers and senior producers find themselves dividing their limited time between phone calls from the beats and story meetings, which take place continually during the course of the day. By the middle of the morning, these producers have already mapped out a potential line-up for that night's broadcast. There is a running list of stories, divided by a line, with the best candidates for broadcast above the line, and those that might make it into the broadcast below the line. A keen interest of beat correspondents and producers is where their stories fall at any given moment of the day.

THE WASHINGTON BEAT: FIRST AMONG EQUALS

While New York producers are quick to say that all news is viewed equally and is equally in play, news out of Washington still dominates the broadcasts.

As Joe Foote of the Southern Illinois University at Carbondale has shown in his yearly analyses, beginning in 1983, Washington correspondents consistently rank among the top correspondents for on-air time.[61] Foote points out that covering the "golden triangle"—the White House, State Department, and Pentagon—has a direct correlation to success in getting on the air. He also notes that about half the networks' evening news comes from Washington.[62]

As would be expected, foreign correspondents' air time goes up in direct relation to action taking place in their regions of coverage. For example, Foote cites the on-air ascension of ABC's Jim Laurie, CBS's Barry Peterson, and NBC's Bob Abernethy as Moscow correspondents during the upheaval in the Soviet Union in 1990 and the upticks in the rankings of correspondents who covered the Gulf War in 1991.[63]

In terms of national security coverage out of Washington, New York producers make it clear that most stories are pretty clearly organized by beat. In other words, where the story emerges is the first indicator of who might cover it. As one New York producer from NBC noted, besides the beat issue, the networks also look at who is best able to do a story, in terms of availability and expertise. In the case of NBC, a national security story could emerge from the Pentagon, State Department, Capitol Hill, the White House, or from another Washington beat, depending on the angle. In each instance, the correspondent assigned to the beat where the news originates is most likely to do the story.

In the case of both ABC and CBS, there are broad "national security" beats not confined to physical geography, though the beat is based at the Pentagon. CBS's David Martin was the first with the title "national security correspondent" and the broad latitude that affords him. He covers a wide range of stories from those traditional Pentagon stories to hearings on Capitol Hill, CIA stories, and some with a foreign angle. ABC's John McWethy is again based at the Pentagon, after having covered the State Department and Pentagon on previous assignments. As ABC "national security correspondent," he, too, can roam across the beats, including doing some foreign coverage from the Pentagon's perspective.

Despite the existence of these national security beats, a fair amount of national security coverage still originates from the White House beat and general Washington beats of all three networks. For example, in the case of NBC, more national security reporting came out of the White House beat than from the Pentagon beat during the periods sampled for this book (see Table 2.1). And while top national security billing on ABC and CBS went to their Pentagon, or national security, correspondents, other beats, including the White House, made sizeable contributions. In the case of both NBC and CBS, other Washington beats, which were made up of Capitol Hill and general assignment correspondents, actually did more national security reporting than the State Department beat did.

THE WHITE HOUSE PRISM

While the networks treat the White House as the pinnacle of beat reporting, in terms of the actual practice of journalism, it does not offer the chance to deal with the range of sources and substantive issues that the Pentagon or State Department does. But because of its visibility, it is not surprising that television journalists rank it higher as an assignment than print reporters do.[64]

Table 2.1

Network Distribution of National Security Reports in Washington by Beat and Number of Reports, Jan.–Apr. 1983, Jan.–Apr. 1985, Jan.–Apr. 1990, Jan.–Feb. 1991, and Jan.–Apr. 1994

Beats	Total Reports	ABC	CBS	NBC
Pentagon	414	147	161	106
White House	308	85	108	115
State	178	78	41	59
Other Wash	190	62	64	64
Total	1090	372	374	344

Source: Author's Database. See appendix 1.

Dealing with cramped quarters, the presidential body watch, and pool coverage is a way of life for the White House reporter.[65] Given the pool restrictions and lack of access, one print reporter has taken to telling journalism classes, "If you want to be lazy, the White House is the best beat in the world."[66] On most days, however, the network correspondents who cover the White House can ill afford to be lazy. Theirs is a life of working White House sources and preparing to fit their reports into the larger broadcast being worked up in New York.[67]

Nevertheless, much of that effort is clearly focused on style and politics over issues and substance. Given the importance of the presidency, there certainly is a place for news about whether he is up or down in his daily political struggles, how he looked, and what he said. But, too often, the White House correspondent, while "interpreting" the president's daily scorecard, wanders into foreign policy issues, decisions about defense, arcane matters relating to arms control, and other complex issues that he or she is ill equipped to handle.

With the kind of talent and expertise all three networks have at the Pentagon and State Department, it is somewhat surprising that the White House becomes the focus of many national security stories. But, as one New York producer explained, the networks often turn to the White House beat because it lends "import" to the story.

Prestige aside, the White House beat is clearly focused on politics, not the issues behind the politics. In fact, the networks traditionally assign the correspondent of the winning presidential campaign to cover the White House, sometimes for as long as the new president is in office.[68] Unfortunately, that correspondent's focus has been the politics of the campaign trail, not substantive issues of state. It is not hard to imagine how the politics of the campaign trail become transformed into the politics of the White House.

The final point, which is only tangential to the issues being examined in this book, has to do with the potential manipulation of the press by the White House, a phenomenon not nearly as easy to accomplish on the more specialized beats, where sources are more plentiful and accessible.[69]

NEW YORK'S WASHINGTON OUTPOST

Besides the beat producers and correspondents, the other key players in network national security reporting are the Washington senior producers for each of the evening newscasts. They are the generalists, located in Washington, who keep track of what is happening on all of the Washington beats. They keep in regular contact with New York and advise the Washington beat correspondents and producers of whether a particular story has a chance that evening, given the way the line-up is shaping up during the day. The Washington senior producers also play a role in actually providing the resources needed to produce stories from Washington, including camera crews, production facilities, editors, and so on.

While on paper there appears to be a chain of command, with New York senior producers dealing with their Washington senior producers, who, in turn deal with the Washington beat producers and correspondents, in practice it is not hierarchical at all, according to Pentagon producers and correspondents.[70] Oftentimes, a Pentagon correspondent will deal directly with the network's executive producer. A Pentagon producer might start with a senior producer in New York and then coordinate with the Washington senior producer for resources. Or a Pentagon producer might start by pitching a story to the Washington senior producer to see what chance it has that day.

These various contacts depend on a number of circumstances, from past relationships between correspondents and New York producers, to the interests of individual producers, to the issue of resources needed to get a story done.

As CBS's David Martin has pointed out, "A print reporter's next interview is only a telephone call away, but a television reporter has to get a camera there and get the tape back in time to be edited for the evening news."[71]

WHAT NEW YORK WANTS

"It's almost impossible to describe how we know what's news and what isn't," CBS senior broadcast producer Bob Crawford explained in a 1989 interview. "But when we grapple with the events of the day we use a yardstick that is, in simple terms: Is it something that the audience should know, something they would like to know, something they haven't heard before?"[72]

Getting more to the point, Crawford, in the same interview, added that "news, as most people in the business define it, is conflict, disasters, violence, war. You won't see any news stories called 'things are going really swell in France.' " On the other hand, he noted that CBS liked to give people something at the end of the broadcast that leaves them with a smile, a practice used by the other networks as well.

CBS News President Eric Ober made a similar point to another interviewer in 1990. He said that news used to be defined as what happened and what viewers needed to know, but viewers began insisting on getting information of greater relevance to their lives. According to Ober, what viewers need to know and what they want to know are both important. "News," Ober said, "is everything from what happened of extreme importance to what is interesting to people."[73]

Jonathan Wald, a senior broadcast producer for NBC, emphasized that timeliness was a major factor in deciding what was news. "It has to have happened today or be important enough to get a spot on NBC Nightly News," he said.[74]

As ABC executive producer Robert Frye stated in 1983, "Network journalism has evolved to the point where we aren't just a headline service." He added that ABC would strive to provide an explanation for events and not just the facts.[75] Looking back from the late 1990s, it is clear that explanation and interpretation can be very useful in helping the audience understand complex events, but they represent a double-edged sword: interpretation and explanation have also opened the door to opinion and bias.

Among the more seasoned beat correspondents and producers in Washington, what New York wants in terms of "news" is well understood. In the cases of Fred Francis, who covered the Pentagon for eight and one-half years for NBC before turning the beat over to Ed Rabel (who later turned it over to James Miklaszewski), and John McWethy at ABC and David Martin at CBS, both of whom have experience in national security going back more than a decade, their scripts normally make the cut with few or no changes from New York. The universal refrain from their producers was that "they know what New York wants."

The changes that do occur often have less to do with substance than with the flow of a given night's broadcast. In one instance, a New York producer might need to take out a line referring to Bosnia from the Pentagon correspondent's script that has already been included in a report from the network's foreign correspondent in Bosnia. One producer described this as "deconflicting" scripts and maintaining the flow. The generalist in New York might also want to see a little clearer explanation of what a heat-seeking missile is, for example. In another case, a report might need to be shortened by 10 to 15 seconds.[76]

In the case of all three networks, a typical national security story coming out of the Pentagon is 1 minute, 40 seconds to 2 minutes, 15 seconds long. As David Martin has explained, in a typical 1 minute, 45 second report, he has room for only two to three sound bites.[77] "The curse is that a 15-second sound bite frequently does not add useful information and is used merely to keep the pace of the story moving so that the correspondent does not drone on with 2 minutes of uninterrupted narration. It is, of course, difficult to express any but the most simplistic thought in 15 seconds. Anything over 15 seconds is considered too long."[78]

Given the curse of brevity, it is remarkable how often the networks do manage to get it right. It is an art and a science, but it is not perfect, as correspondents and producers readily admit.

HANDING OFF THE STORY TO THE ANCHOR

When a story that has been prepared falls below the line or never quite makes it above the line, it is sometimes reduced to an anchor-only report, known as a *tell*. These short items are designed to relay news that, in the network's eyes, the American public needs to know, even if it must be delivered in abbreviated format.

These short anchor reports also contribute to the flow of the broadcast and afford the top-paid anchor stars more visibility. When it comes to national security stories that must be worked into tells, Pentagon and State Department correspondents or producers normally provide notes to writers in New York. Ultimately, however, each anchor has a strong influence on the final copy. In fact, they often rewrite the tells themselves.

While all three anchors are seasoned journalists, their position at the anchor desk in New York often does not allow for firsthand knowledge or the contextual understanding that a beat producer or correspondent could provide. Given the time constraints, however, it is the anchor who makes the crucial editorial decisions, which often have more to do with personal style and the anchor's preconceptions than with context and substance.

For that reason, anchor tells represent some of the most troubling reporting on national security. Brevity and anchor "interpretation" can lead to problems of context. Additionally, the type of "news" selected to be reduced to tells, based on attitudes and network definitions of news, can add up to an unbalanced view of particular national security topics.

THE BEATS AND EXPERTISE: ASSET OR LIABILITY?

In his 1979 book, Gans described how New York saw a danger in the beat correspondents becoming coopted by the institutions they cover.[79] At the same time, in his survey of Washington reporters, Stephen Hess found that expert knowledge and specialization actually led to more autonomy among Washington reporters.[80]

More recent views among producers in New York and Washington suggest that cooptation is not as big an issue as is the perception from New York that the Washington beat reporters can fall into the trap of "Inside the Beltway" thinking. One producer noted on background that some beat reporters "have an exalted view of the areas they cover" and that "Washington people can push very hard for the political angles," which, in his view, can be overplayed in terms of audience interest.

Just the same, in the area of defense and foreign policy, it seemed clear that New York producers had a great appreciation for the expertise of the correspondents who cover national security issues. These correspondents were spoken of highly, and their independent judgment was considered an asset. As CBS's David Martin has pointed out, scoops are what give him credibility. He wrote that the scoops "convince the people I work for that I am plugged into the inner circuits of the Pentagon, and they are more likely to accept my judgments about what is important and what is not. In other words, scoops equal clout."[81] Tom Nagorski, who was serving as the ABC senior producer in New York for foreign news, valued highly the expertise of correspondents on the foreign beats, referring specifically to those who had spent years covering particular regions or countries. His inclination was to take advantage of that expertise as much as possible.

For its part, the State Department beat seems to be the exception. At least in terms of the numbers, the State Department correspondent has a small role in reporting on national security. Part of the explanation might have to do with the central role of foreign correspondents; another part of it seems attributable to the inclination of the networks to turn to the White House correspondent on many national security topics.

BOILING IT ALL DOWN

Overall, given the time constraints and inherent weaknesses of the format, the system does work for the most part. It sifts through mountains of news and eventually boils it all down to about 15 news items covering about five to six major stories.[82]

There are, however, two clear weaknesses when the networks go about boiling down national security news: the regularity with which the anchor can skew the context of national security items; and the regularity with which generalists in Washington, including White House correspondents, end up reporting on national security as a result of location rather than expertise.

Chapter 3

Dissecting Network Coverage of National Security

In that process of boiling down the news, there will be, on average, one to two national security items, or "news reports," on each network evening newscast on any given night.[83] Viewed over time and by topic, this daily dose of news adds up to a fairly clear picture of what aspects of national security the networks consider to be most newsworthy and what they tend to ignore.

In trying to determine the patterns of national security reporting, I looked at the whole range of national security news. I then broke it down into topics. Each news report was then judged not by my standards, but by those set forth by the Society of Professional Journalists.[84]

For purposes of comparison, I selected periods from four presidential administrations—the two Reagan administrations, the Bush administration, and the first Clinton administration. To make the analysis manageable, I limited the periods to the first four months of the year (January–April). In this period, defense budgets are prepared and major policy documents are developed, some of which are made public, including the Department of Defense Annual Report to Congress, which includes policy, strategy, and budget information required by Congress. The two-month Gulf War period (January–February 1991) provided a means of comparing network war coverage with more routine coverage.

In selecting the specific years—1983, 1985, 1990, and 1994—my main goal was to find fairly routine periods without major military operations underway or crises that would not reflect typical coverage of national security issues. Having said that, there are almost no periods when some military operation is not taking place. Nevertheless, the periods selected turned out to be about as routine as can be expected. In fact, only 8 percent of the coverage analyzed involved military operations. That compared with a nearly 60 percent slice of national security coverage devoted to military operations during the Gulf War period.

Apart from the Gulf War, network coverage of military operations included everything from peacekeeping in the Sinai and Lebanon during the two Reagan periods, along with exercises in Honduras, military involvement in El Salvador, and the movement of military forces as tensions mounted with Libya, to the launching of the space shuttle Discovery on a military mission. In the Bush period, there was coverage of troops occupying Panama during the post-invasion period, coverage of the drug war, and coverage of major military training exercises and maneuvers like the Reforger exercise, which involves deploying US forces to Germany to demonstrate the US national commitment to NATO.

The Clinton period included coverage of peacekeeping and peace enforcement, from the withdrawal from Somalia to the enforcement of the no-fly zone over Iraq. News related to the combined Republic of Korea–United States Team Spirit military training exercise, which takes place in Korea, also appeared in the Clinton period. And in all four administrations, military crashes and accidents, which were routinely covered by the networks, were coded under the category of military operations.

On a more general note, during the first four months of 1983, the first Reagan administration was well into its defense buildup, and the battleground in the areas of budgets, arms control, and foreign policy was established. With Reagan's re-election, the first four months of 1985 provided an opportunity for the media to zero in on any changes in previous policies. The 1985 period also marked the height of Reagan-era defense spending levels.

The 1990 Bush administration period represented the first chance for the new administration to put its own mark on the defense budget and the nation's national security strategy. The only anomaly was some postwar reporting on the Panama invasion of 1989, with a heavy dose of reporting on the capture and disposition of Manuel Noriega, along with the international legal issues revolving around that case. Otherwise, it, too, was fairly routine.

As for the Clinton administration, the first four months of 1994 seemed a logical choice, given the bottom-up review of military strategy that had taken place in 1993, along with major changes in the focus of US foreign policy. By 1994, the administration had laid down its overall approach to national security.

The Gulf War period provided only a glimpse of overall network news war coverage, since the networks regularly extended their daily coverage of the war. Nevertheless, the evening newscast provided a good mechanism for sampling what the networks considered the highlights of a given day.

The main goal of this analysis was to target day-to-day national security coverage and to determine whether there were any patterns of coverage that violated basic journalistic standards.

To do this, I needed to find a representative sample of national security coverage that could be analyzed. Such a sample does exist and can be found in the transcripts of national security news items from ABC World News Tonight, CBS Evening News, and NBC Nightly News that are provided to the Pentagon by an outside contractor each day. News items are picked using consistent criteria, and the full transcripts are available in the Pentagon's archives.

Using these daily transcripts, I broke down individual news reports from each of the network evening newscasts into such areas as the name of the anchor, the beat, the name of the correspondent, the length of report, and the date of it. The analysis also included the assignment of topics to the report, a summary of overall content, and the determination of whether the report contained problems related to journalistic standards.[85]

If no such problems were found, the report was coded as *neutral*. If any problems were identified, the report was coded as *problematic* and the problems were noted. The content of each report was summarized in terms of main points made by the correspondent and any sources cited.

The topics assigned included arms control, defense budget, foreign policy, industry, military operations, personnel, policy/strategy, procurement, Soviet Union/Russia, threats, the Strategic Defense Initiative (SDI) and weapons/capabilities. Overall, there were 2,947 individual news reports (or items) in this sample of 18 months' worth of evening newscasts. A *news report* was defined in three ways: a segment delivered by the anchor alone (the anchor *tell*); a segment where the anchor introduced just one correspondent; or a segment where the anchor introduced more than one correspondent up front, followed by their back-to-back reporting. By comparing how the networks approached various national security topics over time and across administrations with similar and dissimilar policies, patterns did emerge.

COVERAGE BY THE NUMBERS

In the 1980s and early 1990s, Americans saw network national security reporting that was dominated by foreign policy news (see Figure 3.1). Along the

Figure 3.1

National Security Reporting by Topic and Number of Reports, Jan.–Apr. 1983, Jan.–Apr. 1985, Jan.–Apr. 1990, Jan.–Feb. 1991, and Jan.–Apr. 1994

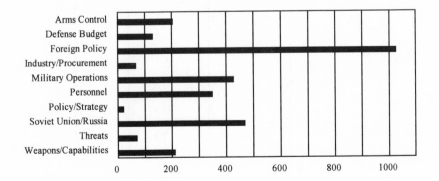

same lines, but often with a defense component added, there was a heavy dose of reporting on Russia and, previously, its former incarnation, the Soviet Union.

Defense topics, like the defense budget, which has consumed on average 18 to 25 percent of the federal budget each year over the last four presidential administrations, or the weapons and capabilities the armed forces must rely upon in war- and peace-time operations, actually did not rate a lot of attention by the networks.

The range of issues covered during the two Reagan administrations and the Bush administration were similar, with reports on foreign policy dominating. Other areas that received attention included the Soviet Union, arms control, personnel-related issues, military operations, the defense budget, and weapons/capabilities, among others. During the Clinton administration, however, foreign policy coverage dominated almost to the exclusion of other areas of national security. In fact, there was no primary coverage of the defense budget, arms control, policy/strategy, and very little coverage of weapons/capabilities (see Table 3.1). Many changes in the patterns of coverage can, of course, be explained by external events, such as the shift from the highly charged arms control negotiations of the Soviet-era taking place during the Reagan years to more cooperation

Table 3.1

Number of Reports by Topic and Administration

Topic	Reagan 1	Reagan 2	Bush	Clinton
Arms Control	128	56	17	0
Defense Budget	63	29	26	0
Foreign Policy	215	173	192	359
Industry	4	31	8	6
Military Operations	72	50	37	53
Personnel	64	75	77	108
Policy/Strategy	8	2	1	0
Procurement	1	5	4	2
SDI	3	13	4	0
Soviet Union/Russia	93	108	232	30
Threats	0	10	21	32
Weapons/Capabilities	62	67	29	11

Source: Author's Database. See appendix 1.

with Russia and mutual efforts to slow nuclear proliferation in former Soviet Republics during part of the Bush and Clinton years. Some areas, on the other hand, like the defense budget and issues related to weapons development or upgrades, have a continuity about them, and why the networks chose to cover or ignore them revealed something about how the networks approached particular topics.

Beyond the extent to which the networks focused upon each topic, it also was important to determine the quality of coverage related to each topic. Since the content of every individual news report was judged in qualitative terms and coded by topics, it was possible to evaluate each topic as a discrete set of news reports (see Table 3.2). Each "set" could also be viewed over select periods of time and be analyzed by beat, correspondent, or even by network.

In the case of news reports that contained problems related to journalistic standards, they, too, could be separated and analyzed as a set. This analysis revealed the existence of six broad problem areas: general lack of balance or context; lack of context as a result of brevity; lack of knowledge on the part of the correspondent; overemphasis on drama or bad news at the expense of substance and context; loaded labeling or advocacy; and bad news judgment.

Table 3.2

Problematic Reporting by Topic and Administration

Topic	Reagan 1	Reagan 2	Bush	Clinton
Arms Control	46.8%	37.5%	41.1%	n/a
Defense Budget	71.4%	75.8%	80.7%	n/a
Foreign Policy	35.8%	47.9%	23.4%	11.4%
Industry	75.0%	100.0%	100.0%	66.6%
Military Operations	15.2%	50.0%	24.3%	43.4%
Personnel	24.2%	26.6%	38.9%	42.5%
Policy/Strategy	100.0%	50.0%	0.0%	n/a
Procurement	100.0%	80.0%	75.0%	100.0%
SDI	100.0%	61.5%	50.0%	n/a
Soviet Union/Russia	15.0%	25.9%	7.7%	13.3%
Threats	0.0%	0.0%	4.7%	18.7%
Weapons/Capabilities	51.6%	47.7%	75.8%	72.7%

Source: Author's Database. See appendix 1.

Overall, the numbers suggest that there is good news and bad news about national security reporting in the 1980s and early 1990s. The good news is that about 70 percent of the time national security reporting was fairly informative, balanced and in context, given the obvious limitations of the medium and the evening newscast format. Out of the 2,947 network news reports analyzed, 886, or 30 percent, had basic problems related to journalistic standards.

The bad news is that, outside of general foreign policy coverage, in a number of key areas, ranging from arms control, to the defense budget, to developments related to defense industry and weapons, there were problems related to journalistic standards anywhere from 37 to 100 percent of the time (see Table 3.2).

The patterns become fairly clear when topics are listed by administration and in terms of the percentage of problematic coverage. The five topical areas where problems were most pronounced were arms control; defense budget; industry and procurement; weapons/capabilities; and some foreign policy coverage during the Reagan periods.

Military operations during these periods, like foreign policy, were subject to wide shifts in the level of problematic reporting based upon how the networks approached each individual operation. But, taken as a whole during the four administrations, the military operations category had about an average rate of problematic coverage, around 32 percent. In contrast, the networks' evening newscasts during the Gulf War were relatively free of problematic coverage, with an overall problematic rating of 6.6 percent in the area of military operations.

Somewhat surprising was the fact that topics like arms control and the defense budget, which were especially controversial and politically charged during the 1980s, received scant attention when viewed in terms of national security coverage as a whole. For example, in the periods analyzed, arms control accounted for only 6.8 percent of all national security coverage. In the case of the defense budget, the slice of the pie amounted to a mere 4.3 percent. Industry and procurement combined represented only 2.1 percent of the coverage, and weapons coverage accounted for only 6.4 percent.

Some might consider it good news that national security reporting containing problems occurred in areas infrequently covered. On the other hand, with the limited attention the networks devote to defense and security issues, those small slices of coverage may be even more important, since television news is one of the public's principal sources of national security information.

The basic numbers and statistics provided some clues about the existence of certain patterns of problematic coverage during the 1980s and, in some cases, the 1990s. They, however, tell only part of the story. The following five chapters will illustrate how the anchors and generalists ended up distorting defense coverage in the five important areas already mentioned: the defense budget; weapons; industry and procurement; arms control; and foreign policy.

Chapter 4

Cut That Defense Budget!

What did expenditures reaching slightly more than a quarter of all federal outlays buy in terms of national defense during the periods sampled in the 1980s and 1990s? How did new weapons systems and technology fit into US military strategy? What are the tradeoffs between incorporating new technology and upgrading older systems? How does the defense budget break down in terms of weapons procurement, operations, and personnel costs, among others? And, how were various decisions reached during the arcane defense budgeting process?

If a typical viewer of the evening news wanted the answers to any of the above questions, he or she would have had to look elsewhere. By and large, the networks covered only one major aspect of the defense budget during the Reagan and Bush administrations: the question of how much the United States should spend on national defense. And that in the most superficial way. Moreover, the story of the defense budget was usually presented as a battle between the president and Congress. Admittedly, the "guns versus butter" debate has always been central to the issue of defense spending. However, so are the rationales behind the arguments for larger or smaller defense budgets, and seldom were they covered.

During the Reagan administration periods sampled and the Bush administration period, the pattern of coverage was clear: the president would submit his budget and network anchors and correspondents would then go about sketching what was going to be spent on defense, how that compared to expenditures on social programs, and how the battle between the White House and Congress was shaping up. The actual budget process, either in terms of the give and take between the Office of Management and Budget (OMB) and the cabinet departments, or in terms of the give and take between the planners from the four military services and those from the Office of the Secretary of Defense, was never really explained to the public. Yet, this process is, in many respects, more important than the so-called "battle" between White House and Congress over various provisions in the budget. As veterans of the budget battles during the years when president and at least one house of Congress were from opposite parties will attest, even though budgets were routinely labeled "dead on arrival," most of what the executive branch proposed, the Congress ultimately accepted.[86]

Unfortunately, the superficial nature of defense budget coverage has done more to misinform than inform. The pictures painted by network news over the years have been almost completely devoid of the most basic context. From watching the evening newscasts alone, it would appear that the Reagan administration misspent billions on national defense without any underlying strategy, that defense spending was the main culprit in soaring deficits, and that this spending was also responsible for cuts to programs for the poor and elderly.[87] Actually, the Reagan defense buildup was not, as one analyst noted, "solely or even primarily responsible" for the sudden growth in the deficit between 1981 and 1985. In fact, defense spending accounted for only about one-third of the nearly $300 billion in outlay growth during that period.[88]

In the Bush period reviewed, the main theme was of a Cold War that ended and a defense budget that was not being cut fast enough to reflect this dramatic change. Directly related to this were a number of references to the search for an elusive, and disappointingly small, "peace dividend."

Of the 128 primary defense budget stories analyzed, 92 contained problems of bias or lack of context, nearly 72 percent. Of the 128, 92 reports were associated with the two periods from the Reagan administrations. Another 26 were associated with the Bush administration, and 10 were aired during the Gulf War period. Isolating problematic coverage of the defense budget by administration, it occurred 71.4 percent of the time in the first Reagan administration, 75.8 percent of the time in the second Reagan administration, and 80.7 percent in the Bush administration sample.

It is interesting to note that the budget issue virtually disappeared off the radar screen during the period surveyed during the Clinton administration. While January–April was the time when the administration's key budget decisions were made, there was no television news reporting on them. Newspapers did cover the debate over Clinton's defense budget, but even print coverage was less intense than during the same period in the Reagan years.

Curiously, the networks completely ignored the debate in Congress in early 1994 over whether the Clinton administration was cutting too much from the defense budget. This contrasts with extensive network coverage of the debate over whether Reagan was increasing the defense budget by too much during the periods sampled from the two Reagan administrations.

While the contrast is quite dramatic when comparing network news coverage of the defense budget between the Reagan/Bush and Clinton periods, the same lack of interest in defense cuts was evident in print coverage of the defense budget during the period sampled from the Clinton administration. The logical conclusion: defense increases are treated as more "newsworthy" than defense cuts.

Of the three network news reports that even mentioned the defense budget during the Clinton period sampled, not one was a "defense budget" story. In the first two cases, the focus was on military operations, and in the third, it was the subject of weapons/capabilities, with only a passing reference to the budget.

By contrast, there were 63 budget stories during the same period sampled from the first Reagan administration, 29 budget stories during the second Reagan administration, and 26 during the Bush administration sample period. Unfortunately, problematic coverage during the Reagan and Bush periods consistently topped 70 percent, with most of it being biased against the Reagan administration's attempts to increase the budget. In the case of the Bush administration, the budget was not being cut fast enough.

Throughout the 128 defense budget reports that appeared on ABC World News Tonight, CBS Evening News, and NBC Nightly News during the periods analyzed, there was an unmistakable, underlying point of view: anchors, correspondents, and producers shaped the news to suggest that the nation was spending too much on defense. While the personal views of network journalists should not really matter, in the case of the defense budget, they were too often at center stage. The following examples help illustrate the general approach the evening newscasts took in their coverage of the defense budget.

REAGAN'S "BULLHEADEDNESS"

Attacks on the defense budget increases advocated by President Reagan and Secretary of Defense Weinberger were a fact of life during the Reagan buildup. Such attacks, whether they came from liberal Democrats or conservative Republicans concerned about the mounting deficit, were news. Over time, however, too many news reports failed to adequately explain the views of those in favor of increases.

A typical example of a stacked report occurred on NBC on January 4, 1983. Anchor Roger Mudd led off by saying, "Here in Washington, there is no sign President Reagan is moving to change his economic policies," a clear suggestion that they *should be changed*. NBC White House correspondent Chris Wallace then added that Republican "senators told Mr. Reagan a budget deficit of more than $180 billion is terrifying, intolerable, that something dramatic has to be done." The solution, the report stated, was freezing defense spending alongside the domestic cuts, according to Sen. Paul Laxalt (R-NV) and others, "some of his [Reagan's] closest supporters."

In the one stab at balance, Wallace quoted White House spokesman Larry Speakes who indicated that the president was committed to his defense buildup, and that the president believed defense was his first responsibility. However, Wallace was quick to add that the only one in the administration who agreed with this "hard line" was Defense Secretary Caspar Weinberger. The final piling on came when Mudd intervened to ask Wallace, "Chris, is the president being a bit bullheaded? Why would he willingly take on a second enormous deficit?"

Wallace then talked of the "core of what the president believes in—buildup

of defenses, keep taxes low—this is really Ronald Reagan unvarnished." Having
said that, Wallace noted that administration officials (obviously the more reasonable ones) see the budget submission as part of "a process, not the end. They
openly expect Congress to change what the president submits."

Nowhere in this report was there any background on Reagan's and
Weinberger's rationale for a defense buildup—no mention of the Soviet Union, no
mention of what they dubbed "years of neglect" in defense modernization—only
the unreasonableness of Reagan's push to increase defense spending, which in
turn would increase the deficit, and his "bullheadedness." Such reporting never
even hinted that Reagan and Weinberger were succeeding at securing real increases in defense spending, despite Congress's unwillingness to give the administration everything it wanted.

This exchange between Mudd and Wallace really captured the total inability
of the network news establishment to consider as a legitimate part of the debate
Reagan's view that a defense buildup was needed to restore military capabilities
that had been neglected during the 1970s. Mudd found Reagan's insistence on
increasing defense spending incomprehensible—and he was not alone.

There was, in fact, a conventional wisdom running through the reporting of
all three networks and a clear tilt toward sources and viewpoints completely at
odds with Reagan and Weinberger. They were the stubborn hard-liners, who,
according to most sources, were out of step with other advisors in the administration and even with conservative Republican allies on Capitol Hill.

The approach taken by the networks toward reporting on the defense budget
is a classic example of what Lichter, Rothman, and Lichter outlined in their 1986
study of how journalists' beliefs and attitudes affect their news products. They
found that journalists cited "a mixture of public and private, partisan and nonparti-
san, liberal and conservative sources. But the liberal side consistently outweighs
the conservative." They were quick to add, however, that there is no "conspiracy
to exclude conservative voices," but merely the "human tendency to turn more
often to those you trust, and to trust most those who think most like you do."[89]

In the case of the defense budget, the sources that seemed to be most trusted
cut across liberal and conservative lines, but they had one thing in common: a
belief that the budget needed to be cut. For their part, congressional liberals were
opposed to defense increases on principle because they believed that the US military was strong enough and that resources needed to be directed elsewhere. Indeed,
the cuts to Reagan's defense requests from 1983 to 1985 were shifted to domestic
spending.[90]

Fiscal conservatives in Congress, on the other hand, were opposed to the
increases for quite another reason: the looming deficits built into Reagan's budget
might have threatened economic recovery by increasing interest rates. While
sympathetic to the need for a strong military, they believed cuts had to be made
across the board, including in defense.[91]

Network news coverage reflected these points of view almost exclusively.
Ignored were points about the neglect of the military during the 1970s, the need

to rebuild in the face of continually expanding Soviet military power, and the importance of technological superiority when it comes to military weapons. Related to the technology issue was the need to prevent the Soviet Union from obtaining advanced technology from the West. These points were made consistently by Weinberger, his aides, some allies on Capitol Hill, and there were outside groups like the Heritage Foundation and other conservative activists saying the same thing.[92] But allies of the Weinberger-Reagan line seldom made it on the air.

EVERYONE IS FOR CUTS

Though Congress passed budgets that contained real increases in defense spending each year through 1985,[93] network defense budget coverage told quite a different story. At the beginning of the budget cycle in January 1983, the main concern of the networks was whether the defense budget would be cut to help reduce the projected deficit. By giving favorable coverage to those advocating defense cuts, both within the administration and in Congress, network coverage created the impression that all parties were opposed to Reagan and Weinberger.

For example, on January 5, 1983, NBC anchor Roger Mudd portrayed Reagan as "isolated from his economic advisors on the coming budget deficit." White House correspondent Chris Wallace added that "there is a growing consensus in business and government that the budget Ronald Reagan is now considering could bring economic disaster." Close advisors, like George Shultz, Donald Regan, David Stockman, and Martin Feldstein, were urging military cuts and tax increases. Wallace also mentioned Congressional Budget Office recommendations to cut defense and entitlements and raise taxes.

On January 6, 1983, CBS White House correspondent Lesley Stahl cited some senators, who said the president was ready to compromise in light of the gloomy forecast for his budget, including estimates of low economic growth and high deficits. Stahl noted that Weinberger left a meeting "armed with billions of newly proposed cuts that he's agreed to consider and report back on tomorrow."

A day later, on January 7, ABC Pentagon correspondent John McWethy said that "all those stories about Caspar Weinberger being willing to cut $10 or $11 billion from his $250 billion budget request are simply wrong." McWethy learned that Weinberger had had a private meeting with Reagan and made a case for minimal cuts. "If there are token cuts, Pentagon sources say, they will not come from big strategic programs." NBC, too, reported that the Pentagon could only find cuts of around $2 billion.

By January 9, ABC reported that the president may have to reverse himself on opposition to defense cuts. Correspondent Mike von Fremd reported from the White House that "even close friends and advisers, like Nevada Senator Paul Laxalt, are telling him that present deficits are terrifying and future deficits are even worse."

On January 11, all three networks reported that the reversal sought by so many had finally come about. NBC's Roger Mudd opened by stating that after "saying any cuts in the defense budget would be a risk to national security," Weinberger "has recommended actual spending cuts of about $8 billion." Then Pentagon correspondent Richard Valeriani outlined the approach to the cuts, which included lowering a planned pay raise, adjustments to fuel costs based on lower inflation, and deferring some military construction and putting off some training exercises. Capping off the report was the "instant disagreement" from Capitol Hill. Sen. Carl Levin (D-MI) said the cuts "are not enough and they appear to be in the wrong place."

ABC anchor Frank Reynolds played up the reversal as well, saying that "for months they said it couldn't be done. But now, with Republicans as well as Democrats clamoring for cuts in defense spending to reduce the deficit, the Reagan administration has found more than $11 billion to take out of the Pentagon's new budget." White House correspondent Sam Donaldson referred to "an unsmiling Defense Secretary Weinberger who met reporters today—and no wonder."

CBS anchor Dan Rather portrayed the news in terms of budget director David Stockman winning "an important round." In all three cases, the networks did present brief sound bites from Weinberger saying that the cuts would hurt, but that the administration was preserving the major programs needed to regain US national security.

After covering this early skirmish and a few side issues, like the overly dramatic reports on how the Joint Chiefs of Staff were unhappy (near "mutiny," said Sam Donaldson of ABC; in "revolt" against the president's policies, said Roger Mudd of NBC) with the proposed pay cuts offered up by Weinberger, the networks turned to congressional calls for even greater cuts in the defense budget.

On January 26, NBC reported a heated meeting between Weinberger and Senate Republicans, who were calling for even bigger cuts. The next day, ABC's John McWethy did a long piece on the loss of public and congressional support for increases in defense spending. In a rare stab at balance, on the same broadcast, ABC anchor Frank Reynolds interviewed Weinberger, who had an opportunity to make a direct case for defense spending.

Yet, the weight of coverage was squarely against a defense increase. On January 28, CBS anchor Dan Rather reported how "a flood of leaks" had revealed that Reagan's fiscal 1984 budget will freeze or cut social programs while boosting defense spending by billions. Rather added that "these proposals assume a fiscal '84 federal deficit of almost $190 billion, and believe it or not, that's $20 billion less than the whopping deficit the White House is now predicting for this year."

A January 31 report from ABC's Frank Reynolds began by quoting Democrats, who said the "strong medicine" applied to the federal budget by the president was mainly intended for "the poor, the elderly, and the sick." Washington correspondent Dan Cordtz then reported on the Pentagon as being the "biggest winner." Spending on weapons would "skyrocket." But, he added, there are even winners and losers within the military. The losers: people in the armed forces who face a pay freeze and retirees who would receive no cost-of-living adjustment. "So this budget is not only tilted toward the military and away from social programs, but toward the purchase of weapons and away from the care and feeding of the people who will use those weapons, a fact that has not gone unnoticed among Mr. Reagan's critics," Cordtz concluded.

Other coverage related to the defense budget included sharp exchanges between Weinberger and congressional critics on all sides. For variety, there was the occasional report about the costs of weapons being underestimated, as occurred on February 3 on NBC, or the report on how every $1 billion spent on defense costs the economy 18,000 jobs, as CBS reported on February 6, citing "an economic consulting firm." Such an assertion was highly questionable, but there was no attempt to validate the claim or cite other economists.[94]

By March 1983, the National Governors Association (NGA) had weighed in, so the networks turned to reporting on its proposals for cuts to the defense budget. ABC anchor Sam Donaldson framed the development this way on February 27: "Meeting here in Washington, the governors moved toward urging the administration to consider tax increases and defense spending cuts in order to reduce federal deficits, deficits they described as ruinous to our economy." For those paying close attention, ABC correspondent Sander Vanocur did mention that the NGA was actually calling for limits to the growth of defense spending to between 4 and 6 percent from fiscal 1984 to 1985, and then to between 3 and 5 percent during the 1984 to 1988 time period.

In very short reports on March 1, NBC anchor Tom Brokaw reported on the NGA's call for "deep cuts" in the president's defense budget, while CBS anchor Dan Rather more correctly stated that "the nation's governors went beyond state lines concerns today, and beyond any position they've taken before to demand a cut in the growth of federal defense spending."

The remainder of the coverage in March focused on the battles between Reagan and the House over his defense budget. Reagan's now famous March 23 speech proposing SDI was actually part of the administration's overall strategy to focus attention on defense spending. Calling for new defensive technology was one way of claiming the high ground. The SDI proposal, however, quickly eclipsed other points in the speech about Soviet military power and military developments in Nicaragua. In April, the networks turned their attention to Reagan's "battles" with the Senate over defense spending. In actuality, an economic recovery was just getting underway, some 55 percent of the American public supported the Reagan administration's policies, and there was a consensus in Congress for an increase in defense spending, just not to the levels requested by the administration.[95] Ultimately, the Senate Budget Committee cut the proposed 10 percent increase in defense spending in half.

DEFENSE INCREASES NOT FAIR

In the second Reagan administration, during the 1985 period analyzed, the networks often used the issue of fairness to attack defense spending. Take NBC and CBS on February 1, 1985. NBC's Tom Brokaw chatted with John Dancy, who was covering Capitol Hill. Brokaw queried him about the chances of military spending going up while domestic spending went down. Dancy's reply: "That is never going to fly here on Capitol Hill. Congress wants a budget that is perceived as fair."

On the same day, CBS's Dan Rather began by saying "green pastures for defense spending, and the expected brown-out of more American farmers." White House correspondent Lesley Stahl then said that eight of the thirteen cabinet departments will be cut, but not defense, which will rise to 35 percent of the budget by 1990. She went on to say that the budget had Congress up in arms. Sen. Charles Grassley (R-IA) was quoted saying that it's unfair to take away the subsidy for farmers and to give it to defense industry.

On February 2, 1985, ABC reported on the budget, noting that only defense would get increases, and that the reining in of government was focused on health care, housing, and other social programs. NBC anchor Connie Chung cited Democrats who said the budget proposal was "dead on arrival," especially "because the Reagan administration refuses to halt increases in defense spending." A day later, CBS anchor Bob Schieffer reported that the proposed increase in defense spending "is getting a bad review from Moscow," as if there were some surprise there.

On February 5, during testimony before Congress, OMB Director David Stockman caused a stir when he called the military retirement system a "scandal" and an "outrage." He said that "the institutional forces in the military are more concerned about protecting their retirement benefits than they are about protecting the security of the American people." All three networks quickly seized on this sound bite, which was certainly newsworthy, since it reflected a serious division between OMB and the Pentagon. However, the finer points of the debate over the military retirement system were never elaborated upon. The follow-up reports focused, predictably, on Stockman's being in hot water, with criticism being leveled from many quarters, and whether he would keep his job, not on whether his view of the retirement system had any merit.

On March 5, the Reagan administration was handed what ABC anchor Peter Jennings called a "stunning defeat," as the Senate Budget Committee froze defense spending at current levels. Jennings did not explain, however, that those "current levels" were at historic highs. CBS anchor Dan Rather made a similar report, saying the Senate committee "took a tentative vote to bury big increases in defense spending."

More heated exchanges between Weinberger and congressional committees during March were covered, along with a few reports on Reagan's jockeying with the Senate over the rate of increase for defense, along with talk of a possible compromise. On April 4, CBS anchor Dan Rather reported that the defense budget approved by the Senate Armed Services Committee, which limited defense spending to a 3 percent increase over inflation, would lead to a "knockdown, drag-out Senate floor fight."

Curiously, these various skirmishes were never really put in context. In all the reports examined, never once was there any explanation of how a particular "defeat" or "victory" fit into the larger budget process. Some committee votes are obviously more important than others. While the Budget Committee in each house sets overall spending ceilings, the Armed Services Committee[96] makes specific authorizations for levels of spending in each category, from weapons procurement to operations and pay, and the Defense subcommittee of the Appropriations Committee in each house, in theory, appropriates monies based on the authorization. Sometimes, however, the process is not that logical and an appropriation may be decided before an authorization.

The other part of the context was how incredibly successful the Reagan administration had been in sustaining a defense buildup for its entire first term. As was pointed out earlier, Weinberger himself believed that the administration would be lucky to maintain increases for more than a few months or a year. What they actually accomplished was, judged by historical standards, remarkable.[97] Moreover, these pitched "battles" the networks described were over a few percentage points of *increase*; the battles were never over real *cuts* in defense spending. There is a rather big distinction between fights over the rate of increase and actual cuts in real terms, a point the 1996 debate over Medicare proved the networks still had not learned.

While viewers of a 22-minute newscast do not need to be fully acquainted with the most esoteric aspects of defense budgeting, it would help for them to know the overall context in which budget numbers are cited. Why not tell viewers that a particular vote may indicate the congressional sentiment of one committee, but it is just a small step in a much larger process (or not cover it at all if it is insignificant)? As it is, it must seem to the network viewer that budgets are being voted upon many times each year, with seeming victories on one side often turning into defeats as the process moves along.

Moreover, the "play-by-play" coverage tends to exaggerate the battles and the jockeying at the expense of actual issue coverage. What is clear about the two periods analyzed during the Reagan administrations is the absence of defenders of the Reagan buildup. It appears, from network coverage, that Reagan and Weinberger were on one side and everyone else was on the other side. If that had really been the case, the defense buildup would have never materialized. In reality, the administration sustained the buildup for four consecutive years *with* congressional support.[98]

That story, however, was never told, nor were stories about the improvements in weapons systems, the quality of personnel, and other mundane areas, like training and spare parts.

THAT ELUSIVE "PEACE DIVIDEND"

The Bush administration was also subjected to incomplete and unbalanced reporting on the defense budget. In the 1990 period analyzed, the networks clearly did not approve of the pace of post–Cold War cuts—these cuts were much too slow for their liking.

Another aspect of coverage during the Bush administration was the quest for a "peace dividend." Unfortunately, the networks tended to raise expectations about such a windfall without the slightest understanding of what it initially costs to close overseas bases, ship whole units back to the United States, and to slow planned weapons purchases, which increases per unit costs and sometimes requires the payment of penalties built into contracts.

To take some specific examples, on January 9, 1990, CBS correspondent Mark Phillips reported on the National Urban League's State of Black America report. The league, he reported, wanted the "peace dividend" spent on America's inner cities. According to the report's estimate of savings from lower military costs in Europe, the peace dividend was going to amount to $50 billion, which could be spent on "education, housing, health care and job care for American minorities."

After outlining all of these possibilities, Phillips then added that the Bush administration said there would be no peace dividend, citing Secretary of Defense Dick Cheney, who said, "There's not going to be a lot of money to spread around the landscape to go spend on other purposes." Phillips never told viewers which of these views was closer to reality. In this instance, some basic research on the costs associated with downsizing forces would have revealed that Cheney's view was correct.

Again, on January 14, the peace dividend was at issue. ABC anchor Carole Simpson said that the dramatic changes in Eastern Europe have "much of official Washington talking about a peace dividend, the idea that defense spending can now be cut back and the money saved put to other uses."

ABC correspondent Cokie Roberts then said that the Bush administration "thinks it's too early to cash in on the thaw in the Cold War." Cheney and former Defense Secretary Weinberger explained that there is no large pot of money to be shifted and that, while the threat has changed, it has not altogether disappeared. On the other side were New York Gov. Mario Cuomo and Sen. James Sasser (D-TN), chairman of the Senate Budget Committee, both calling for faster diversion of defense monies to other purposes. Maybe Simpson should have begun the report by saying that, so far, "official Washington" has proven itself to be sorely uninformed on issues related to the "peace dividend."

Again, as if suddenly surprised, ABC anchor Peter Jennings reported on January 22 that all the talk of a peace dividend "had cold water thrown on it in a report from the Congressional Budget Office. The report says the reduction of American troops in Eastern Europe—or, rather, in Western Europe would, at the very most, save about $3 billion a year. And the Budget Office does not see any other significant savings before the mid-1990s."

In the view of the networks, one reason this peace dividend was not emerging was the failure of the administration to cut big weapons programs. For example, on January 29, 1990, ABC's Diane Sawyer introduced a defense budget story by Pentagon reporter Bob Zelnick. She cited Senator Sasser, who said the Bush budget "was a combination of Cold War leftovers and warmed-over Reagan." Others, she noted, said "it failed to take advantage of the so-called peace dividend."

Zelnick stated that "this budget was the Pentagon's first chance to show how the crumbling of communism in Eastern Europe might affect US military programs. But Secretary Cheney's principal adjustment to the changed world situation is to deactivate two Army tank divisions. . . . Other than that, the budget cut of 2.6 percent after inflation continues a trend that began five years ago to reduce the overall deficit."

Zelnick proceeded to report that Cheney would retire some old weapons and stop buying some others, like the Apache helicopter and M-1 tank, both designed for war in Europe. But Cheney "wants more money for the Strategic Defense Initiative, the C-17 cargo plane, two Seawolf attack submarines, advanced tactical jet fighters, and five Stealth bombers at more than half a billion dollars apiece. Critics charge these weapons were designed for a war against the Soviets and should be reexamined."

Both Sen. Sam Nunn (D-GA) and Rep. Les Aspin (D-WI) then explained why the government could not afford these new weapons. For "balance," Admiral William Crowe was allowed to say that the prospect of war had not gone away altogether before Zelnick concluded that "still, many say Pentagon plans have been overtaken by events."

One aspect of the budget debate was placed in the proper context, probably because it could be explained in terms of politics: Cheney's proposal to close bases to reduce infrastructure costs. CBS Pentagon correspondent David Martin reported on January 24 that these proposals would cause a "firestorm" on Capitol Hill. Martin ran a sound bite by Rep. Richard Armey (R-TX), who said, "You've got to expect a congressman to act like a congressman. And those congressmen that represent the exact locations will probably be resistant." Martin also explained that Cheney was sending a clear message to Congress: if you want a smaller military, this is what it's going to look like.

Even in this area, however, there were some problems in reporting. Take, for example, CBS correspondent Bob Schieffer, who offered this sound bite by Rep. Patricia Schroeder (D-CO): "Ninety-nine percent of civilian personnel that will be laid off by base closures are in Democratic districts." To Schieffer, this was a sign of the "heavy fire" the base closure proposal was drawing. What he and Schroeder seemed oblivious to was the history of conservative southern Democrats' efforts to have bases built in their districts. The idea that Cheney had somehow deliberately targeted Democratic districts was pure nonsense.

Overall, the strongest theme running through defense budget coverage of this period of the Bush administration was the idea that proposed cuts did not go far enough. A February 1 report by NBC correspondent Andrea Mitchell was typical. She reported on Democrats calling for deeper defense cuts and then highlighted an exchange between Sen. Alan Dixon (D-IL) and Cheney, in which Dixon said the administration's cautious approach did not make sense. Mitchell then explained how the "sharpest attack was against Bush's proposal to spend $4 billion more on nuclear weapons: the B-2 bomber, strategic defense, the MX missile to be put on rail cars, new short-range missiles for West Germany, even though the German government has said it won't accept them." (The B-2, of course, is not a nuclear weapon, nor is strategic defense.)

Sen. Ted Kennedy (D-MA) was featured next by Mitchell, whom she said called Bush's budget "preposterous." Kennedy suggested cuts in SDI, the MX missile, and the B-2 bomber programs.

On February 6, CBS White House correspondent Lesley Stahl opened her report by saying, "If you watched President Bush today, you would think the Cold War was colder than ever." Stahl was traveling with Bush, who had gone to California to watch Army exercises. Her interpretation: "Mr. Bush is here to fight for his new military budget, with its expensive arsenal of strategic weapons, as if the Soviet threat hasn't diminished at all." She went on to say that the president's budget would "cut as much out of Medicare as out of defense." Yet, Stahl did not bother to explain what if any connection there was between these two cuts.

On NBC the same day, White House correspondent John Cochran took a similar approach, stating at one point that "Bush at times seemed at war with himself, as he applauded events in Moscow while warning against any letdown in US military preparedness." After referring to Bush's "big-ticket weapons" priorities, Cochran concluded by saying, "Those in Congress who want a big peace dividend say Bush is guilty of what Gorbachev would call old thinking. The president prefers to call it prudent thinking."

A month later, ABC anchor Peter Jennings picked up the budget story again. The twist on March 7, however, was almost an exact repeat of his January 22 report noting that "cold water" had been thrown on the peace dividend, then estimated at only $3 billion. This time, he said there was another "piece of bad news for people who may be expecting a large peace dividend in dollars from the end of the arms race. The Congressional Budget Office says today that even if the US and Soviet Union reach a new strategic arms agreement, the savings could be as little as three billion dollars a year. And none of it coming in fiscal 1991." News about the peace dividend clearly had a life of its own, quite separate from reality.

None of the networks picked up the budget story again until April 20, when Peter Jennings announced that the "enormously influential" Sen. Sam Nunn (D-GA) called for a cut of $6 billion more in the defense budget, a fair description of Nunn, but where were the "influential" opponents of deeper cuts?

On April 26, all three networks put the Pentagon's grudging "deep cuts" in perspective. ABC's Jennings began by saying the Air Force and Navy were "going to lose 457 of the aircraft they want, which would save, at least on paper, $35 billion. Sounds like a lot of money. And the secretary's offer is clearly the result of the diminishing threat of war. Yet it may not be enough for the Pentagon to win the battle of the budget." Jennings then turned to Pentagon correspondent Bob Zelnick, who explained how cutting numbers of weapons and stretching them out actually costs more. In the case of the B-2, Zelnick pointed out that Rep. John Kasich (R-OH) wanted to cut the program even more, from Cheney's proposed 75 aircraft to 16.

CBS Pentagon correspondent David Martin gave a similar report on the weapons cuts and how that drives up costs, citing the B-2 and stating how opponents of the program were disappointed with Cheney's numbers. Then Martin noted that no matter how far Cheney cuts, "Congress will almost certainly make even deeper cuts."

NBC's man at the Pentagon, Fred Francis, told the same story, noting Cheney "enhanced his image as a Cold Warrior," trimming only $2.5 billion from a budget that "critics say ignores the prospect of peace with the Soviets." He, too, noted that the price of the B-2, "the most expensive plane ever built," would "soar" as fewer bombers were built.

The last report during the four-month period came on April 29, when ABC reported that both Sen. Sam Nunn (D-GA) and Rep. Les Aspin (D-WI), the respective chairmen of the Senate and House Armed Services Committees, were calling for deeper cuts.

All in all, coverage of the defense budget during the 1990 budget cycle was skewed in ways very similar to the Reagan periods. Like Weinberger and Reagan, who were "isolated," Bush and Cheney were portrayed as out of step, as "Cold Warriors" in a post–Cold War world. Additionally, cuts that were proposed were never enough, with the bulk of reporting being devoted to those who disagreed with the Bush administration's approach.

As with Reagan and Weinberger, little serious reporting was directed at Bush's and Cheney's rationale for moving cautiously with cuts.

Chapter 5

Weapons That Do Not Work?

Something happened early in 1991. After being misled for at least a decade, Americans saw with their own eyes a few images of military weapons systems that actually worked. From the M1 Abrams tank to the AH-64 Apache helicopter to the various precision-guided munitions that found their marks in Baghdad, these weapons performed well in the hands of trained personnel.

Speaking about the extensive television coverage of the Gulf War, former Secretary of Defense Caspar Weinberger said, "It was important for the public to realize what accurate weapons we had. We had a pretty steady diet of how expensive they were, how they wouldn't work—they wouldn't work in the desert; Aegis cruisers were too heavy and wouldn't float; helicopters wouldn't fly; pilots and sailors didn't have the intelligence needed to handle this sophisticated equipment; and it was all a waste of money."[99]

Unfortunately, outside of war, weapons do not make news when they work, and that has been the problem with network news coverage of weapons systems dating back to the first Reagan administration. In fact, evening news coverage of weapons and their capabilities has been problematic anywhere from 47.7 percent to 75.8 percent of the time. And while weapons coverage was not nearly as extensive in the Bush and Clinton periods sampled as it was in the Reagan periods, the quality of coverage was actually worse, with problematic coverage taking place 75.8 percent of the time in the Bush period and 72.7 percent in the Clinton period. That compares with a problematic rate of 51.6 percent in the first Reagan period and 47.7 percent in the second Reagan period.

Problems in coverage of weapons systems occurred mainly when anchors or correspondents slanted a story, most often to the side of the critics, and when correspondents failed to present adequate context as they characterized problems during the normal weapons development process. Add to this the networks' proclivity to report crashes and other accidents, and the picture of military weapons becomes highly misleading at best.

Most often, the networks chose to cover a weapons system in terms of some problem that had suddenly come to light. It might have been a General Accounting Office report that tipped them off, a congressional staffer, or a Pentagon whistle blower. In any case, the network (or networks) swooped in, covered all the problems or "defects" and then headed on to the next story.

Surprisingly, of the 190 reports covering weapons and their capabilities, only 59 emanated from the Pentagon beat. Nearly half the reports, 71, came from the anchor desk, where any depth and context were precluded by time. Another 51 reports came from the other Washington beats, including the White House. The other 9 were reported by foreign correspondents.

The bottom line: less than a third of the time were weapons issues covered by the Pentagon beat where the real expertise resided. The result is predictable. Collectively, weapons coverage was sensational, uninformed, and very misleading to anyone not intimately familiar with the Pentagon's complicated acquisition process.

F/A-18: $40 BILLION MISFIT?

Take CBS's February 21, 1983, report on the F/A-18 Hornet aircraft. Anchor Dan Rather began by saying, "The flight of the F/A-18 has never been smooth. From drawing board to runway the plane had trouble winning acceptance. . . . Now there are signs this expensive aircraft might have trouble getting off the ground in the next Pentagon budget."

Then Pentagon correspondent Bill Lynch explained how the aircraft went from its original concept of a "light-weight, low-cost" fighter and attack aircraft into "a heavy high technology plane costing three times more." Lynch next cited a former undersecretary of the Navy who tried to kill the program and a Marine Corps colonel who suggested that range was an issue in the plane's ability to perform the attack mission, and that it was very expensive in its role as a fighter plane for the Marines.

Lynch then added more about the F/A-18's limited combat range before allowing two brief sound bites from Marines who were satisfied with the F/A-18. Next came references to the investigation Weinberger had launched to determine hidden cost overruns and to sources who said the Pentagon may cut significant numbers from the total program. Finally, Lynch noted that "killing the Hornet won't be easy," explaining how powerful congressmen have interests in the program because parts are manufactured in their districts and states. The closer: "The F/A-18 seems to be a classic case of a good weapon that doesn't quite match the job it's been given. In today's budget climate, the question is, can the nation afford a $40 billion misfit?"

Apart from the two brief sound bites from the Marine aviators, the deck was stacked here from the beginning. References to the *expensive* aircraft, its problem with range, and the presumption that killing this plane was the noble course of action that had so far been foiled, all add up to an unbalanced approach. Where was a supporter of the program who could address the cost and range issues? And where was someone who could provide context for the dual role of the aircraft: how it fit into the carrier aircraft mix and the close air support role for the Marines? Moreover, nothing Lynch said even hinted at what he termed "a classic case of a *good* weapon that doesn't quite match the job it's been given."

In the end, not only would the F/A-18 survive, but after the Navy botched the A-12 aircraft program, a modified version of the tested and proven F/A-18 would become the Navy's best hope for the future of carrier aviation.

C-5B: ANOTHER EDSEL?

Another target of stacked reporting was what is now the venerable C-5 transport aircraft. In 1983, when the Reagan administration decided to build the C-5B, an improved version of the C-5A, NBC could not find one positive thing to say. Anchor Roger Mudd noted, while introducing an April 25, 1983, report, how the "old C-5A proved unsafe, but now the new C-5B is overrunning its cost."

Pentagon correspondent Richard Valeriani then said that the C-5A Galaxy cargo plane "earned a reputation as the Edsel of the aircraft industry with its cracked wings, expensive maintenance, and a notorious $2 billion cost overrun." He then went on to say that "despite Lockheed's track record," the company was given a contract to build 50 C-5Bs at a fixed price. The final piling on came when Valeriani cited the Project on Military Procurement, a self-appointed watchdog group whose own record was less than spotless.[100]

The significant cost overruns of the C-5A are well documented. Famed whistle blower Ernest Fitzgerald provided his account of what he called "The Great Plane Robbery," referring to the money the government eventually reimbursed the Lockheed Corporation for its cost overruns.[101] But what Fitzgerald and other critics did not dwell upon was the revolutionary nature of the technology involved, along with the difficulty of projecting costs of untested technology. In 1968, the specialized press did explain how the world's largest aircraft revolutionized strategy and technology. Among the technological advances being pursued: the C-5A was the largest aircraft in the world, which introduced a whole range of aerodynamic challenges; its engine was twice as powerful as any transport engine of its day, and involved new design techniques; and its ability to carry the heaviest loads placed special emphasis on new materials and precision tooling. The whole process involved quantum leaps in manufacturing and aerospace technology.[102]

On the strategic level, the C-5A had a profound impact. As one writer put it: "For the first time military planners will be able to move large numbers of troops and their vehicles, artillery, armor, and other equipment and supplies to almost any point in the world within hours—combat ready and without depending on prepositioned supplies. Men and machines arrive together, the so-called 'unit integrity' that has long been a military dream."[103]

Indeed, the C-5A's first operational experience in a combat environment involved the emergency airlift of six 49-ton, M-48 tanks from Yokota Air Base, Japan, to Da Nang Air Base, South Vietnam, on May 3, 1972. On that mission, the crews unloaded the tanks in less time than 7 minutes, and the C-5As took off again within 30 minutes.[104] The newest airlifter also contributed to the success of the airlift that resupplied Israel with urgently needed war materials during the 1973 Yom Kippur War.[105]

Over the following years, the C-5A was steadily improved through a series of modification programs, including one that strengthened its wings. By the time the C-5B program was initiated in order to provide additional heavy airlift, a whole range of improvements were available, including the wings, advanced avionics, an improved engine, and an advanced system for detecting problems.[106]

The bottom line: the case of the C-5B was a far cry from the days when an unproven technology had first been developed. By 1983, the C-5A had been in operation for over a decade, and it had provided the United States with a unique capability, which was put to good use on many occasions.

For his part, Valeriani chose to question Lockheed's track record, which, if anything, is rather distinguished. In the area of transport aircraft, its C-130 Hercules, whose first flight was in 1955, has been the mainstay of air forces around the world. And Lockheed has produced many famous aircraft over the years, including the Hudson bomber, the C-56, C-57, C-59, and C-60 transports, the highly successful P-38 Lightning fighter during World War II, the F-80 Shooting Star jet fighter of Korean War fame, the SR-71 reconnaissance aircraft, and the C-141 airlifter, not to mention more recent aircraft like the F-117 stealth fighter and the F-22 air superiority fighter.[107]

Valeriani's report clearly lacked historical perspective and even a fair understanding of how the C-5A performed after overcoming its development problems, not to mention the unique capability it provided the nation with its ability to transport heavy equipment. Until the introduction of the C-17 in 1995, the C-5 was the only transport capable of moving the largest loads or the heaviest equipment, like tanks.

Valeriani's focus on the C-5's problems, however, was typical of weapons coverage in the 1980s. Other stories analyzed during the 1983 and 1985 Reagan periods featured questions about the basing scheme and need for the MX missile, questions about F-15 and F-16 fighters being cannibalized because spare parts were not reaching field units despite all the money invested, a freak accident at a Pershing II missile site in West Germany, and a series of crashes ranging from the Blackhawk helicopter to the F-16, A-4, and B-52 aircraft. In the same category was the collision of the USS *Coral Sea* carrier with an oil tanker.

In fact, out of the 129 stories during the Reagan periods, only about 6 were what could be deemed stories about a positive development in this area, from a few missile tests that succeeded to a positive note about microelectronic technology. Overall, the distinguishing feature of weapons coverage is the focus on problems reported out of context and bad news.

HUMVEE AND "INVESTIGATIVE REPORTS"

Among "investigative reports" was the story about the Army's "Humvee," a multipurpose vehicle that was being built to replace the tried-and-true jeep. In a long-form segment on March 5, 1985, ABC correspondent Peter Lance portrayed the "Humvee" as a dud that was not up to replacing even the "outmoded" and "unstable" jeep, as anchor Peter Jennings described it in his introduction.

Lance, who discovered problem after problem as he "investigated" the development of the Humvee, relied heavily on the General Accounting Office (GAO), as so many investigative correspondents do. The problem, though, is that the GAO's little blue-covered reports usually trickle out long after the "problems" cited have been found and corrected. Moreover, auditors seem to have little appreciation for the development *process*. Still, print and broadcast news organizations dutifully report on such *newly released* findings, usually without any countervailing viewpoint or overall context.

As it turns out, investigative correspondents seldom investigate. As one of their own has pointed out, what they do is report on what the government has already investigated.[108] And seldom do they have the background and knowledge to put complex investigations into the proper context.

In his report, Lance cited a two-year-old Marine Corps memo that mentioned "excessive tire usage, excessive corrosion, frequent replacement of power steering and power brake systems, and serious problems during missile firing." A year after the Marine memo, the GAO reported that the Humvee's radiator was subject to clogging, that there were air leaks in the fuel system, and that there were frequent frame and body cracks. According to Lance, the Army ignored these reports and went ahead with risky production.

While then Sen. Dan Quayle (R-IN) was allowed to say that all those problems indeed had been fixed, Lance intoned that ABC News had "learned" that a number of these problems have yet to be resolved. Two, in particular, involved the ability of a Blackhawk helicopter to safely transport the Humvee and the ability of the Humvee to ford streams up to 60 inches deep. There were also problems with bolts holding the front axles and with the drive shaft.

In the end, Lance allowed the Army to make the point that, like any other car, you fix what needs to be fixed as you go along. "But," Lance concluded, "the critics insist that a combat vehicle isn't quite the same as a Ford or a Chevy. And if the Humvee breaks down after it's built, it won't be so easy to order a recall, especially if the Humvee, like the Jeep, ever goes to war."

Just two months later, two *Washington Post* reporters, both of whom had covered the military, would come to just the opposite conclusion on the Humvee. They wrote that the Humvee had cleared all hurdles in an extensive development process that did indeed correct the many problems uncovered along the way. Citing independent auditors, they called it "a commendable improvement over its predecessors, despite dozens of nettlesome glitches during development, from faulty brakes to fractured axles." Even the GAO finally came around, they reported.[109] If Lance had done a more thorough "investigation," he might have come to the same conclusion. But, then again, it might not have been considered "news," given the networks' preconceptions and selection process.

A "QUESTIONABLE" F-117

The December 1989 invasion of Panama introduced the first operational appearance of the F-117 stealth fighter. After initial reports that the fighter had hit its targets, then Secretary of Defense Dick Cheney had the embarrassing job of correcting the record. But the networks, which were already having a field day with the $100 million cost of the fighter, never put any of this in context. Stories were slanted toward the price tag and the plane's "questionable" capabilities.

April 1990 saw two "unveilings" of the F-117 on the evening newscasts. The first occurred on April 3, when the Pentagon released videotape of the F-117 in flight. CBS anchor Dan Rather opened by saying the "Defense Department went public today with details of its expensive stealth fighter jet. The Pentagon did so amid questions about what all this stealth technology is costing, whether it actually works, and whether it's needed."

On to David Martin at the Pentagon, who at least provided some background on the program and allowed a Pentagon spokesman to say that the F-117 "tells us that stealth can be developed, can be used on an operational aircraft, is a successful technology, that it works." But the thrust of Martin's report was the price tag. "But at what cost?" was his reply to the spokesman's claims. Martin then outlined the high price of better than $100 million per aircraft and said this could prevent stealth from becoming the technology of the future. The final note by Martin questioned whether the F-117 had a mission after the changes in Eastern Europe and whether another stealth fighter should be developed. The "questions" posited by Rather and Martin as the basis for this report clearly slanted what could have been a fairly straight reporting job, something ABC Pentagon correspondent Bob Zelnick did manage to do on the same evening.

For his part, Zelnick balanced background on the program and the aircraft's capabilities against the fact that the F-117 has not really been tested and that some say its use in Panama was nothing more than an advertisement for stealth. Zelnick also mentioned the cost, but this was his approach: "The Air Force purchased 59 F-117s at a cost of $6.5 billion, just over $100 million a plane, right on budget." Price was not the thrust of this report, but the report itself was still hard-hitting.

Like CBS's Martin, NBC's Pentagon correspondent, Fred Francis, was obsessed with the price tag in his April 3 report. After NBC anchor Jane Pauley's reference to the $106 million price tag, "four times more expensive than a conventional fighter," Francis noted that it was "the slowest, most costly fighter in the Air Force." He added shortly thereafter: "But defense economists are not sure what the taxpayers have bought for the total price of $6.5 billion." Francis did talk about the capabilities and carried the Pentagon spokesman's sound bite, with a balancing and more skeptical sound bite from an outside expert. In the end, however, Francis returned to cost, by citing another stealth project underway, the B-2 bomber, whose half-a-billion price tag had caused "shock" in Congress.

Two days later, in a short anchor report, NBC's Tom Brokaw was first to announce that what Cheney had previously described as the F-117's operational success in Panama had not been accurate. In fact, Brokaw stated, one of the two bombs had fallen way off target and the defense secretary had been kept in the dark by the Air Force.

On April 21, the second "unveiling" of the F-117 took place, this time with the real article displayed before the public on the flight line at Nellis Air Force Base, Nevada. And this time, all three networks zeroed in on questions about the F-117's performance in Panama.

CBS anchor Bob Schieffer opened with reference to "an auspicious event. It involved a state-of-the-art warplane whose accuracy has become the target of some questions." Pentagon correspondent David Martin then described the scene at Nellis, noting that the US Air Force spent $6.5 billion for 59 planes and "it's proud of what it bought." An Air Force spokesman then said the F-117 is the only operational aircraft to employ both stealth and pinpoint accuracy in delivering weapons. This was Martin's cue to talk about the stealth fighter being "under a cloud caused by questions about its performance in last December's invasion of Panama."

After noting that Cheney had initially announced the F-117 "had performed flawlessly," Martin stated that one of the bombs was hundreds of yards off target, "a fact that was kept from the secretary of defense until a reporter for the *New York Times* took pictures of the craters." Martin, at least, did explain that the Air Force "still claims the fighter performed exactly as advertised." He cited an Air Force pilot who said the bombs went exactly where they were aimed. The problem, Martin noted, was that one of the pilots aimed at the wrong point. "And now the Air Force Inspector General is attempting to determine why the bad news never reached the secretary of defense."

Martin's report was the most balanced of the three, even with its premise of "questions" and "clouds" hanging over the aircraft. For its part, ABC began with a note by anchor Carole Simpson about the unprecedented look at the F-117. "But despite today's spectacular ceremony," she added, "there are still serious questions about the new stealth technology."

ABC Pentagon correspondent Bob Zelnick made a brief reference to the plane flying in daylight before he framed the event in terms of the Pentagon seeking public support for other stealth projects, like the B-2 bomber, the A-12 fighter, and what was then called the Advanced Tactical Fighter (now the F-22), which, he noted, "all face serious budgetary pressures." He then turned to the F-117's performance in Panama, where "the Air Force now concedes one of the planes was unable to get a fix on its target." Next he noted a "glitch" in the B-2 program, referring to hairline cracking in the rear section of the plane. He concluded by saying that sources predict that Cheney will not cancel any of the stealth planes but may decide to buy fewer numbers.

The F-117's "big price tag" led off anchor Garrick Utley's introduction of the

NBC report that same evening. Pentagon correspondent Fred Francis then picked up on cost again, before adding that in its only test in combat in Panama one of the fighters missed its target. Francis then said that the "Air Force stuck with its story about the fighter's performance," as he introduced a sound bite from an Air Force spokesman. Then it was the critics' turn. They charged that the Air Force "fudged the truth" to help build a case for the B-2 bombers, which cost $530 million a plane. This "ploy" has angered many congressmen. These congressmen, according to Francis, also said that, even if the F-117 is the greatest aircraft ever built, the nation does not need another stealth plane, the B-2 bomber, "here in the waning days of the Cold War."

This early focus on the F-117 was certainly shallow, but much of the blame goes to the Air Force, for not making public from the start the missed aimpoint. While the networks were reflexively focused on the price tag of the F-117, the Air Force gave them an excuse to muddy the waters with "serious questions" about performance, something that could have been avoided with a simple explanation of the difference between pilot error and aircraft capability.

THE PRE–DESERT STORM APACHE

The Army's AH-64 Apache helicopter was another victim of misleading network reporting. One example was an ABC report on April 18, 1990. Anchor Peter Jennings set the stage, citing "more bad news for the Army's helicopter program." With less tension in Europe, Secretary of Defense Dick Cheney was canceling an order for 168 Apaches. The Apache, with its anti-tank missiles, Jennings explained, was designed to knock out Soviet tanks in Europe. Additionally, the GAO will tell Congress to stop buying any new Apaches "because they are seriously flawed."

On to Pentagon correspondent Bob Zelnick, who proceeded to refer to a new GAO study on the Apache. It cited "enormous maintenance problems," noted that rotor blades have broken down almost ten times more often than the Army expected, and claimed the 30mm cannons repeatedly failed to work. Then Zelnick added this whopper: "What's more, during recent operations in Panama, the Army could not use the Apache to support US troops in close combat with the enemy. The reason? Apache's weapons are so destructive, they could have endangered US forces." It probably did not occur to Zelnick that a helicopter designed as an anti-tank weapon was not going to be directed against a force that had little in the way of armor.

On the other hand, the 11 Apaches deployed in Panama were used to fly against targets at night, taking advantage of the helicopter's forward-looking infrared radar system (FLIR). Noriega's headquarters was virtually destroyed by the Apaches' Hellfire anti-tank missiles, and of the 200 hours flown by Apaches during the Panama invasion, 138 were flown at night.[110]

This report by ABC was another example of the complete failure to provide any context. At the same time Jennings was taking the GAO gospel to heart and declaring the Apache "seriously flawed," Secretary of the Army Michael P. W. Stone, while admitting logistics problems and diagnostic problems, pointed out that on the Army's last Reforger exercises in Europe, the Apache's readiness rate was 85 percent, well over the 75 percent requirement. He also noted that maintenance problems reported from Panama were exaggerated, citing readiness rates of 80 percent if the one Apache damaged in transport was not included.[111]

The Apache is another case of a major technological advance that takes time to mature. Like other new systems, after its introduction in 1984, the Apache had serious growing pains, including problems with the main rotor blade debonding, the main rotor strap pack cracking, design flaws in the shaft-driven compressor, bearing failures in the tail-rotor swashplate, and jamming of the 30mm gun as a result of problems with the ammunition feed system.[112]

Then there are the complex avionics. One technical writer put it this way: "A major problem is the Apache's technical complexity. The Army compares it to the Air Force F-16. Its jet-like cockpits are packed with problems waiting to happen."[113] The Apache also has complex subsystems and components. The Target Acquisition and Designation System (TADS) alone contains 26 major electrical, optical, and mechanical components.[114]

Nevertheless, the complexity was seldom explained, nor were the occasional successes of the Apache in an operational environment, where the system was gradually coming into its own. In October 1990, for example, at the same time the GAO was again blasting the Apache for mission-capable rates below 50 percent, the Army was reporting an overall rate of 75 percent, with an 85 percent rate in Desert Shield.[115] Which report made the news?

That same month, the GAO asserted that the remedies being applied by the McDonnell Douglas Corporation and the Army would likely not be adequate for sustaining sufficient numbers of Apaches in high-intensity combat.[116] Within a few months of this GAO report, the Apache would prove its capabilities in a truly historic air cavalry assault deep into Iraq.[117] By the end of the Gulf War, the Apache achieved an operational readiness rate of 92 percent. The 288 Apaches were responsible for destroying in excess of 500 tanks, 120 armored personnel carriers, 30 air defense units, 120 artillery pieces, 325 miscellaneous vehicles, 10 radar installations, 50 bunker/observation posts, 10 helicopters, and 10 fixed-wing aircraft. The score for the Apache's Hellfire missiles: 107 fired, 102 hits.[118]

Maj. Gen. Barry McCaffery, commander of the US Army's 24th Infantry Division, called the Apache "the single biggest maneuver factor on the battlefield."[119] For his part, Gen. Norman Schwarzkopf, the overall commander of Desert Storm, credited the Apache with "plucking the eyes" out of Iraq's air defense system.[120]

What had the networks missed? Once again, no one was paying attention to the way problems are fixed, both during development and after what the military terms "initial operational capability," or IOC, when a system is first fielded. In the case of the Apache, improvements that had been taking place in the late 1980s were beginning to reach field units in 1990. In the first six months of 1990, for instance, the worldwide mission-capable rate of the Apache was 71 percent, but by the second half it had reached 77 percent, with rates in Saudi Arabia topping 80 percent, a fact that even the GAO accepted after a 10-day trip to the Middle East.[121]

Over the years, deficiencies in the aircraft were fixed, and organizational problems related to reduced numbers of maintenance personnel in Army aviation units were remedied. Additionally, depleted stocks of spare parts were replenished, but few in the media noticed.

THE PATRIOT: A TALE OF NETWORK WEAPONS COVERAGE

The Patriot air defense missile is a case of a weapon with an even more complicated development and operational history, fraught with arcane technical details related to its capability against aircraft and its more limited anti-missile capability. The story line taken by the networks was typically simplistic and sensational. There were essentially four phases: the Patriot's troubled history and lack of capabilities; its "near-perfect" performance in the Gulf War; claims of a considerably less-than-perfect performance in the Gulf War; and the weapon whose performance was questionable in the Gulf War.

Phase 1: Early "Troubles"

NBC's March 10, 1983, report on the Patriot missile is a very typical example of how weapons in the development process or just coming out of the development process are covered. After noting the Patriot's $11 billion price tag, anchor Roger Mudd said, "The Patriot's troubled history raises questions about whether high-tech, high-cost weapons systems really help."

Correspondent John Hart then began, "There goes half a million dollars, the cost of one anti-aircraft missile, the Patriot, the product of 31 years of research and development, and it will never do all that it originally promised." Next came a laundry list of what it could not do. Hart described how the Patriot cannot see 360 degrees around the horizon; it cannot tell a friendly from enemy warplane; it cannot diagnose its own breakdowns by computer; and, as a radar-guided missile, it radiates an electronic signal that tells the enemy exactly where it is.

Hart then turned to an expert who talked about the Patriot's vulnerability. Next, the project director of the Patriot was set up with a brief sound bite saying there are "countermeasures that we are developing that will react to that." Hart then intoned that the countermeasure was a decoy that will cost even more money. Another critic then added that it is doubtful this will ever be a "working weapon system." A few facts followed on the incredible cost growth of the program, along with critical bipartisan sound bites from Rep. Les Aspin (D-WI) and Rep. Newt Gingrich (R-GA), before Hart allowed the project director to admit that there have been "problems."

This report contained no balance at all. Correspondent John Hart traveled all the way to White Sands Missile Range in New Mexico, but he never sought out any military experts who could defend the program or any company or technical experts who could shed light on the development process. Then, two days after this initial report, Hart surfaced in West Germany to report on a planned upgrade to the Patriot that would allow it to shoot down Soviet SS-20 missiles. Hart, however, was not there to explore potentially revolutionary technology but to suggest that the planned Patriot upgrade "might" violate the 1972 Anti-Ballistic Missile Treaty. To buttress this point, he turned to former arms–control negotiator Paul Warnke, who said it was a "flat violation" of the treaty.

What Hart did not say was that the Patriot was not even in the class of strategic missiles the ABM Treaty covers, nor did he say that Warnke was a vocal opponent of strategic defense. Naturally, any success in anti-missile defense on the tactical level with the Patriot would provide arguments for the feasibility of the technology on the strategic level.

Hart's basic approach, however, was far less complicated than that. Like much other weapons coverage, the basic point was that the Patriot was another expensive weapons system that costs too much and does not work as advertised. Within this context, the ABM Treaty aspect was only another complicating reason why this weapons system should not be further developed to defend against missiles.

Phase 2: The Gulf War's "Near-perfect" Hero

Within a few days of the start of the Gulf War, NBC correspondent Mike Boettcher said to his viewers, "Meet the war hero, a boring-looking box on the back of a truck and the crew that fires the Patriot missiles inside. They haven't missed yet." In that January 21, 1991, report, Boettcher then turned to one of the crew, who made the point that he had been on quite a "high" while working the Patriot battery the night before. Anchor Tom Brokaw then turned to correspondent Mike Jensen, who was reporting from the Raytheon Company's plant, where the Patriot is manufactured. He briefly mentioned the "thrilled Raytheon workers," proud of how Patriot missiles were shooting down Iraq's tactical ballistic missiles, known as Scuds. His report was about how the industry might be affected after the war, based on both the performance of various weapons and the need to replenish weapons stocks.

ABC's Bill Redeker also mentioned the Patriot in his January 21 report from Saudi Arabia. He noted that repeated barrages of Scud missiles aimed at Riyadh and Dhahran that day represented the most concentrated attack since the war began. Once again, according to the American command, the Patriot had intercepted all but one Scud, which crashed into the sea. By mid-February, President George Bush would tell a Raytheon audience that there had been "42 Scuds engaged, 41 intercepted." Bush's applause line: "Thank God for the Patriot missile!"

Some of the luster was taken off the Patriot's shine on February 25, however, when a Scud landed on a make-shift US Army barracks near Dhahran, Saudi

Arabia, killing 28 American soldiers and wounding 98. On February 26, 1991, CBS correspondent Harry Smith showed footage of the devastation: "This is what happens when a Scud makes a direct hit, a steel-frame building turned to shambles. The Americans inside never had a chance. Until last night, many people around Saudi Arabia thought themselves virtually Scud-proof. They believed the Patriot missile system was protection enough. But no Patriot was fired to intercept this Scud." Later, it would be determined that a computer problem shut the battery down by mistake.

Just after the war, the US Army's tally was 45 Scuds intercepted out of 47, still a tremendous success, according to media reports. That record, however, would not stand. Like so much reporting during a crisis or war, first reports are seldom totally accurate. The case of the Patriot was no exception.

Phase 3: We Only Thought the Patriot Was Near-perfect

The Patriot's war hero status did not last long. By April 1991, the print media were reporting on congressional testimony by Theodore A. Postol, a professor at the Massachusetts Institute of Technology.[122] He contended that the Patriot had not been as effective as originally thought. He cited Israeli newspaper reports of damage to local apartment complexes, showing that there had been less damage and injury before the Patriots began operating than after. This evidence was a bit weak, to say the least, but it was the first salvo at the Patriot's status as war hero.

Also that spring, the Army completed its initial assessment of the Patriot's performance and reported that the missile had an 80 percent success rate in Saudi Arabia and a 50 percent success rate in Israel. The differences were related to less than optimal deployments of Patriot units in Israel's populated cities and the decision made in Israel to use the "manual" mode as opposed to the "automatic" mode. The manual mode was designed for use against aircraft and was not as efficient when defending against missiles, but after some early automatic firings against Scud debris over Israel, the Israeli operational commander made the decision to switch modes to conserve missiles, a decision that stayed in place even after two software modifications were made to correct the early problem, one on February 4 and one on February 18.

Over the summer and fall of 1991, Postol prepared for another attack. He assembled his case into an article that eventually appeared in the journal *International Security*.[123] In early December, he launched a media campaign by co-authoring an article with an Israeli researcher from the Jaffee Center in Tel Aviv, Reuven Pedatzur, which appeared in *Defense News*.[124] The defense of the Patriot came principally from two experts on anti–ballistic missile defense, Charles Zraket, a former president of Mitre Corporation, who responded[125] to the *Defense News* article, and, later, Peter Zimmerman, of the Center for Strategic and International Studies, who was the counterpoint to Postol on the MacNeil-Lehrer NewsHour on January 27, 1992, and during congressional testimony. Raytheon also was actively engaged in defending the missile's capabilities.

With the battle joined, Postol next took to the airwaves. One of his central pieces of evidence was video footage he had requested from ABC News.[126] On January 16, 1992, ABC World News Tonight entered the fray. Anchor Diane Sawyer began, "We all remember those nights last January and February watching anxiously as Iraqi Scud missiles rained in on Saudi Arabia and Israel, and then the relief as the Patriot missiles shot them down. Or so it seemed." Sawyer then said that correspondent Morton Dean "has been investigating."

Dean's report was based almost entirely on Postol and all-around weapons critic Pierre Sprey. Postol was allowed to go unchallenged as he told ABC's viewers that "the evidence overwhelmingly points to almost a complete failure [of the Patriot] to intercept warheads [during the Gulf War]."

Somehow ABC had missed the debate in the trade press and failed completely to provide any defender of the Patriot. Both the Army and Raytheon had declined to comment. In the end, ABC World News Tonight would just let this story stand.

The closest it came to presenting any balancing viewpoints came on April 7, 1992, when it reported on congressional testimony by the US Army. Anchor Peter Jennings introduced the report: "There was some unfinished business from the Gulf War as the subject of a hearing on Capitol Hill today. The Patriot missile, you'll recall, was hailed as a great success story during the war. But in the year since, a number of studies have questioned whether the Patriot was really as effective as the Pentagon said it was. Today, the Army retreated just a little on its claims." Pentagon correspondent Bob Zelnick then mentioned that the Army lowered its previous estimates of the Patriot's interception rate from 80 percent in Saudi Arabia to 70 percent, and from 50 percent in Israel to 40 percent. "Still," Zelnick said, "[the Army] says Patriot was a big success."

A brief sound bite from an Army representative followed asserting the missile's success. Then Zelnick turned to the Congressional Research Service, which called into question even the Army's "more modest claims," Zelnick added. To his credit, Zelnick also pointed out that the CRS had called Postol's video evidence of misses "equally unreliable." What follows is the only background Zelnick provided about the studies or about how the rate of success was determined: "But to the Army, success includes knocking the Scud slightly off course, even if its warhead remains intact. While that might protect a Saudi airfield, it could mean heavy damage in a city like Tel Aviv." Definitions of "success," however, were at the heart of the disagreements of all the parties engaged in the battle and that issue required far more explanation than ABC provided.

Phase 4: The Lingering Tag of a "Questionable" Performance

Within a year of the end of the Gulf War, the Patriot success story had been punched full of holes. As far as network coverage went, it was a simple story. The US Army had put out false information, others had called them on it, and the Patriot neatly fit into the networks' preconceptions about costly weapons that do not work as advertised.

When the Clinton administration decided to send Patriot missiles to South Korea during the standoff with North Korea over nuclear inspections in early 1994, the "conventional wisdom" about the missile was well established. All three networks reported on the Patriot story on January 26, 1994.

After a very straight report by CBS Pentagon correspondent David Martin on the administration's decision to send the Patriots to North Korea at the request of the US commander in South Korea, anchor Dan Rather made this statement, which certainly could have used more context and background: "Those Patriot missiles, you may recall, were hailed as defensive marvels during the Persian Gulf War, but later on analysts questioned just how effective they really had been in deflecting enemy missiles." End of report.

ABC Pentagon correspondent Bob Zelnick started out by describing the request for the Patriot and the decision to send them. Then, he, too, ended his report on a similar note: "But some in the Pentagon privately note the Patriot's spotty record at intercepting Iraqi Scud missiles during the Gulf War and say they would offer no protection against an estimated 7,000 North Korean artillery pieces."

NBC Pentagon correspondent Ed Rabel, the less experienced of the three, was even more prone to the conventional wisdom. After a sound bite from White House spokeswoman Dee Dee Myers, explaining how the commander in South Korea believed the Patriot would be a "security enhancer," Rabel chimed in with this comment: "Maybe. But the South Korea theater commander, who requested the Patriots, Gen. Gary Luck, also knows this: A post–Gulf War congressional study said American soldiers' lives could be unnecessarily endangered in future conflicts based on inaccurate assessments of the Patriot's capabilities."

Next, Rabel provided a sound bite from a Joe Cirincione, who he said helped produce the congressional GAO study. Cirincione said that sending the Patriot was "better than doing nothing, but it's not much better." Rabel added that Cirincione's "study said probably only 9 percent of Scuds were hit in the Gulf War." After a brief sound bite from a Pentagon spokeswoman, who expressed "a very high degree of confidence in the Patriot," Rabel made the point that former Defense Secretary Les Aspin was fired in part for not sending equipment to a field commander in Somalia, so "no official is likely to turn down a field commander's request for missiles these days, even if they don't work."

Among the many problems with Rabel's report was his failure to identify Joe Cirincione as a former researcher for Rep. John Conyers (D-MI), who chaired the House Government Operations Committee and led the charge against the Patriot.[127] He also failed to mention that the GAO study that Cirincione helped produce actually said that 9 percent of engagements "are supported by the strongest evidence that an engagement resulted in a warhead kill."[128] That is not the same thing as Rabel's saying "only 9 percent of Scuds were hit." Rabel also did not mention that Cirincione's final report for the committee, which included material from the GAO study and other testimony and studies, was so controversial that Conyers had to withdraw it before taking a vote he would have lost, even in a committee he controlled.[129]

Rabel would bring back Cirincione for a February 17, 1994 report. This time he would be identified as having "led a federal government study of the Patriots following the Gulf War." Cirincione said on that occasion: "The Patriot performed poorly in the Gulf War. It performed poorly in its recent tests. I think the Army's looking for a new technology." The overall thrust of Rabel's report was about the Extended Range Interceptor, or ERINT, a theater anti-ballistic missile the Army had selected to develop instead of an upgraded Patriot, but his reliance on a biased source certainly did little to help explain why the Army was moving toward the ERINT system.

What the Networks Missed

Months after the Army's many attempts to adequately explain the role and capabilities of the Patriot, along with trying to explain the nature of the limited data available from the Gulf War, which, alone, will never provide conclusive proof one way or the other, Secretary of the Army Michael P. W. Stone wrote: "Perhaps the most bizarre as well as perplexing element of the success-rate debate has been the accommodating reception given by the press and networks to Patriot critics. No serious examination of the critics' positions was undertaken by either the print or electronic media. The statements of critics have been reported as gospel."[130]

Stone was right. With a little basic research, the networks (and the print media) could have provided some needed context. These are just a few of the points that could have been explained in greater depth:

▸ The Patriot missile was originally designed for the point defense of airfields and field command-and-control headquarters, yet it was criticized for being unable to perform perfectly in an area defense role protecting small cities in Saudi Arabia and Israel;[131]

▸ A point defense capability also means that the Patriot, which works by using a proximity explosion that either detonates an incoming warhead or knocks an enemy missile off course and away from the airfield or headquarters being defended, technically fulfills its mission if it diverts a missile away from the defended area, a critical point that arose in the debate over determining a "successful" intercept, but one which was never explained in detail;

▸ Because of the instability of the modified Scud missiles used by Iraq, some broke up before or during the Patriot intercept, which sometimes foiled the intercept as a Patriot exploded near an errant piece of the Scud, allowing the warhead to pass. Virtually ignored by the media was the remarkable speed with which two software modifications were tested and deployed to correct this problem;

▸ The Patriot batteries did not have any means of collecting data during the intercepts. Until the post–war advances in optical disks, no recording device small enough to fit in Patriot's Engagement Control System was available with the data capacity and bandwidth required. Therefore, neither the Army, nor its critics can make a case based on absolute scientific certainty;

▸ The Army relied upon its Ballistics Research Laboratories for its analysis. BRL based its assessment on examinations of the holes in the ground created when Scuds impacted, estimating the energy transferred to the ground, equating this with explosive force, analyzing pieces of Scud warheads for deformation and the presence of Patriot warhead fragments, determining the presence of large pieces of unengaged Scuds, and so on;

▸ General Accounting Office auditors found such raw data wanting, and said so. GAO also found Postol's video methodology to be flawed, but the networks ignored this—and still do;

▸ The Patriots deployed to the Gulf, known as PAC-2s, were modified with enhanced anti-missile capabilities and were still being tested at the time Iraq invaded Kuwait on August 2, 1990. Moreover, at that time, only three PAC-2s existed, but by January 1991, Raytheon had produced more than 500;

▸ Finally, the debate over Patriot success had political dimensions related to the issue of strategic defense. Many critics of Patriot had a stake in discrediting this system, despite its limited anti-missile capabilities, a connection that was not always made clear when the networks trotted out their experts, like Postol and Cirincione, both opponents of strategic defense.

The story of the Patriot was a complicated one. While Gulf War reports of perfection were misleading, so, too, were the early reports of the program's troubled history. Never explained was the extent to which even the anti-aircraft version of the Patriot was surpassing existing technology. As is often the case, such high-risk development typically encounters problems along the way. What really counts, however, is the end result, which is usually ignored by the media.

As for the anti-missile version of the Patriot, in 1998 it was still the only US operational system capable of intercepting a tactical ballistic missile. In terms of what is on the horizon, Patriot anti-missile capability is primitive, but it still provided a remarkable contribution to the Gulf War, whether its success rate was 9 percent, 40 percent, or 70 percent.

A RECURRING PATTERN

Too often during the 1980s and 1990s, weapons capabilities were misreported because of the overly simplistic focus on cost and development problems unearthed during routine testing. Both the military and industry were regularly portrayed as wasting money and taking too many risks with unproven technology.

It is still amazing to see an almost total lack of appreciation for what it takes to develop the most advanced weapons in the world. This is not to say that the media do not have a role in raising questions about the costs associated with weapons development and the legitimate differences that exist over whether to pursue one weapons system or another. Questioning the need for particular weapons is also a necessary function.

But where is the basic context? Why can't the networks occasionally report on the success story? Why don't they occasionally cover a successful training exercise highlighting just what role different weapons systems play in actual operations? Why not even occasionally talk about how these weapons fit into US military strategy?

Reporting in each of these areas could be compelling and could certainly hold the audience's attention. The problem seems to be that there is a well-established pattern of sensational reporting that takes as a starting point the idea that an advanced weapon always costs too much and seldom works along the lines promised by defense industry.

Chapter 6

The Defense Industry: A Scandalous Business?

While some network news correspondent, producer, or anchor somewhere might have a basic understanding of the process by which the government buys its weapons and industry develops and produces them, such an understanding is certainly not reflected in the news reports that appear on ABC World News Tonight, CBS Evening News, and NBC Nightly News.

In fact, overall reporting on industry and procurement amounts to a grotesque caricature of a system that has successfully produced some of the most advanced technology in the world. Instead of covering a complex process with its share of failures, substantial costs, successes, and a few scandals, network news has focused almost entirely on corruption in the industry and waste and mismanagement by the Pentagon.

In the 1980s' periods reviewed, the basic context related to the superpower competition and a very real Soviet military threat was usually nowhere to be found. In the 1990s' periods reviewed, there was no attempt to explore the implications of the dramatic changes that had taken place in the nature of the threat or to explore how high technology fit into a strategy that pitted a smaller US military against uncertain and unpredictable regional threats. The conventional wisdom was this: the Cold War is over; therefore, costs of weapons should be significantly lower, and the high technology aimed at the former Soviet Union is no longer necessary. It never occurred to the network establishment that high technology might be even more important to a smaller US military.

Nor was there any fundamental explanation of why the United States pursued certain weapons capabilities or how the complicated system of procurement actually worked, a system that involved unique military requirements, an industry whose main—or only—customer was the government, and a Congress whose behavior was often driven by political dictates rather than by logic, military necessity, or efficiency.

Why did the United States invest huge resources to build sophisticated weapons systems in the 1980s? And how had things changed by the early 1990s? Viewers who had relied on network news for answers to those questions would have been completely in the dark. They would have known, however, that the Reagan administration "wasted" money on defense routinely and that the defense industry "ripped off" the government as a general rule.

If the sampling of network news coverage of defense industry and procurement from the periods in 1983, 1985, 1990, and 1994, had to be characterized in a few words, those words would be *lack of context* and *sensationalism*.

THE NETWORK VIEW OF INDUSTRY AND PROCUREMENT

On April 17, 1983, NBC anchor Chris Wallace introduced a piece on Pentagon procurement: "How the Pentagon goes about buying things," he said, "not just weapons and weapon systems, but also the thousands of small parts they need, has long been a subject of concern. And some people, like the whistle blowers who talked to George Lewis, say the whole procedure is riddled with waste, fraud and abuse."

Correspondent George Lewis jumped in by stating how the "Reagan defense budget is filled with all sorts of sophisticated and expensive weapons." He then got to the point: "There are thousands of small parts, like this electronic circuit chip, that go into those big weapons. All too often, through carelessness or because of fraud, the Pentagon pays too much for these parts."

What followed was a laundry list of examples, from the $2.16 gaskets that cost the Pentagon $14.66, to the $442 walkie-talkies that the Pentagon bought for $31,000 each because of an error, which was later caught. "The sloppy bookkeeping sometimes makes the Defense Department an easy mark for swindlers," Lewis said.

One of his sources said the Pentagon was considered "a huge warehouse of money." Another told him of the kickback schemes between defense companies and their parts suppliers. Such a scheme cost Emerson Electric Company, a maker of guidance systems, a million dollars. And guess who pays for it? The government (and by extension the taxpayer). Lewis concluded this report by explaining how the Defense Department hotline, set up to combat fraud, waste, and abuse, had not yet led to a prosecution. And the department has only 100 investigators. The closer: "So it appears the unscrupulous operators will continue to regard this place as nothing more than a huge warehouse of money."

On April 21, 1985, ABC focused on Pentagon spending practices. Anchor Sam Donaldson set it up by saying how "investigations into Pentagon spending practices and the practices of defense contractors have recently centered on cost overruns and contract overcharges. But now an Air Force study finds that taxpayer money is also being misspent through plain old inefficiency." On to correspondent Dennis Troute at the Pentagon.

Troute opened with the case of the Tomahawk missile, whose $3 million price would be much lower if the manufacturer, General Dynamics Corporation, "could meet its own efficiency standards." And that is the case with other weapons systems, according to the Air Force study. Contractors, it was reported, were operating at only 46 percent efficiency, "requiring twice the time that their own engineers thought necessary," Troute said. "The taxpayer picks up the extra cost of inefficiency, because virtually all contracts with the military guarantee a profit."

Troute then threw in his one attempt at balance: "Responding to such criticism, contractors, including General Dynamics and Hughes, say their efficiency is improving, but critics in Congress say the Pentagon should take a stronger hand in cutting weapons costs." To conclude, he said, "Some reform was underway in the Air Force and Navy contracts. Pentagon officials say it is too early to tell if these efforts will work where past measures did not."

As these two reports seem to suggest, in the eyes of the networks, Pentagon ineptitude, combined with industry corruption and inefficiency, costs taxpayers a lot of money. This is the basic conventional wisdom buried in almost all network reporting on industry and procurement. And the focus is most often on cost increases during weapons development and improper charges by defense contractors.

Take the CBS Evening News broadcast of January 28, 1983. After focusing a budget story on the fact that the Defense Department would get a boost of "billions" if Reagan's spending plan were approved, anchor Dan Rather turned to the misuse of government funds: "Posh parties in Florida and jaunts to Europe. Not unusual for the jet set, but as Fred Graham reports tonight, these are some of the allegations involving a maker of jet engines and your tax dollars at work."

Correspondent Fred Graham introduced exhibit one: "The Pratt & Whitney jet engines in this Air Force fighter cost the American taxpayers $2 million." He then added, "CBS News has learned that the FBI is investigating allegations that the price includes corporate executives' family trips to Europe, a congressional junket to South America, and visits to massage parlors in Denmark." At issue: whether Pratt & Whitney officials "fraudulently tacked on to the price of the engines what one source said was millions of dollars in lavish entertainment costs."

After a list of the various allegations about $50,000 parties and world tours, Graham said that a company spokesman said the allegations of impropriety were false. Graham then turned to a government auditor, "who would make only a general comment." The auditor then said, "The defense budget is so huge, that there is so much money to be spread around—again, this is my personal opinion—that excesses, abuses, will take place." Graham concluded by saying a grand jury was focusing on allegations that company officials misused government funds and that "some Pentagon officials learned about the improprieties as far back as 1976 but did nothing to stop them."

Sensational stories about industry misuse of government funds were the rule of network coverage, not the exception. In 1985, for example, General Dynamics, then the largest defense contractor, incurred the Pentagon's wrath for passing on charges for trips to vacation homes, bar bills, country club memberships, and even the kennel charges for one executive's dog. On March 5, 1985, the Pentagon suspended payments to General Dynamics, pending a review of these charges. This was a noteworthy story. But the tone of the networks seemed to stretch the limits of objectivity. For instance, ABC anchor Peter Jennings began his report this way: "The Pentagon has now decided—and some people are bound to say, 'Finally'—to get tough with some of America's biggest military contractors." ABC correspondent Dean Reynolds then did a fairly straight report on Defense Secretary Caspar Weinberger's action and the reaction in Congress. At the end, however, Reynolds made this observation: "Still, General Dynamics' competitors had better not gloat. The Pentagon has made it clear that all major defense contractors are being reviewed and all will have to certify that their bills are for business, or they'll face charges of perjury." The underlying presumption in both Jennings's opening and Reynold's closing is that the industry is basically corrupt and that tough measures are in order.

On the same day, CBS anchor Dan Rather was less obvious, but the basic message was there: "After repeated allegations that General Dynamics has been living high on the hog, even kenneling a dog at taxpayer expense, the Defense Department today put millions of dollars in payments to the nation's largest defense contractor on a month-long hold. They will stay on hold pending an audit. Other defense contractors were put on notice, too."

For its part, NBC let John Chancellor loose with one his "commentaries." Chancellor complained about how defense companies do not pay any taxes and then cited other cases of abuse, like Boeing's charges to the government for political contributions, a claim the company eventually withdrew. Chancellor concluded with the "irony" of a story about contractors "padding their expense accounts" right in the middle of budget season. "Some of the companies which profit most from defense may be helping to get the budget cut even more," he said.

That same month, on March 26, 1985, General Electric, the nation's fourth largest contractor, had troubles of its own. The company was indicted on more than 100 counts of defrauding the government. ABC's Peter Jennings said GE was "accused of bilking the government on a $47 million contract to develop a nuclear warhead system." ABC correspondent Dennis Troute then described what federal agents claimed was a scheme to tamper with time cards and overbill the government to the tune of $800,000, a charge GE denied.

NBC aired a similar report, but both ABC's Troute and NBC correspondent James Polk twisted the end of their reports to suggest that the Pentagon should ban GE from future defense work. They then noted that it would probably not happen because the company was too big a supplier of goods to the Pentagon. Was this to suggest that the Pentagon would work with "corrupt" contractors just because it already did a lot of business with them?

CBS correspondent Ray Brady ended the CBS coverage with a similarly bizarre aside: "The Defense Department told CBS News today that it's currently conducting more criminal investigations of defense companies than ever before. Defense industry insiders, meanwhile, say that crackdowns like the one announced today are part of an administration strategy, one designed to make increases in defense spending more acceptable to Congress." So, in Brady's view, it was all a cynical attempt by the Reagan administration to placate Congress and gain more defense funding, not to punish wrongdoing.

Another aspect of industry and procurement reporting that lived on, fueled by ignorance and publicity-seeking congressmen, were the stories of the Pentagon paying outrageous prices for parts most Americans could seemingly buy at corner hardware stores for a fraction of the price the government was paying. One example was the case of the $748 pliers. By the summer of 1984, a whole range of "horror stories" had been reported, from these pliers to $640 "toilet seats." Congressmen had a field day making these charges. And the media lapped them up.

In the 1985 period reviewed, there were two follow-up reports on the Boeing charges for pliers. It is worth looking at each anchor tell in full. First, there was NBC's report on March 22, 1985. Tom Brokaw had this to say: "Last summer there was an uproar, you'll remember, when it was reported that Boeing was selling pliers to the Air Force at the price of 748 dollars a pair. Boeing quickly announced at the time that the price of the pliers would be only 90 dollars. Now a senator, who looked into the deal, said that the money Boeing knocked off of the price of the pliers, it added to the contract as so-called administrative costs. The Air Force ended up spending just as much. But Boeing insisted that it did absolutely nothing underhanded."

CBS coverage on the same day was similar. Anchor Charles Kuralt reported: "There was a great national outcry last June, when a Boeing contract with the Air Force, worth $557,500 to Boeing, was found to include pliers at $748 a pair, much like the $8 pliers you find at the hardware store. Boeing dropped its price to $90 a pair, and cut prices on 50 other tools in the contract. Now it turns out that Boeing added $95,000 for what it called "support equipment management charges," bringing the contract cost to the Air Force back to $557,500. A Boeing spokesman said today there was absolutely nothing underhanded here."

Both of these reports implied that Boeing was doing some fancy footwork to cover overcharges to the government. But there were two aspects to all of these stories that never made the airwaves. First, sometimes high prices for single items reflected how the industry was directed to allocate its overhead charges.[132] Secondly, in cases where prices were inflated, it was usually government auditors who caught such charges early on.[133]

In the case of the Boeing pliers, Secretary of Defense Caspar Weinberger wrote at the time that not only did the Department of Defense find and correct the problem, but it also purchased most of its pliers for $3.10. As for the "support equipment management charges," this was one of the breakdowns the Department of Defense required in order to more easily spot overcharges.[134]

When asked about television news coverage of these "horror stories," Weinberger said, "It's a big interesting, exciting, funny story that the Defense Department paid $100 for a hammer. The facts are much duller, much less exciting, much less interesting, so they don't get presented."[135]

WHAT THE NETWORKS NEVER TOLD US

As one writer with years of experience in acquisition pointed out, many of the news reports of "horror stories" contained "outright distortions." He noted, for example, that the famous $3,046 coffee pot was actually designed for the huge C-5A aircraft, which carries as many as 365 people. Major airlines, he pointed out, had purchased similar coffee makers for about the same price, $3,107. On another highly publicized overcharge: "The $640 toilet seat was, in fact, a large molded plastic cover for the entire toilet system of a P-3 aircraft."[136]

This same writer concluded that possible explanations for the inaccurate and incomplete reporting and the "theatrics" of congressmen were "dismaying." While some, he suggested, might have been well-intentioned but poorly informed, most, he believed, were motivated by a desire to discredit the defense buildup.[137]

To put the Pentagon's "waste" and "mismanagement" into perspective, another writer argued that, based on comparative studies by the GAO and the House Government Operations Committee, the Defense Department is one of the best-managed federal agencies. According to his analysis, the Department of Defense was implementing over 15 million contracts a year in the 1980s, around 52,000 contracts a day, spending around $300 billion a year. Analyzing statistics from 1984 and 1985, he found that there were roughly 1,500 illegalities out of 15 million procurement actions. That comes out to .01 percent.[138]

In addition to distorting the Pentagon's management practices, the networks regularly ignored the role Congress played (and still does) in driving up weapons costs. Instability in funding from year to year routinely increased unit costs, the same costs congressmen then ridiculed in public.[139]

The networks and, to a lesser extent, print reporters also failed to explain what goes into the cost of weapons systems and how that differs from "costs" associated with consumer goods. Take the case of the B-2, which will be described in greater detail in chapter 10. Cost was an obsession, the main focus of all three networks' reporting, but seldom was it properly explained. Even in recent years, the per unit cost of the B-2 has been regularly cited as over $2 billion per aircraft. Network whiz kids arrived at this figure by simply dividing the total cost of the program, $44.4 billion, by the 21 aircraft the Pentagon finally decided to procure (down from the original planned buy of 132).

The problem with this type of approach is that research and development (R&D) costs get lumped in with production costs. In reality, R&D is the cost of pursuing the newest technology. It is also the riskiest part of the proposition, since some technologies just do not pan out. In the case of the B-2, research, development, testing, and evaluation ate up $24.8 billion. The per unit price tag of the final product, however, is better measured by using the costs involved in actually producing it, including start-up costs associated with production tooling, salaries of workers, materials, and so on. In the case of the B-2, this cost was $19.6 billion for the 21 aircraft finally approved by Congress. So a more accurate reflection of the actual per unit cost would be under $1 billion a copy, still a hefty price, but less than half the cost still being routinely reported by the media.

By way of comparison, take the Saturn automobile produced by General Motors Corporation. According to press reports, GM sank anywhere from $3 billion to $5 billion into development costs alone. If the lower development estimate of $3 billion were used, without taking into consideration any production costs, by the same logic used by the networks to price weapons, the first 100 Saturns would have cost more than $30 million a piece.

While it still cost the American taxpayer $44.4 billion to procure the original 20 B-2s (and a bit more to convert 1 test aircraft into an operational configuration), how cost per aircraft is determined matters most when considering future production. Having already sunk the R&D costs, for example, the actual production cost of additional B-2s was estimated at $630 million per aircraft by the Air Force during the debate that took place in 1995. Critics, however, still went around calling it a $2 billion bomber.

The other aspect of cost that is ignored has to do with capability and trade-offs. In the B-2 debate, critics who argued against building more B-2s said that older bombers using cruise missiles could do the same job for a fraction of the price. In reality, as one analyst pointed out, if the Gulf War were used as an example, it would take 40,000 cruise missiles at $1 million a piece to strike all the aim points hit during the war, or $40 billion.[140] And once launched, the cruise missile is gone forever.

For its part, one B-2 can hit 16 aim points with gravity bombs which each cost 10 times less than one cruise missile.[141] That same B-2 can return time and again with these inexpensive bombs. In terms of simple arithmetic, the B-2, then, can be quite cost effective in war, even when compared with the less expensive cruise missile. Moreover, one B-2, with 2 crew members, can strike as many targets as a force package of 75 aircraft, with 147 personnel, did during the Gulf War.[142] That means that fewer aircraft are put in harm's way, and fewer pilots' lives are at risk, a tough commodity to put a price on.

The main point, here, is that cost is not a simple matter. The government is not buying some off-the-shelf item in the commercial marketplace. Military requirements are often unique, and military specifications have historically driven up costs, one reason why commercial practices, where possible, are in vogue today.

When price tags are put on weapons systems to make them seem wildly expensive, this grossly distorts the entire process that took place from concept to fielding a particular weapons system. It fails to take into account the unique military requirements that led the Defense Department to invest funds in what were often unproven technologies. And it never really explains the link between a new technology and the capabilities it might translate into on some future battlefield.

A final note on cost has to do with the defense budget as a whole. Often enough, the MX missile was cited as an expensive strategic system. The same was true of other programs, like SDI. Frequently, correspondents talked about the $11 billion Patriot anti-aircraft missile system, the $14 billion MX missile basing plan, or the $26 billion research program for "Star Wars," all in the aggregate. This sounds shocking without an explanation of how many years such program funds are spread over. Expenditures for SDI, or Star Wars to the networks, for example, only reached slightly more than 1 percent of the defense budget in the peak year of spending on the program in the 1980s. To listen to the hype on the networks, many Americans must have thought the program was going to break the bank. And when the "expensive" strategic weapons were discussed, network correspondents rarely pointed out that total spending on all strategic forces seldom exceeded 9 or 10 percent of the defense budget during the height of the Reagan buildup.[143]

Context is important in the area of weapons acquisition. It is a complicated business, and the resources devoted to it are substantial. Moreover, there are legitimate debates over the level of resources devoted to defense and over how those resources are spent within the defense budget. The acquisition process is far from perfect, as the many attempts at reform suggest. But given the many successful results, it is not the corrupt, incompetent, and wasteful system that has been portrayed over time in network news reports.

WATCHING OUT FOR TAXPAYERS' MONEY?

Judging from the many stories about defense contractors overcharging the government and the Pentagon wasting money, it would seem that the networks were trying to ferret out corruption and report to the American public on how its government was spending taxpayers' money. In many cases, the networks made a big deal of contractors overcharging by thousands of dollars, even millions in some cases. Yet, when Secretary of Defense Dick Cheney reported that he had a plan to save taxpayers $39 billion, the networks yawned.

On January 11, 1990, ABC anchor Peter Jennings delivered this report: "The Defense Secretary announced today that he is imposing management reforms at the Pentagon. Dick Cheney says they will save $39 billion in Pentagon spending over the next five years. It will also reduce the number of civilian and military service jobs by 42,000." End of report. There was no flourish, no background on what the secretary of defense proposed, or even any criticism of whether the number was achievable.

NBC, for its part, tied its report to pressure for defense cuts and to job losses. Anchor Tom Brokaw reported in full: "Reforms in the Soviet Union and in Eastern Europe are creating new pressure at home, here in the United States, for more defense cuts, of course. Well, today Defense Secretary Dick Cheney said he'll propose a plan to save $39 billion over the next five years. The jobs of 42,000 people who buy weapons will be cut. Cheney said he would recommend extensive military base closings as well."

Surely there was more to this story than ABC and NBC were willing to report. How was the Pentagon going to find such savings? Were they likely to succeed? What about the track record of similar attempts in the past? What part of the workforce was going to be cut, and why? And so on.

The most curious part about the network decision to ignore broader aspects of this story has to do with scope. When it comes to real money, the savings proposed by Cheney dwarfed the nickels and dimes in industry overcharges that the networks hyped so much during the 1980s. Yet, there was little interest in this story. Apparently, savings by the Pentagon did not fit into the network paradigm for deciding what's news.

THE SCORECARD

It is not hard to understand why the networks suffer from problems of context and sensationalism when covering industry and procurement. For one thing, the networks seldom devote enough time to explain the problems that occur during weapons development. In all of the periods reviewed, 33 out of the 63 reports tagged as either industry or procurement were anchor tells. That means that over half of these complicated issues were dispensed with in a few short sentences by the anchors.

Moreover, as is the case overall, Pentagon correspondents accounted only for a small fraction of the reporting on these arcane issues, 8 out of 63 reports in an area they are the best qualified to analyze and explain—that's about 13 percent of the time. Once again, generalists dominated coverage, in this case a whopping 87 percent of the time.

Not surprisingly, the biggest problem areas identified in the coverage of industry and procurement were overdramatizing the news (read sensationalism), lack of knowledge (read generalists), and context problems related to brevity (read anchor tells). As far as the networks go, CBS and NBC each had twice as much problematic coverage as ABC. Of the 57 problematic reports, NBC had 24, CBS 22, and ABC 11. Overall, industry and procurement reporting by the networks was warped and out of context 67 to 100 percent of the time.

Chapter 7

Arms Control: Let's Make a Deal

The Reagan administration's approach to arms control was a novel one. It aimed at actually reducing nuclear weapons, something the Strategic Arms Limitations Talks of the 1970s had failed to do. Indeed, SALT II, the unratified 1979 treaty to which both superpowers were adhering in principle, may have capped the growth of nuclear weapons, but it also locked in historically high levels of nuclear arms on both sides. While introducing *stability* into the process, arms control, as practiced by previous Republican and Democratic administrations, had allowed the superpowers to arm themselves to the teeth, albeit with mutual agreement.[144]

By the late 1970s, security specialists in both Democratic and Republican camps began questioning the status quo. This set the stage for a highly political strategic debate in the early 1980s. On one side, there was an arms control establishment with core beliefs about the importance of arms control and real stakes in past agreements. This establishment, from high-visibility members of the Arms Control Association in Washington, D.C., like Paul Warnke, to former arms negotiator Gerard Smith and the academic nexus along the Charles River in Cambridge, Massachusetts, where those out of power took refuge at Harvard and MIT, was grounded in the strong view that arms control was at the center of any strategic relationship with the Soviet Union. It added stability to the deterrent equation, and anything that threatened the web of agreements was seen as *destabilizing*.[145]

Another group, which included members of the Committee on the Present Danger, like Paul Nitze and Eugene Rostow, was less enamored of the arms control agreements that the United States had negotiated with the Soviet Union. Indeed, Nitze helped torpedo ratification of the SALT II agreement because he and others saw it as fundamentally flawed. Many of the limitations enshrined in these arms control agreements, they reasoned, had locked the United States into an inferior strategic position.[146] This crowd of *hard-liners*, including conservative Democrats like Richard Perle, who had worked for Sen. Henry "Scoop" Jackson

(D-WA); academics like William Van Cleave; former military men like Edward Rowny; and old hands in the national security field like Nitze, who had worked for Democrat and Republican alike, saw arms control as less important than the need to ensure increased US military strength.[147]

After the election of Ronald Reagan in 1980, many of those advocating a shift in the arms control dynamic toward a tougher negotiating stance with the Soviets alongside a strategic modernization program ended up in key posts in the new administration, setting the stage for a volatile strategic debate,[148] part of which was still raging in 1998 over issues like missile defense and the sanctity of the 1972 Anti-Ballistic Missile Treaty.

The problem for the media, especially the networks, was that these issues were arcane and difficult to communicate, from concepts like deterrence by denial and deterrence by punishment, to terms like *counterforce, countervalue, circular error probable*, and *throw weight*.

The Reagan administration's harder line also involved changing traditional approaches to nuclear deterrent posture, especially in pursuing strategic defense and strategic weapons systems that might be viewed in the *warfighting* versus *deterrence* categories, artificial as these distinctions were in light of Soviet military doctrine at the time, which spelled out in no uncertain terms how to actually fight a nuclear war.[149] Of course, when officials in the Reagan administration made such points, they created an uproar over the idea that they, too, were dabbling with the notion of actually fighting a nuclear war.[150]

By 1983, the Reagan administration was on a path toward deploying intermediate-range nuclear missiles, including Pershing II and cruise missiles, in Western Europe, in order to counter Soviet SS-20s capable of reaching most European capitals in a matter of minutes. On the other hand, there was also an arms control proposal on the table known as the zero-zero option. If the Soviets would remove the SS-20s aimed at Europe, the United States would not deploy its own intermediate-range nuclear missiles.

Network coverage of this period had several themes:

▸   There was a continuing battle in the administration between the *hard-liners* and those who would take a more *flexible* and reasonable approach toward dealing with the Soviets on the missile question.

▸   The administration's hard line had the Europeans worried, who, after all, were the ones closest to the SS-20s. The networks also made it clear that the United States should make a deal with the Soviets as soon as possible.

▸   Another angle involved drawing attention to Soviet statements that said, if the United States did not come to reasonable terms with the Soviets, there could be dire consequences.

By 1985, the focus was on the framework for strategic arms reduction talks (START) in Geneva. The network themes for this period were similar but with differences in emphasis:

- ▸ The hard-liners were continually foiling efforts by those who were serious about arms control.
- ▸ The Strategic Defense Initiative was complicating efforts to reach a strategic arms control agreement.
- ▸ The world would be worse off if an arms control agreement could not be reached.

THE INTERNAL STRUGGLES OVER ARMS CONTROL

In early 1983, Eugene Rostow, the director of the Arms Control and Disarmament Agency, and no dove toward the Soviet Union, found himself on the way out, after a series of problems with Reagan's White House. When Rostow was forced to resign on January 12, 1983, all three networks took the opportunity to explore the divisions in the administration over arms control. CBS anchor Dan Rather portrayed Rostow's dismissal as a "rift" in arms control policy that "almost rivals the one between the United States and the Soviet Union."

CBS State Department correspondent Bob Schieffer then said, "There has been considerable friction between Rostow and the White House in recent weeks. Rostow felt the White House bowed to pressure from the Republican right-wing when it refused to support the nomination of Robert Gray—a man that many conservatives felt was not enough of a hard-liner to negotiate an arms deal."

Schieffer then turned to "a larger dispute" over strategic policy. At the heart of it was the zero-zero option proposed by the Reagan administration in 1981 but rejected by the Soviets in 1982. At present, he continued, "Pentagon hard-liners say hang tough with the original zero-zero offer, but Paul Nitze, the chief US negotiator at Geneva, is known to be pushing for more flexibility."

Meanwhile, in light of the Soviet propaganda offensive in Europe, explained Schieffer, which was aimed at influencing the West German elections in March, "many officials" at the State Department "consider public relations aspects of the situation crucial. They worry that an appearance of inflexibility on the part of the United States will only help the Soviet Union to make its case in West Germany. Now the confusing situation has been thrown into even more disarray."

NBC State Department correspondent Marvin Kalb stated that Rostow had major problems with congressional conservatives led by Sen. Jesse Helms (R-NC), mainly over personnel issues. He then turned to Sen. Paul Tsongas (D-MA), who said, "In my view arms control is dead and it will take a major reversal of attitude by the president to change that. I don't see that reversal taking place." Kalb concluded by saying, "It's known that Rostow feared that the Russians might even think that extremists were taking control of America's arms policy. Obviously the president and his aides cared less about Rostow's fears than they did about offending conservative allies."

ABC's coverage was the least apocalyptic. Anchor Frank Reynolds announced that a "shakeup" had taken place at the Arms Control and Disarmament Agency. White House correspondent Mike von Fremd then made it clear that Rostow was fired over differences with the White House staff. Rostow was viewed by the White House as "stubborn and at times a loose cannon." The bottom line: the president (read White House) wanted someone else. Von Fremd also said that the departure "will not have a great effect on arms control negotiations because, for the past few months, he [Rostow] has not played the dominant role, but his departure may be seen by our European allies as more confusion in Ronald Reagan's attempts to negotiate arms reductions."

As these reports suggested, there were different viewpoints within the Reagan administration over arms control policy. Reporting those differences was never the problem with network coverage; however, leaning to one side of the debate was—nearly half the time.

For instance, the very next day, January 13, 1983, the networks did follow-up reports on the Rostow firing and arms control policy. CBS State Department correspondent Bob Schieffer began his report by saying "the administration's arms control policy appears in complete disarray." Then he reported that Secretary of State George Shultz, "who's hardly said boo to reporters since coming to the State Department," personally conducted the daily briefing "to say not to worry."

The message from Shultz: the president is in control of US arms control policy. Moreover, US policy is strong and firm, calling for "dramatic reductions in armaments, for the removal of a whole class of weapons from European soil, and for the reductions in many others." That was Schieffer's cue to cite Rostow's departing remarks, during which he said that "without flexibility as well as firmness, there would be serious consequences." After a quick note on the hard-line views of Rostow's successor, Kenneth Adelman, who was serving as the deputy to UN Ambassador Jeane Kirkpatrick, Schieffer concluded by saying that Shultz is actually emerging as the key figure on arms control, and, in the end, he will be more flexible than Rostow ever was.

ABC's coverage on the same day made the point about Shultz being in control even more strongly than CBS had. After reporting on Shultz's appearance in the State Department briefing room, ABC State Department correspondent Barrie Dunsmore concluded this way: "The big question is whether the US is now better or less able to deal with arms control. The early answer from arms control advocates within the administration is that George Shultz's new involvement is an asset and they predict he will ultimately persuade Ronald Reagan to take a more flexible course."

The networks, many times without even realizing it, seemed to subscribe to the arms control establishment's view of the centrality of arms control. They reported with approval on those who would be more flexible. Hard-liners, on the other hand, were usually described as obstacles to real progress.

Take as an example a long report on ABC at the start of the second Reagan administration. Anchor Peter Jennings introduced the January 2, 1985, report by citing Henry Kissinger, who said that there were "few people, including heads of state and government, who understood all the complications of arms control and weapons systems." ABC, Jennings noted, was going to help remedy that problem by running a series of reports. The first, prepared by Pentagon correspondent Rick Inderfurth, focused on the question, does the Reagan administration yet have a coherent arms control policy? (Not too loaded.) In what otherwise could have been an informative analysis of the competing arms control groups within the administration, Inderfurth chose instead to turn to Strobe Talbott and Paul Warnke to tutor the American public on these weighty matters. Talbott began by stating that sharp differences over the US approach to dealing with the Soviet Union had split the administration, noting that one side believed, incorrectly, that we should get out of arms control as it had existed since the whole process started, an idea that was clearly foreign to him. Warnke basically suggested that Reagan's previous approaches had been unfair to the Soviets. "We were asking for cuts in the heart of the Soviet strategic retaliatory force, while accepting only token cuts in our own forces. The Soviets could not accept them because they would be worse off than if they had no agreement at all."

Inderfurth then added, "Now, however, President Reagan has signaled his intention to break that impasse over US arms control policy by appointing his *most flexible* negotiator, Paul Nitze, to be Secretary Shultz's senior advisor for the talks in Geneva. Some see that appointment as a victory over the *hard-liners*. Others are not so sure." (Emphasis added.) Enter Talbott for the second time: "Those people [the hard-liners] are still there. They still have an opportunity to influence policy, and indeed *to thwart* what Shultz and Nitze try to do." (Emphasis added.)

Message: beware the hard-liners. They could mess it all up again.

THE EUROPEANS ARE WORRIED

On January 13, 1983, NBC anchor Tom Brokaw introduced a report on arms control after the Rostow firing by stating that in Western Europe "many people have been concerned about the Reagan administration's attitude toward nuclear weapons," and "the Rostow firing only adds to their concerns."

NBC correspondent James Compton then outlined how the Europeans had an "impression of incoherence in the White House" and of "American mismanagement of the arms talks." America was out of touch with Europe at the same time that Soviet leader Yuri Andropov "has repeatedly taken positions more conciliatory than Reagan," Compton continued. And, even though the governments of West Germany and Britain have sided with the president's line, "Reagan foreign policy is getting harder to defend as more and more Europeans demand that America not ignore their interests when it deals with the Soviet Union."

Besides inferences that the Reagan administration was out of touch, there was periodic coverage of protests and demonstrations in Europe, usually delivered without any context or background material, especially when it came to the positions of the governments of key US allies. West Germany, under the leadership of Helmut Schmidt, for instance, played a central role in urging the United States to deploy missiles in Europe, a point that was never made when the networks reported on these very protests and demonstrations.

Network coverage of the complicated situation in Europe was too often shallow. On January 17, 1983, for instance, ABC anchor Peter Jennings delivered a short clip on a protest in Britain, noting that this is "the year of the missile" there and in Western Europe. On that day, 100 women lined up outside of Parliament. As Jennings put it, "Their intention was to get inside, which they did without cameras, to protest the planned deployment in Britain later this year of the cruise missile. They sat down inside Parliament's Central Hall, demanded a public debate on NATO's decision to deploy the cruise. They were detained, later released, and made their point." That was the extent of the substance of Jenning's report. While it may have highlighted the controversial nature of planned US missile deployments in Britain, it did nothing to explain the broader context, including the reasons for the British government's support of the deployments.

The main theme of arms control reporting, however, was the need to compromise. On March 15, 1983, CBS anchor Dan Rather made this point after a brief note about the possibility of an interim proposal being developed for arms reduction talks in Geneva. "President Reagan is under increasing pressure from European allies to compromise in those negotiations, but he has been holding fast to his so-called zero-zero option." While there is nothing fundamentally wrong with the premise of this report, it once again illustrates the framework of the network paradigm: Reagan's hard-line approach is all that stands in the way of compromise and an agreement, details be damned.

The Soviets, of course, were doing all they could to make the Europeans nervous, and their efforts to do so were often presented to the American public without any context or US response. For example, after referring to Soviet propagandist Georgi Arbatov's "pointed message to the United States warning that stationing new American missiles in Western Europe later this year could undermine the chances for success on talks to control all nuclear weapons," NBC anchor Tom Brokaw, on March 17, 1983, got to the real point: "In an interview with the *New York Times* today, the chief of the Soviet General Staff, Marshal Nikolai Ogarkov, had an even more ominous message. He said any conflict involving the new missiles, which are intermediate in range, would inevitably lead to an all-out nuclear war." End of report. What Brokaw could have explained was that such a view among the military was not unusual at all. The American military, too, continually talked of escalation from even the tactical level to all-out nuclear war if nuclear weapons were ever introduced into conflict. Indeed, the overall premise of the US reliance on tactical nuclear missiles for defense against a Warsaw Pact army that would outnumber NATO forces was based on high stakes, namely escalation to all-out nuclear war. These high stakes contributed to deterring such an attack in the first place. In Brokaw's formulation, however, Ogarkov's words were "ominous"—and out of context.

SDI: THE GREAT IMPEDIMENT

Within days of President Reagan's March 23, 1983, SDI speech, Soviet leader Yuri Andropov gave the networks a dramatic reply. On March 26, 1983, CBS and NBC devoted reports to his response to SDI. CBS State Department correspondent

Bill McLaughlin reported, "The Reagan bid for new high-tech weapons, says Andropov, would actually open the floodgates to a runaway race of all types of strategic arms." The path Reagan was pursuing was "extremely dangerous." And, Andropov said, "It is time they stopped devising one option after another in the search for the best ways of unleashing nuclear war in the hope of winning it. Engaging in this is not just irresponsible; it is insane." That report was followed by a note from CBS anchor Bob Schieffer on how two key Pentagon officials, Richard Perle and Fred Ikle, had expressed doubts about the SDI plan, and at least one White House aide "had also been leery of the idea."

NBC's approach was similar, as Moscow correspondent Stan Bernard said Andropov resorted to name-calling, "saying Mr. Reagan told a deliberate lie when he said the Soviets are not observing their own moratorium on deployment of medium-range missiles."

The problem with these reports had nothing to do with the fact that the rhetoric between the Reagan administration and the Soviet leadership was volatile and heated on many occasions. Charges were leveled by each side routinely. The problem here was again context. In fact, there was seldom any attempt to explain how such rhetoric fit into the ongoing negotiations or how it might influence various audiences in Europe and the United States.

On the other hand, the networks were quite capable at times of presenting complex analysis and balanced reports. For example, ABC's second installment of its arms control series, cited earlier, focused on the Strategic Defense Initiative. On January 3, 1985, ABC State Department correspondent John McWethy outlined both sides of the SDI issue, interspersing the views of Secretary of Defense Caspar Weinberger and Reagan Science Advisor George Keyworth with those of SDI opponent Robert McNamara and arms control specialist Michael Krepon.

While Weinberger and Keyworth explained the aim of making strategic missiles obsolete through a series of technologies, which McWethy had already outlined, McNamara blasted the notion, stating that the nation's technical community says "there's no prospect whatever" of developing a leak-proof defense and making nuclear missiles obsolete. McWethy also stated that the Soviets were taking SDI quite seriously, and that it had become a powerful bargaining tool. While Secretary of State Shultz might be putting it on the table in Geneva, Reagan himself seems determined to at least keep up the research program, McWethy concluded.

McWethy's report was balanced, fair, informative—and unusual when it came to SDI. As often, the reporting on SDI as it related to arms control was unbalanced. On January 12, 1985, for example, CBS Pentagon correspondent Bill Lynch reported on a symposium held in Washington, DC. Lynch opened by saying that the conference showed that "the nation's top scientists" were "still sharply divided over so-called Star Wars missile defenses. The debate is only partly about whether a twenty-first-century Maginot line against thousands of Soviet missiles is feasible. It is also about the political wisdom of space weapons and their staggering costs."

With that setup, Lynch turned to "administration critics" who say "the Star Wars program threatens to destroy the ABM Treaty." The result, according to one critic: "We are catapulted into an unconstrained and increasingly dangerous arms race as to both offensive and defensive weapons."

A Pentagon scientist was then cited. He said the ABM Treaty permitted defensive research. He also noted that a defensive system against ballistic missiles was unlikely to be perfect. Lynch then chimed in with this: "Not just imperfect, say the critics, downright impossible." Physicist Richard Garwin then focused on how the software was out of reach. A Soviet scientist called the whole concept "a risky situation," especially from the budgetary standpoint. Nevertheless, added, Lynch, President Reagan still "wants the research to go ahead full steam."

Lynch's report, like others, was skewed toward the critics from start to finish. It also was flawed in terms of the reference to the "Maginot line," the impenetrable shield notion that the administration started moving away from shortly after the president's March 23, 1983, speech. And he failed to present any background on what was permitted by the ABM Treaty or on how even a limited defense challenged the conventional wisdom of the doctrine of Mutual Assured Destruction and how it could have complicated Soviet strategic calculations, thus enhancing deterrence rather than detracting from it. These arguments were being made regularly by SDI supporters, but they were seldom explored in detail by the networks.

On that same day, ABC chose to focus part of its broadcast on how SDI could complicate the arms control process begun in Geneva. ABC Moscow correspondent Walter Rodgers reported on a news conference by Soviet Foreign Minister Andrei Gromyko, who "warned that without progress on banning space weapons in the next round of Soviet-American negotiations, there would be no point in talking further about reducing superpower nuclear arsenals." Gromyko's other points included how he would "fight to the end to prevent the militarization of space," how "questions of strategic nuclear arms cannot be considered in isolation from space," and how ridiculous was "Reagan's claim that Star Wars is not an offensive weapons program."

In a stab at some balance, ABC followed with a report by Dennis Troute at the State Department, who focused only on the issue of linkage between nuclear arms talks and SDI. Secretary Shultz, according to Troute, "left the door open to an accommodation with Soviet views." Secretary Weinberger, however, "reflecting the hard-line approach of the Pentagon, had a somewhat different view." He did not see any degree of linkage.

Troute concluded by saying this "ambiguity" over linkage will be the source of continued jockeying until Reagan makes his decision as to who will lead the negotiating team. Missing from Troute's report was any countervailing views on the key point Gromyko made about "militarization of space" or the characterization of Star Wars as offensive in nature, both rather central points that an administration official could have easily rebutted.

Other periodic Soviet charges also went unanswered, often in the short anchor tell format. For example, on March 4, 1985, NBC anchor Tom Brokaw made this report: "The Soviet Union tonight is putting some new pressure on West Germany to stay out of American-sponsored research on space weapons, the so-called Star Wars. Soviet Foreign Minister Andrei Gromyko warned Germany today that such research would make it an accomplice to a violation of the 1972 anti-missile treaty."

The network apparently did not feel any need to provide the context for the Gromyko charge, which would have involved explaining the limitations imposed by the ABM Treaty and then determining whether the SDI research proposed would actually violate the treaty, which at that stage in the program was highly unlikely.

The Soviets were not the only ones whose views were presented on occasion in a one-sided fashion. Take this full anchor tell by Bob Schieffer on February 9, 1985: "With Defense Secretary Weinberger in Europe trying to generate support for the Star Wars concept among the NATO allies, France's Defense Minister said today that he had serious misgivings about the space weapons system. He said it would probably help start a new arms race." End of report.

And even in other, longer reporting that was more balanced, references to SDI often included the idea that it was the main obstacle to arms control. On March 8, 1985, for example, CBS White House correspondent Bill Plante reported that the administration might be flexible on the issue of long-range strategic missiles, but on Reagan's "pet," SDI, "research must go forward." Plante concluded his report by stating, "Despite all the talk of flexibility, US officials concede that convincing the Soviets to accept the Star Wars research program is the only real key to progress as far as they're concerned."

THE WORLD WANTS ARMS CONTROL

On January 4, 1985, the eve of the Geneva arms talks at the beginning of the second Reagan administration, ABC anchor Peter Jennings summed up the world's collective sigh of relief: "In this capital city tonight and all across Europe, millions of people are focusing their hopes on the Soviet-American meetings which will take place in Geneva on Monday and Tuesday. Europeans, just like Americans, want nuclear arms controlled, and they have sighed with relief that the superpowers are finally returning to the negotiating table." Beyond stating the obvious—that most people wanted nuclear arms controlled—Jennings had captured the networks' real focus when it came to arms control: getting to the table and, hopefully, getting an agreement.

In all the problematic and nonproblematic reporting on arms control and SDI, one thing seemed clear: The networks were largely captives of the arms control establishment and its conventional wisdom. The lack of specialized expertise, even among State Department correspondents, meant that the unconventional approach of holding out for deep cuts in nuclear weapons in the Strategic Arms Reduction Talks and in the talks focusing on intermediate-range nuclear missiles could never really be treated with seriousness or explained cogently. Instead, the Reagan administration was viewed as either not serious about arms control or as anti-arms control altogether.

When it came to strategic defense, another unconventional idea that involved shifting the strategic calculus of the nuclear era from total reliance on offensive systems and mutual assured destruction to a combination of offensive and defensive systems, the networks were as ill equipped in terms of expertise. They saw SDI simply as a ploy used by the administration's hard-liners to avoid entering into a serious arms control agreement with the Soviets. Complicating the networks' efforts were arcane policy differences within the administration itself over SDI and arms control. If the networks did capture one thing quite accurately, it was the lack of a clear consensus on these issues among the key players at the State Department, the Pentagon, the Arms Control and Disarmament Agency (ACDA), the National Security Council, and the Joint Chiefs of Staff.

Overall, as a result of this confusion, the serious issues surrounding a complicated arms control process were never treated in any depth. A group within the Reagan administration clearly believed that a series of arms control agreements had locked in levels of nuclear weapons that, in themselves, were dangerous and becoming more so as new and improved versions of strategic missiles kept appearing on the Soviet side, all within the legal limits of previous treaties. This same group also thought the Soviets' extensive efforts in the area of missile defense should be answered. This was the case even before the announcement of SDI.[151] For many of the reasons cited above, that side of the debate never came across in network reporting.

Table 7.1

Problematic Arms Control Reporting by Beat, Number, and Percentage for sample periods Jan.–Apr. 1983, Jan.–Apr. 1985, and Jan.–Apr. 1990

Beats	# of Reports	% Arms Control Coverage	# of Prob. Reports	% Coverage w/ Problems
Wash/Gen	22	10.9%	14	63.6%
State	22	10.9%	14	63.6%
White House	29	14.4%	16	55.1%
Pentagon	8	3.9%	3	37.5%
Anchor	79	39.3%	29	36.7%
Foreign	41	20.4%	12	29.2%
Total	201	99.8%	88	43.7%

Source: Author's Database. See appendix 1.

The overall pattern of arms control coverage was clearly lacking in balance and context. Not surprisingly, taken together, the Pentagon and State Department beats played a relatively minor role in covering arms control (see Table 7.1). Once again, the White House, other general beats, and the anchors reported on this complex area the majority of the time. In terms of problematic coverage, all the beats had higher than average rates, reflecting how deeply embedded the conventional wisdom was.

Chapter 8

The Foreign Policy Scorecard

When it came to foreign policy coverage during the periods sampled, the networks were much less prone to the kind of bias and distortion that crept into coverage of arms control, the defense budget, weapons, and industry. For the sample periods from the four administrations and the Gulf War, foreign policy coverage was problematic just 25.1 percent of the time. And, in many areas, it was even lower: Middle East coverage was problematic only 13.6 percent of the time; coverage of Europe, only 21.4 percent of the time; Asia/Pacific coverage, 22.7 percent of the time; Africa, 18.7 percent; Soviet Union/Russia, 13.7 percent; and Bosnia, a mere 11.3 percent of the time.

Having said that, it should be noted that the constraints of the 22-minute format seldom allow for more than a quick overview of developments abroad. Still, as several recent studies have suggested, within these limitations, the evening newscasts have made a consistent effort to provide foreign policy coverage in spite of the fact that it does not rank high with viewers, and the networks do at times compare favorably with midsize daily newspapers when covering major foreign stories.[152]

Few would suggest, however, that network evening news coverage even comes close to the depth and context that major newspapers like the *New York Times* or the *Washington Post* provide in their coverage of foreign policy. In fact, a study that tracked international news coverage on the networks found that "no country, with the possible exception of Russia, was explained and presented coherently enough so that attentive viewers could believe they understood how life was lived there."[153] It also noted that international coverage was also narrower in scope than was domestic, with violence being the subject of half of all international stories.

The foreign policy coverage analyzed here from the Reagan, Bush, Clinton administrations, and the Gulf War had a similar tilt, with more than half of the coverage being devoted to the guerrilla wars in Central America, violence in the Middle East, and the war in Bosnia. Out of the total 1,022 foreign policy reports from the ABC, CBS, and NBC evening newscasts, 324 were devoted to Central America, 117 to the Middle East, and 220 to Bosnia.

As for level of effort, the Soviet Union/Russia, which was treated as a separate category, received the most attention from the networks, with a total of 465 reports, more than any other country or region. This coverage also stood out for its high quality, with a mere 13.7 percent being problematic.

The reasons for the high quality of this coverage are instructive. First of all, as the principal adversary during the Cold War and a significant military power even after the breakup of its empire, the Soviet Union and Russia drew sustained, in-depth coverage, ranging from the military and political to social developments. Second, the networks turned to their Moscow correspondents and their correspondents at the State Department and Pentagon 58 percent of the time when covering the Soviet Union/Russia. The generalists, including the anchor, White House correspondent, and other Washington beats, accounted for 41.9 percent of the coverage. Not surprisingly, the generalists were also responsible for three times as much problematic coverage in this category, 48 out of the 64 problematic reports.

CENTRAL AMERICA: FOREIGN POLICY COVERAGE WITH A POLITICAL EDGE

Despite the low problematic rate for foreign policy coverage taken as a whole from all of the sample periods analyzed, it was not always balanced and full of context. In fact, network coverage of the Reagan administration's Central America policies in each of the periods sampled stood out as the most problematic of all foreign policy coverage, with a rate of 46 percent. That problematic coverage of Central America during the two Reagan periods tended to skew the problematic rating for Central America coverage as a whole, which ended up averaging just over 40 percent for all four administration periods sampled (see Figure 8.1).

The main problem during the Reagan periods was related to the networks' lack of balance and context. In fact, there was a clear inclination to emphasize the points of view of critics of the administration.

NBC's back-to-back reports on January 24, 1983, were not unusual. Roger Mudd first delivered a short anchor tell on "a group of congressmen, academics, human rights activists, and celebrities," who held a news conference "to protest the Reagan administration's certification of human rights progress in El Salvador and to demand a halt to US military aid. Meanwhile, in front of the State Department, about 123 demonstrators protesting certification were arrested. The demonstrators said each of them represented one of the thousands who have disappeared in El Salvador."

Mudd then introduced a second report from correspondent Bonnie Anderson on the quarter of a million people left homeless as a result of the intense fighting

Figure 8.1

Problematic Foreign Policy Coverage by Region and Percentage for Jan.–Apr. 1983, Jan.–Apr. 1985, Jan.–Apr. 1990, and Jan.–Apr. 1994

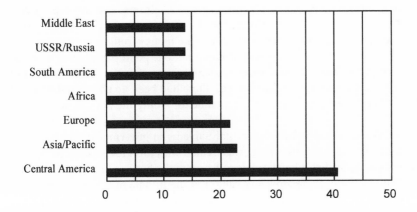

in El Salvador. Anderson visited a group of refugees being supported by the Catholic Church. The situation was a sad one, and her report was poignant in a number of spots. For example, she explained that "dozens of women spend their day washing clothes or cooking for their neighbors, but the people of San Jose de la Montagne share more than food, clothing and shelter. They share collective memories of brutality and terror and loss. Ten-year-old Rosendo Sato saw her father dragged away by government troops and later found his body in an open field."

What Anderson did not tell her viewers was that the Salvadoran guerrillas had also managed to displace innocent civilians and that they, too, had committed "brutal" acts of terror. For his part, Mudd had no references to why Reagan certified El Salvador for making progress in human rights.

On February 27, 1983, CBS anchor Morton Dean noted how the "war in El Salvador has triggered a battle in Washington; a battle over how far the US should go; how deep a commitment the US should make to help the government of El Salvador defend itself. President Reagan wants to dispatch increased military aid to that troubled ally."

Correspondent John Ferrugia then explained how Reagan was requesting $60 million in additional military aid, which he said was critical to the Salvadoran's fight against leftist guerrillas. "That amount would bring total aid this year to nearly four times what Congress has already appropriated," Ferrugia added. After noting that Reagan would try to convince key committee chairmen to support the request, Ferrugia, to his credit, pointed out that the level of aid in 1982 was $82 million, compared with the $26 million authorized for 1983.

"But," Ferrugia said, "Mr. Reagan is facing tough opposition from many in Congress who won't support a government they see as lacking in popular support because it's brutal to its own people." To illustrate this point, a sound bite followed from Rep. Stephen Solarz (D-NY), a vocal critic of the administration's policy. Solarz said the United States should not support the government there "because right now it's like money going down a rat hole." Finally, Ferrugia described Reagan's various strategems for getting around Congress: one was reprogramming funds, which only the Appropriations Committee has to approve; the other was to "bypass Congress completely by taking the money from emergency contingency funds which he alone controls." Other than one point paraphrased from an administration official about the need to supply new weapons, ammunition and spare parts to the Salvadoran government, there had been no effort on the part of CBS to explain the administration's rationale for aiding the Salvadoran government.

In contrast to the portrait of a brutal Salvadoran government, in the case of Nicaragua, the Marxist government was treated with kid gloves. And, unlike the regular focus on the Salvadoran people suffering at the hands of their government, from human rights abuses to being caught in the middle of the war, there were few, if any, stories about hardships imposed on the Nicaraguan people by the Sandinistas, who had taken power in Nicaragua in 1979. To the contrary, it was mostly the contras (from the Spanish for counter-revolutionaries, the group seeking to oust the Sandinistas from power) who were to blame for human rights abuses and for the dislocation of Nicaraguan civilians. And, unlike the case of the Salvadoran government, which was portrayed as the "troubled ally" and a right-wing dictatorship, few judgments were rendered on the Sandinistas, whose charges against the US government often went unanswered and whose policies toward their own people were infrequently scrutinized.

Take this example of coverage on January 9, 1983. NBC anchor Chris Wallace reported, in full: "Nicaragua sent a letter of protest to Washington this weekend charging the US with criminal acts and a policy of aggression against Nicaragua. It also accused the US of backing right-wing raids into Nicaragua. Meanwhile, the foreign ministers of Mexico, Colombia, Panama, and Venezuela today called for an end to foreign meddling in Central America. They said the region should solve its own problems." It would seem like the seriousness of such charges would have demanded more explanation. There was none.

On March 22, 1983, CBS devoted considerable air time to a report on Nicaragua's charges about a US-backed rebel invasion across the Honduran border, but there was little in the way of balance. After a short introduction by anchor Dan Rather, CBS correspondent Charles Gomez reported on fighting between contras and Sandinistas in the country's central province. He then described how Sandinista Defense Minister Humberto Ortega had denounced the Reagan administration for "pushing Nicaragua to the edge of war with neighboring Honduras."

Gomez continued, pointing out all the charges leveled by the Sandinistas about CIA involvement with the contras inside Honduras. Anchor Dan Rather then added that the State Department spokesman refused to discuss the Nicaraguan charge of a US-backed invasion, "but he said there is increasing opposition in Nicaragua to the Sandinista government." Since Rather had given the administration a chance to comment (and reported it), he and CBS were quite satisfied that they had done their part in checking off the box for balance. Yet, somehow, the networks always managed to find a critic of administration policy when needed, whether it was a congressional representative or a think tank expert brought forth to make the point. Washington, of course, is full of experts and representatives who take positions on all sides of every issue. For some reason, the defenders of administration policies on Central America were not sought out very often.

Another example of reporting on Nicaragua demonstrated the sympathetic approach the networks took toward the Sandinista regime, an approach rarely taken when they reported on the Salvadoran government or military.

On March 26, 1983, CBS anchor Bob Schieffer led off with this introduction: "Rebels who are trying to overthrow Nicaragua's revolutionary Sandinista government claimed tonight they have opened a second front near the border with Costa Rica. The government says the rebellion, which it claims is financed by the US Central Intelligence Agency, has been crushed. In an effort to build new support for the government, officials today organized a funeral march for war casualties." Correspondent Charles Gomez then reported on the funeral of Emilio Cruz, "one of the new heroes of the revolution, a hero in a battle against familiar enemies. . . . Children led cheers," Gomez reported. "The crowd shouted 'power to the people.' "

While Gomez did note that not more than 1,000 people showed up to cheer the Sandinistas, he also made clear that the crowd there "still enthusiastically supports the revolution." And there was the Sandinista commander Alonso Poras, who said, "We know this aggression is the result of Yankee imperialism." Gomez also explained at the end of his report that the cross-border attacks by the contras have "left many Nicaraguans less eager to back a revolution which now is forced to be on the defensive." But overall, the report, with its strong visual images of the funeral procession and the denunciations of Yankee imperialism, played heavily on emotions and lacked broader context, not unlike the report on the hardships of Salvadoran refugees.

A few days later, on March 31, 1983, NBC carried two reports on Central America. The first was a short anchor tell by Tom Brokaw: "Guerrillas fighting in El Salvador are claiming a major victory tonight. They say they killed more than 70, perhaps as many as 84 government soldiers, northeast of San Salvador today. Many of the government troops were said to be part of elite units trained by the United States. The El Salvador government will only say that there was heavy fighting in that area." What Brokaw did not tell his viewers was that Salvadoran guerrilla-supplied casualty numbers were notoriously unreliable. Radio Vinceremos, which is likely where these numbers came from, was skillfully used by the guerrilla movement as a propaganda arm of its war efforts.

In the same evening newscast, Brokaw turned to Nicaragua, where the Sandinistas claimed "their army beat back an attempt by right-wing rebels to establish a stronghold along the Atlantic Ocean." NBC correspondent George Lewis then reported on the Nicaraguan government claims of "a huge US-supported invasion force" massed on the Honduran border. Though Lewis himself said that journalists on both sides have "found no signs of an imminent invasion," he continued to describe the Nicaraguan defense minister's claims that 2,000 invaders had been pushed back. Though the Sandinistas would not take journalists to the scene of any big battles, they did take them to the scene of "a small battle where two days ago right-wing guerrillas, known as contras, had burned down a coffee warehouse."

Such attacks by the contras, Lewis explained, were further eroding a crippled Nicaraguan economy. The need for "vigilance" has been "costly for the Nicaraguans, more money for arms, less for consumer goods. Empty supermarket shelves. Gas lines in the middle of a worldwide oil glut. And the continuing cost in human lives." And so Lewis concluded his report. Even though he and NBC recognized that the entire premise of the report was false, namely, that there was no big battle, they were led along by the Sandinistas to report on a skirmish that resulted in a burned-down coffee warehouse, all so Lewis could make the broader points about the contras causing hardship to the people of Nicaragua.

ONE BRIGHT SPOT FOR REAGAN'S POLICIES

One of the few times that coverage tilted in favor of the Reagan administration's policies came near the end of April 1983. On April 20, all three networks carried reports on Libyan cargo planes destined for Nicaragua that had been detained in Brazil. The cargo, however, was not medical supplies as the pilots had claimed. Instead, the planes were loaded with arms for the Sandinistas and possibly the Salvadoran guerrillas.

CBS Pentagon correspondent David Martin took the opportunity to explain that the Nicaraguans had been taking a number of steps in the military realm, including extending airfields for the possible delivery of Soviet MiG fighter aircraft. NBC anchor Roger Mudd called it "a public relations bonus" for the administration. NBC Pentagon correspondent Fred Francis reported that the Brazilians had discovered enough arms for a small army. And ABC Pentagon correspondent John McWethy revealed that there were several Russians aboard the aircraft, lending credence to the administration's claims that the Soviet Union had been supplying Nicaragua through such middle men as Cuba and Libya. But incidents like this were rare, and so was reporting that adequately explained the administration's aims in taking covert action against the Sandinistas, which quickly became overt, and in supporting the Salvadoran military in its guerrilla war.

THE GOOD GUYS AND THE BAD GUYS

In the 1985 period analyzed during the second Reagan administration, there was more sympathetic coverage of the Sandinistas and negative coverage of the contras, while the situation was reversed in the case of El Salvador, with the government taking the brunt of the negative coverage while the guerrillas were seldom taken to task. On January 10, 1985, for instance, ABC anchor Peter Jennings announced in all seriousness that "Sandinista leader Daniel Ortega [Saavedra] was sworn in as Nicaragua's first elected president in nearly five years." Where Jennings's reference to "five years" came from was puzzling. The Sandinistas had seized power in July 1979. A little over a year later, in August 1980, they announced there would be no elections until 1985, this after promising elections as early as possible.

ABC's own Peter Collins would follow Jennings and say that Ortega's election was part of "a Sandinista campaign to persuade the world that Nicaragua now has a legitimate, elected government." He would also carry one sound bite from an opposition leader who called the November election a fraud. On the other hand, Collins spent half of his report talking about the hardship of ordinary Nicaraguans, for which the Sandinistas blamed the United States, and about the contras' continuing to spread their attacks, even though Congress cut off funding to them.

Collins went on to say that "dozens of people have been killed in ambushes recently. In one this week, the contras seized but then released an American Maryknoll nun, Nancy Donovan. She says 14 other persons traveling with her were killed." To conclude, Collins noted that the "opposition" says Nicaragua seems headed "toward one-party control, but with a limited degree of opposition tolerated." Of course, Collins failed to point out that Nicaragua had been a one-party state since the day the Sandinistas seized power and that the political opposition was in the same category as that which the deposed Anastacio Somoza Debayle "tolerated" for most of his reign. Collins did, however, manage to spotlight how the contras were the ones wreaking havoc on Nicaragua.

On January 28, 1985, ABC took on the contras once again. ABC anchor Peter Jennings began the report by saying that there was evidence that the contras might be responsible for the deaths or disappearances of 250 opponents of the pro-American government in Honduras. ABC correspondent Mark Potter had been "investigating." First there was a former contra intelligence agent, who claimed he was ordered to kill innocent civilians in nearby Guatemala and Honduras. Also, "past and present members of the FDN [the contras based in the north of Nicaragua] now in the United States have told ABC News of criminal activities within the organization that had nothing to do with the military fight. Fearing for their lives, they would speak only under cover." Potter then described contract murders, armed robberies, and executions, making links to those who were currently in charge of the FDN. He also described the innocent victims of these abuses. For balance, he stated that "repeated attempts by ABC News to reach these men [contra leaders] for comment were unsuccessful." According to Potter, another FDN leader, Adolfo Calero, declined to comment on television, but disputed the allegations by phone, "calling them a smear campaign."

As a reference by Potter to the State Department's efforts to pressure the FDN to "clean out what it calls the rotten apples" suggested, it was no secret that some of the 15,000 contras belonging to the FDN had either violated human rights or committed crimes. But ABC's repeated focus on human rights problems and the contras showed a level of scrutiny by the networks that was far greater than that applied to the Sandinistas or the Salvadoran guerrillas.

In one of the few cases where a massacre by the Salvadoran guerrillas was the subject of a network report, NBC left it to an anchor introduction and then shifted the focus of the report to the tragedies on both sides of the Nicaraguan war. This particular report aired on April 10, 1985. NBC anchor Tom Brokaw first described in vivid detail, including references to women and children with their throats slit, a "surprise attack" by "300 leftist guerrillas" against the Salvadoran village of Santa Cruz Loma. Some of the people described it as a massacre, he said. Brokaw also stated, "It's not clear why the village was attacked, nor why the Salvadoran army sent no troops to defend it" (so much for the notion of "surprise attack").

Brokaw then suddenly concluded his introduction by shifting to US maneuvers in Honduras, known as the Big Pine III war games. That was NBC correspondent Mike Boettcher's cue to launch into a discussion of "the real war" (as opposed to war games) going on across the border in Nicaragua, where the war between US-supported contras and Nicaragua's Sandinistas had deposited its latest victims. As he continued, Boettcher made clear that both the contras and Sandinistas were responsible for these Nicaraguan victims. "Only the Sandinista army and the contras are left here to kill one another. That is what's beyond the sight of the American tanks and Hondurans. . . . In Nicaragua, it's all too real. Here, it is still just a game."

For their part, the other two networks focused entirely on the US-Honduran exercises, ignoring the Salvadoran guerrilla attack on civilians. ABC correspondent Peter Collins provided a solid report on the purpose of the maneuvers, which was to reassure Honduras, given the possibility of the Sandinistas pursuing contras across the border, and pointed out that this was part of a series of such exercises.

CBS, however, featured a bizarre report from correspondent Martha Teichner, who laced her coverage of the Texas National Guard with references to its Hispanic makeup and a possible racist motive behind the deployment of this unit. She even suggested that someday there could be "Hispanic fighting Hispanic here," in spite of the fact that the deployed guardsmen basically told her they were just doing their jobs.

The issue of guard deployments would only become politicized a year later, when a number of governors challenged the Pentagon's authority to send guard units out of the country for training.[154] Teichner's strange point about the race of guardsmen serving in Central America was not even related to the ultimate controversy over the guard.

As for the periodic coverage of El Salvador in 1985, it continued to focus on the Salvadoran government's problems. A March 31 NBC report, for instance, was laced with references to the situation being "not encouraging" from a US point of view, the situation in El Salvador being "grim," and the issue of millions of dollars in US aid going down "the rat hole."

CENTRAL AMERICA AND VIETNAM

Avoiding another "Vietnam" was a regular theme of critics of the Reagan administration's policies in the region. On January 15, 1985, CBS found a rather creative way to make this point. Out of the entire two-million-strong Veterans of Foreign Wars (VFW), CBS had managed to turn up the one local post that was criticizing the Reagan administration for its intervention in Central America.

CBS anchor Dan Rather, in his usual melodramatic way, pointed out that since the VFW's founding in 1913, no VFW post, "reportedly, has ever disputed the national organization on a major foreign policy matter. But now, David Dow reports, one post has triggered a war of words." Correspondent Dow began by saying how unusual it was for a commander in chief like Reagan not to be able to depend on the VFW for support. But local post 5888 in Santa Cruz, California, he added, was a small post "composed largely of Vietnam veterans."

Cut to sound bite by a veteran: "The war in Vietnam was dead wrong. And the same kind of mentality is getting us in Central America." Next, Dow told his viewers how the post had sent an unofficial resolution to the Sandinista government endorsing nonintervention in Central America, "criticizing US policy for escalating rather than resolving such conflicts." More sound bites from post members about their right to speak out—"out of conscience," Dow added.

For balance, Dow inserted a point about older VFW members grumbling and a national leader saying this was not the position of the VFW. The concluding kicker: "Meanwhile, back in Santa Cruz, the leaders of Post 5888 say they are not alone, that similar incidents could happen elsewhere, as more and more of the boys of Vietnam become the grown-up leaders of civic groups, civic groups such as the Veterans of Foreign Wars." End of report.

This was just one of a number of references to the specter of Vietnam in coverage of Central America. In fact, in the process of analyzing the several hundred reports on this topic, it was hard to ignore the collective urge of the networks to insert themselves in what seemed to be an attempt to avoid another Vietnam.

A NETWORK POSTSCRIPT ON NICARAGUA

Moving beyond the Central America coverage of the Reagan periods, network coverage of Nicaragua's 1990 election brought the Central American story full circle.[155] Somehow, the ballot box had miraculously accomplished what years of war could not. Polls leading up to the February 25, 1990, Nicaraguan election all suggested that Daniel Ortega would finally become Nicaragua's popularly elected president. On February 21, 1990, the last day of campaigning, ABC correspondent David Ensor described Ortega as "parading his popularity with young voters." His campaign featured rock music and was "slick and sexy," according to Ensor. Though Ortega had two weaknesses—the miserable economy and the unpopularity of the draft—"the Sandinistas are already proclaiming victory." One of Ensor's main points: Daniel Ortega has made the switch from "Commandante Ortega" to "Daniel the Swinger."

On the same day, NBC correspondent Ed Rabel was even less circumspect. With images of Daniel Ortega behind him, Rabel began: "This is the man, pollsters say, who will be elected overwhelmingly this weekend, six more years as President of Nicaragua, the man President Reagan promised would cry uncle." Rabel continued: "The United States spent hundreds of millions of dollars on the contras, the so-called freedom fighters, to do the job. They failed. Election observers say the Bush administration may have itself to blame for Daniel Ortega's rise in popularity among the voters. The reason, they say, is the US military invasion in Panama. That was a move that was widely denounced here in Nicaragua."

Two days before the election, on February 23, Rabel emphasized Ortega's "dramatic transformation" on the campaign trail, "taking on a fresh persona just as his government enters a brand new political era." Rabel talked as if Ortega was the winner: "Ortega's supporters hope his new, non-threatening image will help pull in desperately needed foreign aid." Back at the White House, NBC correspondent John Cochran told NBC viewers that "the White House is already preparing public opinion in this country for a Sandinista victory."

On the eve of the election, February 24, ABC anchor Jack Smith began by saying, "Nicaraguan President Daniel Ortega says he'll invite President Bush to his inauguration, predicting he'll win tomorrow's national elections in Nicaragua. A decade of US hostility to the ruling Marxist Sandinista Party is at stake in Sunday's vote." ABC correspondent David Ensor then trotted out his formulations of the commandante transformed into rock star versus Violetta Barrios de Chamorro, who "has the quiet blessing of the church and of the United States." The bottom line: "Ortega doesn't expect to lose."

On election day, February 25, NBC's Rabel covered the voting of the candidates and then said, "The widespread belief that the Sandinistas will prevail has shifted thinking far beyond the ballot box." ABC's election day coverage contained this nugget from David Ensor: "For many Nicaraguans, the question today is who do they blame for the miserable state of their economy? The Sandinistas, for mismanaging it, or the US for the trade embargo and for backing the contras?" What was striking was the fact that, while hailing the "democratic process," the networks never suggested that freedom and democracy themselves might be at issue in this election.

After Ortega's surprising loss, ABC anchor Peter Jennings made this observation in his February 26 broadcast: "For ten years the US supported the military attempt to overthrow the Sandinista government in Nicaragua. It never succeeded. Today the Sandinista government has been overthrown at the ballot box. Tonight the president-elect of Nicaragua is Violeta Chamorro, who led the coalition of political parties united in their opposition to the Sandinista record." NBC's Tom Brokaw took a similar tack: "The people of Nicaragua and their ballots did to Daniel Ortega what ten years of guerrilla war waged by the contras could not do. They drove him from power."

In their reports, both ABC and NBC correspondents in Managua then focused mainly on issues related to a transition and possible economic assistance from the

United States. Each also made brief references to who deserved credit, carrying balancing sound bites from those, like Reagan and Oliver North (the Marine lieutenant colonel who served on Reagan's National Security Council and was partly responsible for the Iran-contra scandal), who believed that the struggle by the contras made the difference, and congressional critics of Reagan's policies, who believed that the move toward negotiations was what made the difference.

NBC, however, went one step further with a long analysis by John Dancy. His report was remarkable in terms of how coherently it captured the three networks' conventional wisdom over the years. While making reference to how the Sandinista movement turned more Marxist and repressive, he stated that Ortega, who was a mere "irritant" to Carter, became an obsession to Reagan, "who saw him as an instrument of Moscow." The contras, Dancy noted, were Reagan's "blunt instrument" against the Sandinistas. Reagan's support for the contras would ultimately "scar" his foreign policy. A Reagan quote calling the contras "the moral equal of our Founding Fathers" or akin to "the brave men and women of the French Resistance" followed, mainly to illustrate his "obsession." Many of these contras, Dancy continued, were former members of "the Nicaraguan National Guard, Somoza's enforcers. They were often brutal, often inept."

Then there were references to the aid given to the contras, the CIA's "illegally and secretly" mining Nicaraguan harbors, the scheme to secretly fund the contras without the knowledge of Congress. President Reagan just would not accept a Marxist regime in Nicaragua, Dancy added, using another Reagan quote on how "it would be a major defeat for democracy in our hemisphere."

"But," Dancy continued, "poll after poll showed the American people did not support Reagan in his devotion to the contras." This was followed by a sound bite from Sen. Dale Bumpers (D-AR), who labeled Reagan "the consummate ideologue" who submitted to the proposition that "we can overthrow this communist down there." Of course, Dancy never hinted at whether media coverage of Nicaragua had anything to do with the lack of support for Reagan's policy. Dancy's conclusion: "It has been one of the longest and most traumatic chapters in US history in Latin America. And tonight it seems to be ending, and ending in a way that Ronald Reagan never could have imagined."

CAUSE AND EFFECT

In a few short minutes, NBC's Dancy had revealed more about the nearsightedness of the networks themselves than he did about Reagan's so-called "obsession" with the contras. To the networks, it was a simple story. There were bad guys and good guys, and, once labeled, it was hard to break the mold. In the two periods analyzed, there was never any serious attempt to explore in depth the administration's efforts to encourage democracy in the region or the overall strategic context concerning US versus Soviet influence in the region.

As the Nicaragua "postscript" suggests, the networks had missed entirely the basic relationship of cause and effect. Had these elections suddenly appeared out of the blue and solved the problems between the various factions in Nicaragua? Hardly. As former UN Ambassador Jeane Kirkpatrick observed, the Nicaraguan regime of Daniel Ortega did not fall because of one simple reason. She suggested it was a combination of Reagan policies, the "terrible incompetence" of Nicaraguan economic managers, stagnation and repression, pressure from the other Central American presidents and encouragement for the electoral process from President Mikhail S. Gorbachev of the Soviet Union.[156]

Moreover, it was not only, as ABC's Ensor had boiled it down to, a simple choice between whom to blame more, the incompetent Sandinista economic managers or the US policies of backing the contras and depriving Nicaragua of aid. As corny as it may sound to network producers and correspondents, there were certainly issues of political and economic freedom involved. The networks never seemed to understand that, from the start, the Sandinistas had it within their own power to liberalize their country, have free elections, and to simultaneously build good relations with the United States. They chose to do none of the above and, thus, not only made an enemy of the United States, but also of many of the Sandinista movement's original supporters, Violetta Chamorro included.

For their part, the networks preferred to view the United States and its support of the unseemlier elements of Somoza's old guard as the real cause of Nicaragua's problems. That is not to say that the United States did not make a concerted effort to overthrow the Sandinista regime. It did, and all the reports about those policies were grounded in fact. What the networks never took seriously, however, was Reagan's strong belief in democracy, whether it was taunting Mikhail Gorbachev to tear down the Berlin Wall, or describing the Soviet Union as the "evil empire," or believing that groups opposing a repressive, Marxist regime in Nicaragua were engaged in a noble cause, despite their own warts.

The same nearsighted view was evident in coverage of El Salvador. The networks focused on the warts of the government, but never really thought through whether democracy had a better chance of succeeding with the US government prodding a Salvadoran government dominated by the military or whether a Salvadoran state governed by Marxist-Leninist guerrillas would have ultimately moved toward democracy and bettered the lives of the country's disaffected citizens.

The problem with network reporting on highly politicized issues like Central America does not come down to individual reports. It comes down to a collective whole, with underlying beliefs in the correctness of one side versus the other, with innuendo and cynicism about approaches that do not conform to the conventional—and, often, the liberal—wisdom. A large part of the problem also came down to the choices the networks made on what to cover, choices strongly influenced by their own preconceptions.

Given the same tools at their disposal and the identical situation, the networks could have undoubtedly made the Salvadoran rebels into the bad guys and the Salvadoran government into a model of democratic change. Similarly, they could have portrayed the Sandinistas as the totalitarians and the contras as the heros of the people. The trouble is, that approach would have been just as flawed as the approach that was taken. What was clearly needed was the full picture of these conflicts and their root causes, with all the plots and subplots.

Chapter 9

Why Network Coverage Fell Short

Behind the patterns of distorted coverage was a news process, as well as a set of practices and standards, that governed the way it operated. On the most basic level, journalists subscribe to the credo of fairness, accuracy, and objectivity. But while reporting on the defense component of national security, network correspondents and anchors often fell down in these areas, particularly when it came to reporting on the defense budget, weapons, defense industry and procurement, arms control, and foreign policy coverage of Central America.

To the extent that the patterns of problematic coverage existed, they seemed to reflect two institutional aspects of the news process. The first involves the process of selection, assignment, and presentation; and the second is directly related to the lapses in adherence to journalistic standards at various points within the news process.

On the first aspect, one writer observed, "The conventions of choosing 'the news' are so familiar, and so much of the process happens by learned and in-grained habits, that it is easy for journalists to forget that the result reflects *decisions*, rather than some kind of neutral truth."[157] There is indeed a series of decisions that affect the quality of national security news, beginning with the basic decisions about what the news will be on any given day. Those decisions emanate from the interaction between producers and correspondents in Washington and those in New York who accept pitches from the beats or assign stories to the beats and particular correspondents. Decisions are also made as to the time each news report will be allotted, from the one- to two-sentence anchor tell to the "longer" several-minute news report introduced by the anchor with back-to-back reporting from different beat correspondents. In the case of a topic like defense industry, by choosing only news about scandals and then relegating most of it to the anchor tell format, there was little chance for any context to be added and a big chance that the cumulative effect of such news coverage over time would lead to distortion and public confusion. Assigning generalist correspondents without the expertise in complex matters, like weapons development, is another example of how problems sometimes reflect decisions within the process.

Lapses in adherence to journalistic standards constitute the other side of the coin. The main issue here is whether network anchors and correspondents were fair and objective in presenting the news. It is certainly understood that *objectivity* and *neutrality* are ideals. In fact, one writer has argued that it is unrealistic to think that journalists can or should reach for these ideals: "Journalism needs to help people understand increasingly complex issues that affect their political and social decisions, and this is impossible to do without making judgments of fact and value."[158] This same writer did, however, still hold journalists to what he called the higher standard of "intellectual honesty," which "means that in presenting a news report a journalist may draw certain conclusions and make certain predictions about the consequences of a particular event, but it also imposes a duty to do justice to the areas of legitimate debate."[159]

In my analysis of network news reports, it became clear that there were sins of omission and sins of commission when it came to doing justice to the areas of legitimate debate. To get to the bottom of why some coverage fell short, "problematic" reports were grouped into six broad categories. Naturally, there was some overlap among the categories, but most often one problem area stood out in each report. While there might have been other ways to organize and analyze the coverage identified as "problematic," the conclusions would likely be the same: either there was a departure from basic journalistic standards or something went wrong in the decisions made within the news process. Problems most directly related to journalistic standards included (1) lack of balance or context, (2) overemphasis on drama and bad news, or (3) loaded labeling or advocacy; and problems most directly related to the news process—in terms of news selection, assignment, and presentation—included (4) lack of context as a result of brevity, (5) lack of knowledge on the part of the correspondent, or (6) bad news judgment. Overall, about 60 percent of the problems identified related to lapses in journalistic standards and about 40 percent were related to flaws in the decisions taken in the course of the news process itself (see Table 9.1).

LACK OF BALANCE OR CONTEXT

Lack of balance or context can result from a failure to frame a news report in terms of where it fits into the broader picture, or it can result from leaving out critical information, whether intentionally or unintentionally. Failing to provide balance or context was the most prevalent problem in national security reporting.

By way of example, on February 25, 1983, both CBS and ABC focused on testimony by Pentagon analyst Chuck Spinney, who contended that the budget for weapons was grossly underestimated. CBS correspondent Bill Lynch began his report this way: "The Senate caucus room was packed with worried looking Pentagon officials and defense industry lobbyists from companies like GE, Raytheon,

Table 9.1

Categories of Problematic Coverage by Number and Percentage for Jan.–Apr. 1983, Jan.–Apr. 1985, Jan.–Apr. 1990, Jan.–Feb. 1991, and Jan.–Apr. 1994

Journalistic Standards	# of Reports	% of Prob. Coverage
Lack of Balance or Context	248	27.9
Overemphasis on Drama, Bad News	185	20.8
Loaded Labeling or Advocacy	98	11
Total	531	59.7
Issues Related to the Process	# of Reports	% of Prob. Coverage
Brevity and Context	180	20.3
Lack of Knowledge	112	12.6
Bad News Judgment	63	7.1
Total	355	40

Source: Author's Database. See appendix 1.

and Northrop." Lynch then explained that the Pentagon "tried to keep [Spinney's] findings under wraps."

The message from Spinney: weapons programs were running twice the early projections and there is no way to bring them down. Spinney went through the mismatch of previous estimates of where modernization costs were supposed to be at different points in the defense program, and some were off by 100 percent. Lynch concluded by stating that Spinney did agree that more money was needed for the defense program, "but without realistic budgeting, he warns, more money will continue buying less. . . . With Congress approaching critical decisions on Pentagon cuts, today's briefing may bring added skepticism as the generals and admirals present their shopping lists."

ABC's John McWethy also made a point about the Pentagon's reluctance to have Spinney testify and then turned to Sen. Charles Grassley (R-IA), who said this was no way to operate a government. McWethy wrapped his report up by saying that, if Spinney's estimates are correct, the Reagan budget could be underestimated by $70 to $80 billion. But, "the Pentagon has been working for the last two years to make sure that doesn't happen." End of report.

Neither CBS nor ABC bothered to adequately frame the cost issue or even describe how weapons costs get underestimated. As often as not, the costs of weapons rise as a result of cuts in the overall number of weapons being bought, which leads to per unit cost increases. Stretching out programs, saving small amounts of money in the current year, can also cause increased costs as inefficiencies are introduced into the production process. In both instances, Congress plays a central role.[160] Another factor involves changes in inflation as these programs are stretched out, often making it necessary to spend more dollars because they are worth less.

The reports also failed to point out important information about Spinney's testimony. Contrary to the impression given, Spinney was not discussing the current weapons estimates of the Reagan administration. He was actually describing an historical study he conducted by examining 30 years of cost data. It documented the consistently overly optimistic projections of the military budget planners. This was all fair game for congressional scrutiny and media attention.

But what the networks failed to tell viewers, except for the oblique reference by ABC's McWethy, was that the Pentagon had taken steps to correct the way cost estimates were being developed. In fact, Secretary of Defense Caspar Weinberger had already testified that the administration had eliminated the problem.[161] Not surprisingly, the Weinberger testimony never made the evening newscasts.

On the exaggerated point about the Pentagon wanting to keep Spinney "under wraps," the reluctance of the Pentagon to have Spinney testify was not that unusual. Mid-level analysts seldom represent the Department of Defense on budget matters, and Spinney's study did not include any references to the steps that had been taken to address the problem, something his boss, David S. C. Chu, the director of the Office of Program Analysis and Evaluation, was far better qualified to explain. For this reason, the Pentagon insisted that Chu accompany Spinney to the hearing, another point that did not come up in the ABC and CBS news reports.[162]

The final detail conveniently omitted, which would have lent context, was the role of Senator Grassley, whose sound bite was included in ABC's report. Grassley was responsible for forcing the Pentagon to let Spinney testify. Neither this point, nor Grassley's own political agenda was mentioned by ABC or CBS.

Context mattered in this case. Without it, these reports left the clear impression that the Pentagon was trying to muzzle Spinney and hide underestimates of weapons systems it was buying. In reality, Spinney's testimony was far more complicated than the networks let on.

OVEREMPHASIS ON DRAMA, BAD NEWS

Network news naturally tilts toward drama, emotion, controversy, and bad news over news of a less provocative nature. Rather than explain a "dull," complicated issue, the focus will be on the weapons test that failed, the sharp exchange at a hearing, the industry scandal, or the plight of the campesino being repressed because of US policies abroad. The network formula for these reports involves finding a simple angle, incorporating dramatic or emotionally charged footage, and avoiding any complicated explanations that might take away from the drama.

Dramatic Focus and Tone

The networks create drama by their language and general approach to news as conflict and struggle. For example, on February 4, 1985, NBC anchor Tom Brokaw and White House correspondent Chris Wallace covered the back-and-forth posturing between the White House and Congress over the budget as a battle between two sports teams, citing the play-by-play action of Reagan making his case for increases and congressional opponents trying to alter some of the administration's controversial programs. Unfortunately, their sports metaphors never extended to the key elements of disagreement and the actual issues on each side.

In March 1985, a series of network reports on whether Congress would vote for the building of 21 more MX missiles again illustrated the propensity to frame things in terms of the drama of a game, with winners and losers. Votes on the MX were to take place in the Senate and House of Representatives. The way the networks reported it, the story was about presidential persuasion and whether the vote would go his way. Little was said about the role of the MX missile in the nation's nuclear deterrent posture, which in itself was controversial, or the complicated link the Reagan administration was making to arms control involving the idea that a commitment to build more MXs would show resolve and help further the arms talks that were taking place in Geneva at the time with the Soviets.

On March 18, NBC anchor Tom Brokaw opened his report saying Reagan "is deeply involved in his own selling job tonight, trying to sell the MX missile to the Senate." Washington correspondent John Dancy then reported on how the MX vote was a major political test for Reagan, noting which senators were coming around and who was opposing the president. Only in passing did Dancy mention the connection to arms talks taking place in Geneva and how the MX was supposed to replace the Minuteman missile. He did, however, manage to fit in the point that many experts were saying the MX would be too vulnerable to Soviet attack.

ABC's approach was similar, beginning with the news of a favorable committee vote in the Senate, but noting the deep divisions that existed as the MX was to be considered by the full Senate. White House correspondent Brit Hume led with this incisive analysis: "The MX has become almost a metaphor for the arms race itself: frightening, unpopular, and fabulously expensive. But a succession of presidents has said we have to have it." Hume's thrust was clearly whether the president might win this one. He noted the intense lobbying all around, but spent little time on the real issue: the MX as it fit into the US nuclear posture and as a factor in arms negotiations. Hume never even bothered to explore why a succession of presidents said we have to have it.

CBS only mentioned the president's preliminary victory on the MX in the Republican-controlled Senate Armed Services Committee.

When, on March 20, the Senate voted for the president's plan, ABC's Charles Gibson said the administration "won big." The whole report focused on how the president won, not on what the 21 MXs meant to US national defense. The same evening, NBC turned its attention to how the MX was faring in the House (not well), and CBS ignored the story.

On March 26, ABC's Peter Jennings and Washington correspondent Brit Hume were able to analyze another big congressional win for Reagan when the House also voted in favor of the MX. NBC ignored the story, and CBS anchor Dan Rather called it a major victory for Reagan. What is striking about all of these reports is the drama of the legislative *game*. The nuclear *issue* was treated only in passing, if at all.

Besides the play-by-play action on Capitol Hill, the clash between administration witnesses and lawmakers is another favorite network story where drama usually replaces substance. On February 3, 1983, Secretary of Defense Caspar Weinberger came under attack by Sen. Donald Riegle (D-MI). NBC's Roger Mudd introduced the segment on defense budget hearings by reporting that Senate Budget Committee chairman Sen. Pete Domenici (R-NM) said "he favors cutting the Pentagon by half, but also Defense Secretary Weinberger reluctantly agreed to supply lists showing budget increases of 4, 6, and 8 percent rather than the 10 percent he wants." Mudd then said, "[NBC correspondent] Richard Valeriani reports that Weinberger agreed to that only after a very rough hearing."

Rather than clarifying Mudd's confusing assertion that Domenici wanted to cut the Pentagon "by half," when what Mudd should have said was cut the *rate of increase* by half, Valeriani launched into the exchange between Weinberger and Riegle, who called the defense secretary "an inflexible ideologue, whose basic judgment is dangerous to the country and more," reported Valeriani.

The exchange was dramatic:

> *Riegle*: By your really fanatical insistence on defense increases that are larger than needed, larger than we can afford, I believe that you're damaging our national security.
>
> *Weinberger*: Well, Senator, I have to say I think . . .
>
> *Riegle*: I did not interrupt you. When I finish . . .
>
> *Weinberger*: That's right but you're . . .
>
> *Riegle*: I have the floor. I think you're making America weaker, not stronger and I think this perverts reality, is actually serving the interests of the Soviet Union, which is the most dangerous irony of it all.
>
> *Weinberger*: Well Senator, you've, I think, accomplished your principal purpose which was to launch a demagogic attack on me in time for the afternoon and evening editions and I want to tell you that I think that everything you've said is both insulting and wrong. The simple fact of the matter is I have certain responsibilities. I do not have the luxury of sitting up there and guessing at what might happen. I have the responsibility of looking at the threat as I see it, and looking at how that threat has grown, and looking at what is necessary in my opinion to advise the Congress and the President what we must do about it.

CBS anchor Dan Rather introduced an almost identical piece that same night by correspondent Bill Lynch, who focused half of his report on Congress's intention to cut defense and the other half on the angry exchange.

Give NBC and CBS credit for carrying Weinberger's response to Riegle, but what happened to the real issue in both reports: The Senate committee chairman's view that the rate of increase in the defense budget would have to be halved? Answer: the exchange was far more dramatic than a report about the proposed rate of increase and the various tradeoffs required to cut it.

On February 27, 1985, the issue was aid to the Nicaraguan contras. Secretary of State George Shultz was testifying before a House subcommittee. CBS anchor Dan Rather started by saying the administration was charging that the Sandinistas were providing training to hundreds of leftists in Latin America, then said, "US policy on Nicaragua, specifically the Reagan administration's support of anti-Sandinista rebels, generated some words of another sort today at a House subcommittee hearing, as Lesley Stahl reports."

Stahl's report focused on an exchange between Shultz and Reps. Ted Weiss (D-NY) and Peter Kostmayer (D-PA). Weiss said, "It reminds me of the Army-McCarthy hearings in 1954. It seems to me that the administration's policy toward Nicaragua has been an exercise in twisting facts, in distorting facts, in misstating facts." Shultz responded, "When you compare me with Senator Joe McCarthy, I resent it deeply. And I will have no part of it and I will have further comment to make."

Kostmayer then added, "There's been a lot of red-baiting going on in the administration. And I think it began with the White House, and I hope it will end fairly soon." That prompted Shultz to suggest that if the committee wanted to withdraw the invitation it gave him to testify, he had other things he could do. To which, Kostmayer said, "Well, you're the secretary of state, and there's nothing we can do about it."

Stahl then shifted to another issue entirely, Nicaraguan President Daniel Ortega's invitation to a bipartisan congressional delegation to visit Nicaragua to see that his military buildup was strictly defensive. She noted that the White House at first welcomed it then had second thoughts, given the likelihood of a "show-and-tell propaganda offensive."

This CBS report jumped between three issues without providing context or background for even one of them. First, there was Rather's point on Nicaraguans training other leftists. Then, at the center, there was the exchange between Shultz and the representatives, and last, the invitation by Ortega. Not one of these issues was adequately reported, yet viewers did see sparks fly.

Anchors also account for a dramatic element by their tone and their presence at the scene of a major news story, from war to earthquakes. Among them, CBS anchor Dan Rather is the hands-down winner for overstatement and manufactured drama. Rather's melodrama is present in almost every newscast he does. One example comes from the opening of his February 1, 1990, newscast: "In the dark days of the Russian winter, a political storm is gathering that could shake the foundations of the Soviet Union and the world. This is the CBS Evening News. Dan Rather, reporting tonight from Red Square in Moscow."

Rather went on to describe an important Central Committee meeting, where Gorbachev's reforms were the main topic. Speculation about Gorbachev's future as Soviet leader was indeed rampant, but Gorbachev proved he was securely in control, at least until later in the year, when an attempted coup would take place, paving the way for the dramatic entrance and accession of Boris Yeltsin.

The Bad News Conundrum

That there is too much bad news is a complaint made regularly about all news.[163] Murder on the street, plane crashes, and earthquakes seem to dominate the news in general. These stories also tend to be followed closely by the public, leaving lasting impressions.[164] In the area of national security coverage, bad news, from test failures of weapons, crashes of aircraft, and misdeeds to indictments of defense industry officials or the sentencing of a soldier who committed murder, naturally makes the evening news. The problem is not that these stories are out there and warrant coverage. The frequency with which bad news is covered does, however, put a premium on covering the bad news with some sense of context.

For example, military crash stories often draw attention to the aircraft itself, and this, in turn, can lead to problems of sensationalism and lack of context. This type of coverage, like that of the crash of a civilian jet liner, focuses on the safety of the aircraft in question and the circumstances surrounding the accident, both of which demand technical knowledge and context by the correspondent or his or her sources.

A case in point occurred on April 14, 1983. CBS anchor Dan Rather led with this: "Air Force investigators are sifting through what remains of a B-52 bomber that crashed last Monday on a training flight in Utah. It was the fourth major B-52 accident in the last five months. This B-52, Jerry Bowen reports, didn't have a chance."

Bowen started with the wreckage and how the B-52 "disintegrated on impact." Then a military spokesman said that the aircraft had been right on track for its low-level route. The report quickly shifted to flags at half staff at Robins Air Force Base and a quick note about the training mission, which "called for the plane to fly anywhere from 200 to 2000 feet above the ground. And it was flying in bad weather, steady rain, blowing snow at the higher elevations."

Next came the miracle of file footage. CBS had interviewed this very crew the previous February. Sound bite, Capt. Donald Heibert: "Well, sir, this airplane flies like no other airplane in the military or civilian inventory and it's a handful of an airplane." The next point CBS's Bowen made was that Heibert had confidence in this plane. Another sound bite from Heibert, who spoke admiringly of the aircraft. Then we were told by Bowen that it was to have been Heibert's last flight. "He was going to celebrate when he returned to Georgia. His wife was going to be waiting at the airfield with a bottle of champagne. Captain Heibert had a desk job waiting for him at the Pentagon."

Emotion over substance. Bowen never explained the reasons for the low-level flying tactics the B-52 was practicing in order to be able to evade Soviet radar or the danger involved or the importance of the particular mission. There was, however, dramatic footage (the wreckage), innuendo about the safety of the aircraft with three other recent accidents, emotion tied to the family, and the irony of it being the captain's last flight. And, of course, there was the piece de resistance, the twist about the desk job. Bowen may or may not have known many pilots, but the last thing a pilot will celebrate is going to a desk job at the Pentagon.

Individual crash incidents come and go. And certainly, some reports are better than others, but there is, inevitably, a cumulative effect that tends to distort reality. In February 1996, for example, Rep. Ike Skelton (D-MO) released a General Accounting Office report that found aircraft crashes down 75 percent in the last 21 years, from 309 in 1975 to 76 in 1995. The death toll, too, had declined from 285 to 85 in the same period. In releasing the report, Skelton said, "The increased media coverage of these accidents left an impression we were seeing higher numbers of crashes and deaths."[165] Skelton's conclusion: "It shows that military aviation safety has improved."

Another area where the cumulative effect of news selection tended to distort was the coverage of defense industry. Indictments and scandals were the only thing the networks covered during the periods sampled. While such news clearly deserved coverage, the networks seldom framed this news in the broader context nor did they tend to cover other aspects of weapons systems or industry that might have provided some balancing perspectives over time.

Bad news will likely continue to be a regular feature of network news, and so will drama. Nevertheless, a little context from time to time could go a long way toward countering the inherent distorting effects of this type of reporting.

LOADED LABELING OR ADVOCACY

Though anchors, correspondents, and producers profess objectivity, their very words sometimes betray a bias. Other times, the way they approach a story suggests a point of view.

Labels and the Liberal Tilt

For some reason, *liberal* and *left-wing* were adjectives the networks tended to avoid, while *conservative*, *right-wing*, *hard-line* and others seemed easy to come by. This was done either innocently based on the biases of the reporters and anchors,[166] or it was deliberately calculated. Oftentimes, people were openly labeled and subtly typecast as the good guys or the bad guys. Usually the *conservatives* or *hard-liners* were the bad guys and the liberals were the good guys.

On January 7, 1983, for example, NBC anchor Roger Mudd reported a brief note on Nicaragua: "There is further unrest in the area. Nicaragua says it's bracing for an attack against its government from *right-wing* commandos across the Honduran border. The attacks are aimed at disrupting a meeting next week in

Managua of non-aligned nations." (Emphasis added.) This was Mudd's entire report. Curiously, the "commandos" were labeled as *right-wing* while the government was not labeled. Why not *left-wing* for balance?

Throughout the two Reagan periods analyzed, there were repeated instances of *right-wing* labels on the Nicaraguan contras and the Salvadoran government. Conversely, there were seldom any mentions of the *left-wing* Sandinista government or the *left-wing* Salvadoran guerrillas. In the case of Central America, congressional and administration officials who supported US policy were the *conservatives* or *hard-liners*. Opponents were typically not labeled.

The same was true in the area of arms control. Take the January 12, 1983, report described in chapter 7. Viewers learned from CBS that Arms Control and Disarmament Agency director Eugene Rostow "was forced out by President Reagan and Senate *conservatives*." Correspondent Bob Schieffer then added that "Rostow felt the White House bowed to pressure from the Republican *right wing* when it refused to support the nomination of Robert Gray, a career diplomat that Rostow wanted for his deputy in the agency—a man that many *conservatives* felt was not enough of a *hard-liner* to negotiate an arms deal." (Emphasis added.)

After finally making the few substantive points about the competing policy views within the administration, Schieffer then stated, "Pentagon *hard-liners* say hang tough with the original zero-zero offer, but Paul Nitze, the chief US negotiator at Geneva, is known to be pushing for more *flexibility*." (Emphasis added.) In a short anchor report following this report by Schieffer, Dan Rather noted that the president was nominating Kenneth Adelman to succeed Rostow. "He is considered a *pragmatist* and Capitol Hill sources say he too may face *conservative* opposition." (Emphasis added.)

In the NBC report on the same day, correspondent Marvin Kalb described Rostow as "a *hard-line* Democrat who had few political allies in this administration." (Emphasis added.) He also noted the president did not want to offend his "*conservative* allies." (Emphasis added.) Only ABC refrained from the loaded labels in this case.

In truth, Rostow, Nitze, and Adelman all had been members of the Committee on the Present Danger, a group that was formed to alert Americans to the unfavorable trends in US-Soviet relations and to espouse the need for a strong national defense. On arms control, the group had opposed the SALT II treaty, which it found to favor the Soviet Union by restricting the United States's ability to maintain a qualitative superiority needed to offset Soviet quantitative advantages.[167]

Rostow's problems had less to do with whether he subscribed to *conservative* views than with his personality and differences with the White House over approach. If labels had been correctly applied on all sides, it could have been argued that they might have provided a form of shorthand that helped viewers understand competing positions. Too often, however, the labels were applied only to one side and sometimes not accurately, as in the case of Rostow. Nitze, too, who was regularly labeled as Mr. Flexibility, had *hard-line* credentials that were well established.

Advocacy and Commentary Disguised as News

There were also occasions when the network reporter or anchor gave up all appearances of striving for objectivity. In style, tone, and substance the report contained a point of view or "call to action" masquerading as news. Key background and contextual details were sacrificed for personal opinion.

For example, while covering a presidential speech in Orlando on March 8, 1983, ABC White House correspondent Sam Donaldson had this to say about the president's remarks pertaining to defense: "Meanwhile, reporters here were given a new Pentagon assessment of Soviet military power, which portrays the Soviet arms buildup as impressive and threatening, and through the use of charts and graphs suggests that the United States is falling dangerously behind." He continued:

> This, along with the president's remarks today, is just another part of the administration's effort to convince Congress to forget about a nuclear freeze and just vote all the money the president wants for defense.

Donaldson, without any expertise in defense or Soviet military affairs, simply expressed his opinion that the Pentagon assessment was nothing but a political tool for the administration to use in its quest for higher defense spending. If Donaldson had bothered to consult independent assessments of the US-Soviet military balance, like the one published by the International Institute of Strategic Studies, based in London, he would have found their conclusions to be very close to those in the Pentagon publication.[168]

Another example occurred on February 7, 1990, when CBS White House correspondent Lesley Stahl was openly critical of President George Bush while traveling with him on a tour of defense facilities. Her report began with a few notes on positive points Bush made about Soviet leader Mikhail Gorbachev's efforts at peaceful change in the Soviet Union. They were followed by a Bush sound bite. Next, Stahl put forth this commentary:

> But in symbolic terms, the president's timing could not be worse. He finds himself on the warpath, so to speak, promoting Star Wars and a strong nuclear deterrent against the Soviet Union at the very moment Gorbachev is promoting democracy.

She then added that "many in Congress just aren't buying" Bush's line that the United States has to continue to modernize.

Rather than injecting themselves into these reports, network correspondents would have been better off using experts on both sides of the issues to present different perspectives.

Besides the subtle commentary, there are also instances of outright advocacy by network reporters. Take the report by CBS correspondent Susan Spencer on January 7, 1990. The issue was women in combat, and Spencer had only one theme running throughout her report: it is time to jettison the absurd distinction between combat and noncombat and let women serve in all combat positions.

Capt. Linda Bray, who had led a platoon of military police that got into a fire fight with Panamanian soldiers and prevailed, was featured describing the brief battle, along with one of her female troops. Next, Spencer turned to Rep. Patricia Schroeder (D-CO), who called for equal opportunity for women in the military. Army Gen. Maxwell Thurman's sound bite then made the point that, in the whole issue of women in combat, nobody "ever said that women would not see combat." On to Lawrence Korb, a former assistant secretary of defense, who said we need to "get rid of this absurd situation." A few more tidbits from Bray and her subordinate were added before Spencer concluded that congressional hearings were coming up and forces opposing change were lining up to keep things the way they were. Her whole report was like a legal brief for abandoning restrictions on women in combat. Surely, there were some other viewpoints out there. What about those very opponents who were marshaling their forces to oppose change?

Another form of advocacy is obvious when reporters agitate for the president to take some decisive action overseas. While nothing like the yellow journalism that preceded the Spanish-American War in 1898, the media drumbeat for action is sometimes still there.

President Bill Clinton got a dose of this on February 5, 1994, from ABC. The day before, both CBS and ABC had carried short reports on the shelling of the western suburb of Sarajevo by Bosnian Serb forces, and the resulting civilian casualties. On February 5, ABC's Aaron Brown was sitting in as anchor: "For 22 months the world has watched and often tried to ignore the bloody civil war in Bosnia," Brown said. "It is hard to watch and impossible to ignore what happened there today. At least 60 civilians, men, women, and children, were killed, at least 200 injured when a market full of Saturday shoppers was shelled."

Coincidentally, ABC's Peter Jennings happened to be in Sarajevo. Jennings filed a long report full of emotion:

> It was a disaster. . . . Sarajevans are helpless in the face of such shelling. . . . This will count as one of the worst attacks since this war began. . . . The dead—and many of them were in pieces—were eased onto trucks. . . . Against civilians, this is not war. This is terrorism. . . . And the biggest difference for me is how people in Sarajevo absolutely are convinced the United States is not going to come to their aid. . . . The Bosnian Prime Minister said once again tonight, "The West is simply watching us die."

After Jennings, ABC correspondent Michele Norris reported from the White House that "today's massacre in Sarajevo has turned up the pressure in Washington to take action to help end the bloodshed in Bosnia." She added that "Republicans and Democrats in Congress say the Clinton administration can no longer afford to turn its back on Bosnia." What really *turned up the pressure* was this one-sided news coverage. Nowhere to be found were any defenders of Clinton's caution.

This kind of advocacy is as much a result of the particular anchors' and correspondents' viewpoints as it is the nature of network news, always ready to paint things in terms of drama, struggles, and competing pressures. Naturally, straight reporting of such an event as the Sarajevo mortar attack would just as surely have raised emotions in Congress and among the public, but ABC chose to add its own voice to the frenzy.

BREVITY AND CONTEXT: THE SPECIAL CASE OF THE ANCHOR

The issue of context is of particular importance when it comes to anchor reports, since time limitations allow only glimpses of different sides of an issue. In many of the instances when the networks relegated news to anchor tells, the complex subjects being addressed simply were not well suited to the abbreviated anchor format. The other aspect of anchor reports had to do with the cumulative effects related to which side of particular issues was actually being reported in the one to two sentences the anchor format allows. Based on the numbers, there is little doubt that the anchor played an important role in presenting distorted national security news to the public during the sample periods in 1983, 1985, 1990, 1991, and 1994.

In the areas of defense reporting where the pattern of distorted coverage was the most pronounced—arms control, defense budget, industry/procurement, and weapons—anchor reports accounted for a sizeable portion of the coverage and the problems (see Table 9.2). Unlike the longer news reports, which were tagged problematic when clear issues of balance, context, and related areas were evident, anchor reports were tagged problematic most often when the report was missing context or explanation. Questions related to balance in the larger scheme of distorted coverage then had to be answered by looking at the problematic anchor reports as a set. The results were revealing.

For example, of the 37 anchor reports on the defense budget, 24 were cited for problems related to lack of context. On the question of balance, every one of these reports was weighted against increases in the defense budget.

On the issue of weapons, 39 of the 71 anchor reports did not have sufficient context. Of the 39, 27 were about negative aspects of weapons, from them costing too much to crashes, to tests failing. On the other side, 12 reflected positive developments, like a test that succeeded.

On arms control, 29 out of 79 anchor reports were cited for contextual problems. Of the 29, 26 reflected the views of opponents of Reagan's hard-line views, from the nuclear freeze movement to the Catholic bishops to experts advocating the need for compromise in arms control negotiations with the Soviets. Only 3 reports brought up views that reflected the other side of the debate.

The story was the same when it came to industry. Of the 27 reports cited for context problems, 25 were about negative aspects of the industry, from scandals to indictments and charges of abuse.

Table 9.2

Anchor Reports by Topic, Number, and Percentage of Total Reports for Jan.–Apr. 1983, Jan.–Apr. 1985, Jan.–Apr. 1990, Jan.–Feb. 1991, and Jan.–Apr. 1994

Topic	Total Reports	Anchor Reports	Percent
Arms Control	201	79	39.3%
Budget	128	37	28.9%
Foreign Policy	1022	253	24.7%
Industry	51	27	52.9%
Military Operations	423	106	25.0%
Personnel	348	115	33.0%
Policy/Strategy	18	5	27.7%
Procurement	12	6	50.0%
SDI	20	9	45.0%
Soviet Union/Russia	465	120	25.8%
Threats	69	28	40.5%
Weapons/Capabilities	190	71	37.3%
Total	2947	856	29.0%

Source: Author's Database. See appendix 1.

Anchor reports that were not cited for context problems, some 537 out of a total of 856, were most often summary statements of basic facts. A commission was formed. A foreign leader made a statement. A treaty was signed. The vote in Congress was close. Fortunately, most anchor reports do not address the most complex topics or the most politically charged issues. But when they do, they often leave the viewer either with a question or a false impression.

Overall, when it came to reporting on defense developments in the periods sampled from 1980s and 1990s, the cumulative effect of anchor tells fit right into the overall pattern of distorted coverage.

LACK OF KNOWLEDGE

News reports singled out over questions related to knowledge and expertise featured simplistic approaches to complex national security issues, including sensationalism, exaggeration, and ignorance. One time, it was a general assignment reporter "investigating" a problem and blowing it out of proportion; another time it was an overly glowing report from a Pentagon beat reporter who should have known better; then there was the report by a White House reporter who treated an issue only in terms of whether the president was up or down; another example involved a softball interview by an anchor ill equipped in terms of substance and knowledge. In most instances, this category reflects lack of knowledge and poor judgment on the part of anchors or correspondents—the ignorance factor. In general, so-called "investigative" pieces on national security topics should be viewed with caution. They are often reported by generalist correspondents who lack expertise and tend to exaggerate.

A case in point occurred on January 10 and 11, 1985, in a two-part special segment on NBC. Correspondent Mark Nykanen investigated military medicine. Anchor Tom Brokaw introduced the series by stating that "some military medicine is so bad, it is no exaggeration to say that people who survive combat could not survive treatment at the hands of military doctors."

Nykanen then trotted out a number of tragic stories, all of them undoubtedly true. One Marine died of a simple strep throat infection that went undetected. Another veteran was in a coma and almost brain-dead because he was given an incorrect dose of anesthesia by an imposter posing as a doctor. A retired Air Force sergeant was killed during surgery because the oxygen supply was routed to his stomach and intestines instead of his lungs. Since he was retired, his wife was able to sue and win $400,000 from the government, but for active duty servicemen who suffer from medical malpractice there is not the same recourse. The government is protected from liability, something one lawyer was trying to change, Nykanen said with approval.

Nykanen certainly did assemble some sensational cases and statistics, which revealed 1100 medical military malpractice claims in the four previous years. But except for a *60 Minutes*-style interview of a senior military doctor made to look silly and uninformed, Nykanen made no attempt to provide overall context—how, for instance, do these military problems compare to similar problems in civilian hospitals?—or to elaborate on steps that the senior military doctor said had been implemented to improve the situation, which might have provided some needed balance.

Another uninformed report came from Lynn Sherr who had been on special assignment for ABC. Sherr's January 22, 1985, report purported to explain how NASA's shuttle program had suddenly become "militarized," contrary to President Dwight D. Eisenhower's insistence that NASA be oriented to the peaceful uses of space. The launching point for the report was the fact that the time of the space shuttle Discovery's liftoff and details of its classified payload had been kept secret. While such a practice is commonplace for classified payloads launched by military rockets, the fact that Discovery was carrying a military payload seemed to shock the network news establishment. Sherr's job was to expose the sinister—and growing—link between the military and NASA.

Faced with a shrinking budget, Sherr told her viewers, NASA became dependent on the military. In fact, shuttle capabilities in the military sphere saved it from President Jimmy Carter's budget ax, she said. Worse still, about a third of future shuttle flights will be masked in secrecy because of military missions. And, Sherr added, the shuttle may one day be used in conjunction with the "Star Wars" program. "This is not the peaceful goal originally set for NASA," she concluded.

Unfortunately, Sherr had a complete lack of understanding of the early ICBM program and many other dimensions of early military space efforts that eventually led to manned space flight. Nor was there any appreciation of the fact that the race to the moon was part and parcel of the superpower competition. The false dichotomy of the civilian versus the military space programs, which underpinned Sherr's report, was sheer nonsense.

Nor was this nonsense limited to ABC. Dan Rather of CBS made a similar point on January 24, 1985: "When the great space shuttle Discovery took off today, it took this nation's civilian space program in a whole new direction. For the first time ever, flying by rules of military secrecy, an all-military crew, and carrying into orbit a new-generation spy satellite." Correspondent Bruce Hall then went on to describe "the most unusual launch day." While less breathless than Sherr's reporting, Hall, too, left the impression that all this military secrecy was somehow sinister and unprecedented.

Apart from pure ignorance, another variation of this category of reporting falls into the area of "the reporter should have known better." Take the report on gee-whiz technology aired by ABC on February 3, 1983. Pentagon correspondent John McWethy did a lengthy report on microelectronic technology that "can instantly transform a hazy picture, like this, into one of exquisite detail." He was discussing developments at a company called the ITEK Corporation, which works on photographic imagery systems for US spy planes. While McWethy can be commended for putting a rare positive spin on a US weapons capability and the industry that produced it, his report came off like a paid infomercial.

"The people at ITEK who are trying to sell this system to the Pentagon for a million dollars a unit are no strangers to this business," McWethy gushed. "They built the camera systems that took these pictures on Mars. But most of what they do is top secret. Their cameras fly aboard American spy planes and satellites. Some of their cameras, which were not shown to ABC News, and which they refuse to discuss, are reportedly so good that from 150 miles above the earth they can read newspaper headlines at a newsstand in the Kremlin."

He concluded with a point about how time will no longer be a factor in identifying imagery targets, given the resolution capability of the ITEK system. But in the whole report, there was not one question about whether the technology was as good as advertised, whether there were competing technologies, or how the million-dollar-per-unit cost compared to other, less capable systems.

The likely reason that this report was aired at all was access: ABC was given an exclusive peek at a top-secret capability. No matter that broader context and balance were sacrificed. Too often, in network correspondents' and producers' minds, having exclusive pictures or access is synonymous with having "news." Unfortunately, the correlation is not always that clear and simple.

Take the example of NBC correspondent Jon Alpert's visit to a Vietnamese reeducation camp. Anchor Tom Brokaw introduced the March 4, 1985, report by saying, "As you will see, it was a carefully orchestrated tour, but Alpert manages to get some unrehearsed answers." Alpert was then shown wandering around the camp with his Vietnamese escort, poking his head in dormitories, pointing out the obvious. "This is the clinic here? These are the patients here. . . . You were a soldier. Uh-huh. . . . This is the music group, huh? Hit it fellas. [Music]"

Alpert eventually got a few prisoners to tell him they do not get enough food. Perhaps that was what Brokaw referred to as unrehearsed answers. Then to show all his viewers what access he had, Alpert turned to his escort and said: "Listen, Major, the people in the United States want to make sure that you're not taking me on like a guided tour. So can I go to any of these other dormitories? Anything I want. All right." Alpert gleefully went through a few more dormitories and even learned the number of years some prisoners had been there. Then he asked one of the prisoners, "It's pretty hard in here, isn't it? It's a tough life? It's a tough life?" His conclusion: "A lot of people feel abandoned by the Americans."

What did viewers learn? That NBC was able to get inside a reeducation camp. And who would not expect prison to be a hard life? Perhaps the real insight was that these people feel abandoned by the Americans, a point that was never explained.

The next month, it was Brokaw's turn. On April 23, 1985, NBC viewers were treated to his interview with Daniel Ortega, president of Nicaragua. Ortega gave Brokaw a peek at his daily routine and expounded on his revolutionary roots. Brokaw noted that even revolutionaries jog, joking that Ortega decided to leave his gun behind today since "that would not win friends in the United States."

After painting Ortega's revolutionary credentials, Brokaw did allow that the Sandinistas have made a mess of the economy, but then added that Ortega blames most of the problems on the United States. For balance, Brokaw stipulated that some of Ortega's American friends think that the Sandinistas carry that theme too far. Brokaw drew attention to the party anthem refrain: "Yankees, the enemies of humanity."

Over lunch, Brokaw asked Ortega about whether he could see Soviet attack helicopters and was rebuffed. He also asked why Libyans are in the country and was quite satisfied with Ortega's response: "We have the right to have relations with every country or movement in the world. We want to insist on that." Ortega also insisted he would never allow a Cuban or Soviet base in Nicaragua. Brokaw was satisfied in every instance. To conclude this probing interview, Brokaw showed Ortega the family man at the dinner table, where "he has limited power." From there, Brokaw mentioned the kinship of Ortega with Sandinista troops returning from the front. "If they win that war," Brokaw added, "Ortega may be able to realize his dream of a Nicaraguan Marxist state, free of American influence. And for the Reagan administration, that would be a nightmare."

Such is the type of "news" that special access often engenders. Straight ignorance, however, is still the biggest sin in this category of problematic reporting.

Coverage of the awarding of the Combat Infantryman Badge to soldiers who had served in Panama is one case in point. On January 10, 1990, ABC's Jim Wooten seemed perplexed that female Military Police (MP) would not be awarded the Combat Infantryman Badge. And, he added, the ruling applies to both men and women. What ruling? one is tempted to ask. MPs have never been eligible for a badge given only to soldiers in the Infantry Branch. Moreover, infantry soldiers don't wear law enforcement badges like MPs.

This apparently was too complicated an issue for ABC and for Rep. Patricia Schroeder (D-CO), who was featured complaining about women not getting any of the glory. Wooten did correctly point out that women could have received the Bronze and Silver Stars, the Distinguished Service Cross, and even the Medal of Honor. So why not waive the rule that one has to be in the Infantry Branch to receive the Combat Infantryman Badge? Wooten intoned, after explaining that women can't serve in the infantry because of the combat restriction.

Finally, he gave the answer: "The real issue here is, to pin it on women is to further erode the Army's position on their presence in combat. Which, of course, didn't seem to matter much in Panama, anyway." There it was. Jim Wooten seemed to suggest that wearing or not wearing a badge was at the heart of the women in combat controversy.

NBC's Fred Francis, more knowledgeable in the ways of the military, used the issue of the Combat Infantryman Badge to launch into a report on the controversy over what is combat and what is not. He explored the distinctions between women in the rear area being attacked and not technically being in combat. But unlike Wooten, Francis clearly understood the real issue. Yet, he still misled NBC viewers by using the badge as a prop, spotlighting a female MP not getting a badge reserved for soldiers in the infantry.

Another example of uninformed reporting occurred on January 16, 1990. In an anchor report, NBC's Tom Brokaw said, "Imagine this: the top brass of the Warsaw Pact and NATO discussing cuts in their respective forces. Well, today in Vienna it happened for the first time." He then reported that the chairman of the Joint Chiefs of Staff (JCS), the top US military officer, met with his counterparts from the Soviet Union and 33 other countries. What Brokaw did not report was that talks in Vienna between lower-level NATO and Warsaw Pact officials had been going on for years under several different names, from Mutual and Balanced Force Reduction talks to Conventional Forces in Europe talks.

Finally, in this category, take the January 13, 1994, CBS report from its White House correspondent. It was a triumph of style over substance. The report was aired during a summit between President Bill Clinton and Russian President Boris Yeltsin. Anchor Dan Rather set up the report by noting that the first day of the summit was "choreographed to show off a working partnership between two powerful leaders." Enter White House correspondent Rita Braver. After talking about the splendor of the Grand Palace of the Kremlin, Braver made this observation: "There is no burning issue to be settled in these sessions. The presidents will talk about US economic aid already in the pipeline for Russia. They will probably announce a military agreement, including one to aim their nuclear missiles toward the ocean instead of at each other's countries. But the real story here is that even though Yeltsin has recently lost political ground in Russia, President Clinton is pumping him up."

Braver never mentioned why the Clinton administration was trying to pump up Yeltsin, whose success was a key component of the administration's Russia policy, nor did she take the opportunity to explain how the military agreement to shift the targeting of Russian nuclear missiles away from the United States, though largely symbolic, marked yet another step in a remarkable post–Cold War evolution of the US-Soviet and, later, US-Russian, strategic relationship.

BAD NEWS JUDGMENT

News is in the eye of the beholder, but there are times when stories are highly speculative or of a nature that might compromise military operations or endanger lives. To be fair, this is a very rare category, affecting about 2 percent of the entire sample of national security news. Moreover, reports that potentially endanger lives account for an even smaller percentage of coverage. Though the examples in this category are few, they are very instructive.

When "News" Fails the Common Sense Test

Take, first, the case of secrecy diplomacy in the Bush administration. In 1990, the networks got wind of potential contacts between US government officials and Iranians on a possible release of US hostages in Lebanon. Though Bush denied the reports, CBS ran a long, speculative report on March 1, 1990, by White House correspondent Lesley Stahl, which she ended by saying, "The administration is anxious to dampen any new wave of optimism. They say they've had no sign of an imminent hostage release." Somehow reporting that the administration was anxious to dampen optimism seemed to defy common sense.

Another instance of poor judgment took place on March 23, 1985. This time, CBS Pentagon correspondent David Martin reported on a secret US airlift of Ethiopian Jews out of Africa to Israel. The Ethiopian Jews were living among refugees in Sudan, where they were picked up by American C-130 transport aircraft. A previous secret airlift by Israel had been compromised and had to be discontinued, given the political position of Sudan, a Moslem country that did not want to cooperate publicly with Israel for fear of retaliation by hard-line Arab states.

After the Israelis were forced to stop their operation, Vice President George Bush met with Sudan President Jaafar Numeiri during an Africa trip and arranged to have the United States take over the operation and keep it secret. All of this Martin reported. And he even gave us his rationale for reporting the story: "US officials say they are concerned that news of the airlift may jeopardize any future attempts to bring out more falashas [a member of highland Ethiopian people who practice Judaism]. But these same officials acknowledge they did not expect the movement of so many planes and people to remain secret for long." Apparently, Martin decided that he would be the one to make sure that it did not remain secret for long.

A few days later, Martin, a generally superb Pentagon reporter, had more sensitive information to pass out. On March 26, 1985, he used the president's legislative victory assuring the building of 21 more MX missiles as a springboard to report on the nation's nuclear weapons arsenal, a highly sensitive topic whose news value is questionable at best, harmful at worst. Citing nuclear expert William Arkin, then of the Institute for Policy Studies (known for its radical views), Martin detailed the number of nuclear weapons in the US arsenal, an estimated 26,000 warheads, and then noted that 28 states store the weapons. He reported from a depot in the San Francisco bay area that Arkin said stores 300 nuclear weapons. He also reported from a bunker the military would reportedly use in Pennsylvania as a command center if the Pentagon were destroyed.

Martin even told his viewers that the soon-to-be-published book by Arkin is an exhaustive catalog of the nuclear network, "a catalog which Pentagon officials denounce as a road map for everybody from Russian war planners to terrorists to anti-nuclear demonstrators." But that didn't seem to faze Martin, who gave it more publicity than it ever would have garnered among Washington policy wonks and security specialists.

Finally, there are a few examples of sensitive information broadcast during the Gulf War. While Saddam Hussein may not have noticed or even believed that US television networks would be allowed to broadcast sensitive military information, the basic outline of the ground campaign was there for the taking. On January 24, 1991, for example, ABC's hired military expert, Anthony Cordesman, sketched out how the air campaign was moving along and how things were changing on the ground. Pointing to his map, he noted the buildup of Marine Corps forces in specific areas where they would "punch through the forward lines," how the Saudi line was withdrawing in specific areas so US and British divisions could move forward, and how the US, French, and Egyptian forces were preparing for the flanking attack, again shown with specificity on the map.

The next day, January 25, CBS correspondent David Martin also referred to the famous flanking attack that was supposedly kept secret throughout the war: "On the other side of the battle front, press pool reports now place American units far to the west of Kuwait, indicating at least the preparations for a flanking attack across the desert."

Then on February 7, 1991, ABC chimed in again. Sam Donaldson had been interviewing Gen. Norman Schwarzkopf all day. After Donaldson's report on Schwarzkopf's view of the state of the Republican Guards, anchor Peter Jennings asked him, "Sam, did the general talk at all about how he might fight such a war, if it does begin?"

"Yes, he did," Donaldson responded. "In our interview, of course, he didn't give us an order of battle. But he talked about the tactics. He said he'd hit 'em hard, he'd not stop. He'd minimize casualties by keeping on. And he said it would be stupid to hit them frontally. Which certainly suggests some sort of end run."

CBS's Martin was more specific the next day, on February 8, 1991. He noted that the potential battlefield extends far beyond the Kuwaiti theater of operations. "US Army units are deployed hundreds of miles west of Kuwait. Any further west and they would run into impassable terrain." He also noted that "the Iraqis may not know exactly where the American Army is and what it's up to, but they can read the terrain and have moved two divisions out west to block an end run."

NBC held its fire until just a few days before the ground campaign began. On February 20, 1991, Pentagon correspondent Fred Francis noted that US forces must avoid attacking through northern Kuwait. "And while American tank units might try to swing to the west and around the Republican Guards, which is called an envelopment, some sources say a grander strategy is possible: sending US tank divisions deep into Iraq, in what is called a turning movement, forcing Saddam's tanks to come north to meet them."

For the most part, the seasoned Pentagon correspondents Fred Francis, David Martin, and Bob Zelnick did understand exactly what could and could not be reported. Nevertheless, the anchors interrogating them did not, which, to some extent, explains how basic operational plans were outlined on the air. Thanks to the US military's ability to destroy Iraq's communications links, these lapses fortunately meant very little to Saddam Hussein, who might not have believed the information in any event.

All in all, whether in war- or peacetime operations, network correspondents and anchors need to be more careful about sensitive information. In most instances, such news should be able to pass the common-sense test. If it does not, it should not be reported.

FROM ANCHOR CHAIR TO BEATS: WHERE THE SYSTEM IS WEAK

Not surprisingly, some of the problems related to the pattern of distorted defense coverage can be traced to a system that favors generalists over those with specialized knowledge. Predictably, correspondents from the foreign, Pentagon, and State Department beats were the most reliable sources of national security news.

By contrast, the worst national security reporting came from correspondents on the generalist Washington beats and those on general assignment, most of whom usually do not have the background and knowledge to put national security issues in the proper context (see Figure 9.1). The result: stories that present a distorted picture of important defense and security issues.

Of all beat reporters covering national security topics, the foreign correspondent seemed to be the least disposed to problems of balance and context. Only 103 of 772 reports filed by foreign correspondents contained problems, or a mere 13.3 percent. The isolation of the foreign correspondent from domestic issues may be

Figure 9.1

Problematic National Security Reporting by Beat and Percentage for Jan.–Apr. 1983, Jan.–Apr. 1985, Jan.–Apr. 1990, Jan.–Feb. 1991, and Jan.–Apr. 1994

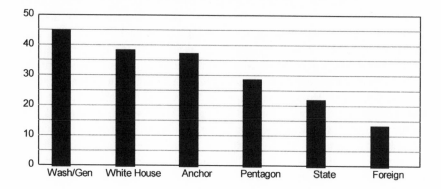

part of the explanation. Yet despite the concentration of problematic coverage among the nonspecialists, they tend to report on a large share of national security issues (see Figure 9.2). As it turns out, anchors, White House correspondents, and the generalists from Washington bureaus and other beats accounted for 53.6 percent of all the national security reporting sampled, with the anchor holding the dominant place with a total of 29 percent of all national security reporting.

Among the specialized beats, foreign correspondents were responsible for a respectable 26.2 percent of all national security reporting. But the Pentagon correspondent accounted for only 14 percent, and the State Department correspondent

Figure 9.2

National Security Reporting by Beat and Number of Reports for Jan.–Apr. 1983, Jan.–Apr. 1985, Jan.–Apr. 1990, Jan.–Feb. 1991, and Jan.–Apr. 1994

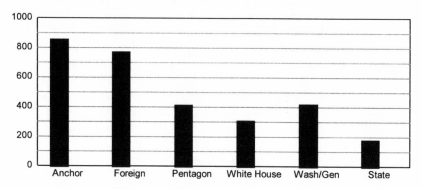

barely registered with 6 percent of total coverage. In fact, both the White House beat, which reported 10.4 percent of national security news, and the Washington bureau and other beat correspondents, which as a group came in at 14.2 percent, actually did considerably more reporting on national security than the State Department beat.

The issue of nonspecialists reporting on national security becomes even more obvious if problematic reports are correlated with topics and beats. In Figure 9.3, anchors, White House correspondents, Washington beat generalists, and general assignment correspondents constituted the "generalists." Correspondents who covered the Pentagon, State Department, and foreign beats were grouped as "specialists." As it turns out, with the one exception of reporting on threats, "generalists" are routinely responsible for anywhere from 64 percent to 90 percent of the problematic coverage. In the area of arms control, for example, the generalists accounted for 67 percent of the problematic coverage; in the budget category, it was 79 percent; in the industry category 89 percent; in the weapons/capabilities category 68 percent, and in the area of foreign policy, it was 64 percent.

It is striking not only to realize that generalists are largely responsible for the worst national security reporting, but also to note to what extent these generalist

Figure 9.3

Problematic Reporting of Generalists and Specialists by Topic and Percentage for Jan.–Apr. 1983, Jan.–Apr. 1985, Jan.–Apr. 1990, Jan.–Feb. 1991, and Jan.–Apr. 1994

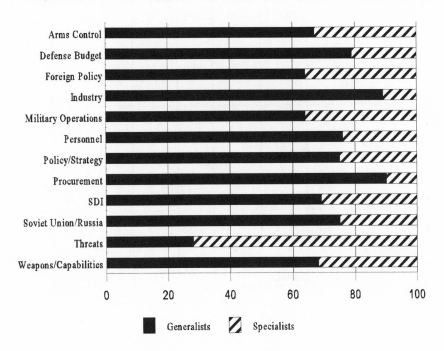

beats dominate coverage of this highly specialized field. As Table 9.3 illustrates, anchor reports dominated coverage of arms control, the defense budget, industry, policy/strategy, procurement, SDI, threats, and weapons/capabilities.

Foreign correspondents dominated foreign policy reporting and coverage of the Soviet Union/Russia; however, anchor tells accounted for about 25 percent of foreign policy coverage, and White House reports accounted for nearly 15 percent. This left a mere 8 percent of foreign policy reports to the State Department correspondent. In the area of military operations, both Pentagon and foreign correspondents dominated, though anchor tells were not far behind.

Similarly, in the area of weapons/capabilities, the generalists account for 64 percent of all reports. The Pentagon correspondent reports on this supposed area of expertise only 31 percent of the time.

Table 9.3

Breakdown of Total Reports by Beat and Topic for Jan.–Apr. 1983, Jan.–Apr. 1985, Jan.–Apr. 1990, Jan.–Feb. 1991, and Jan.–Apr. 1994

Topic	Total	Wash-/Gen	WH	State	Pent	For	ANC
Arms Control	201	22	29	22	8	41	79
Budget	128	32	32	0	27	0	37
Foreign Policy	1022	100	150	83	81	355	253
Industry	51	19	0	0	5	0	27
Military Operations	423	48	11	14	126	118	106
Personnel	348	119	16	9	52	37	115
Policy/Strategy	18	4	2	1	4	2	5
Procurement	12	3	0	0	3	0	6
SDI	20	3	3	1	1	3	9
Soviet Union/Russia	465	29	46	44	33	193	120
Threats	69	4	4	4	15	14	28
Weapons/Capabilities	190	36	15	0	59	9	71
Total	2947	419	308	178	414	772	856

Wash/Gen=Washington bureau and other beats; WH=White House; State=State Department; Pent=Pentagon; For=foreign beat; ANC=anchor.

Overall, the dominant role of the anchor in reporting on national security is troubling. In fact, most of the time it is virtually impossible for the anchor to provide any meaningful context or background.

HOW THE NETWORKS STACKED UP

In terms of the overall numbers, ABC World News Tonight had the fewest instances of problematic reporting, followed by the CBS Evening News and NBC Nightly News, which edged out CBS for the highest number of problematic reports (see Table 9.4). It should be noted, however, that CBS dominated problematic coverage in four of the six areas: lack of balance or context; brevity and context; overemphasis on drama, bad news; and bad news judgment. For its part, NBC had the worst record in the areas of lack of knowledge and loaded labeling or advocacy.

DISTORTING COMPLEX ISSUES

Overall, much of the pattern of distorted coverage related to the networks' unwillingness to provide sufficient time, and, thus, context, for the explanation of complex issues, on the one hand, and their propensity to turn to generalist correspondents, who knew little about the subject matter, on the other.

Table 9.4

Types of Problems Broken Down by Network and Number of Reports for Jan.–Apr. 1983, Jan.–Apr. 1985, Jan.–Apr. 1990, Jan.–Feb. 1991, and Jan.–Apr. 1994

Types of Problems	Total Reports	ABC	CBS	NBC
1) Lack of Balance or Context	248	80	88	80
2) Overemphasis on Drama and Bad News	185	50	70	65
3) Loaded Labeling or Advocacy	98	29	25	44
4) Lack of Context as a Result of Brevity	180	45	72	63
5) Lack of Knowledge	112	34	31	47
6) Bad News Judgment	63	19	24	20
Total	886	257	310	319

Source: Author's Database. See appendix 1.

What follows in chapters 10 and 11 are two case studies that highlight these two inherent flaws in the networks' approach to national security reporting. The case of the B-2 bomber illustrates how a simplistic approach devoid of complicated explanations can distort coverage of a highly complex issue. The case of the Romanian revolution demonstrates, above all, how lack of expertise and knowledge can lead to false conclusions and, in this instance, false images.

On a more positive note, chapter 12 will reveal how anchors successfully turned to outside experts and their own experts in New York and Washington during the Gulf War. The more informative coverage provides a stark contrast to the normal approach the networks take when reporting on national security issues.

Chapter 10

The B-2 and Network News: A Case Study in Distortion

When it comes to the history of television news, few passages are cited as often as this famous paragraph written in 1963 by Reuven Frank, then executive producer of the NBC Evening News: "Every news story should, without any sacrifice of probity or responsibility, display the attributes of fiction, of drama. It should have structure and conflict, action, a beginning, a middle and an end. These are not only the essentials of drama; they are the essentials of narrative."[169]

At its best, television news uses its dramatic nature to convey important information to the public "without any sacrifice of probity or responsibility," as Frank suggested. But that assumes that the correspondent understands the issue and has enough time to explain it in the most basic terms. By its very nature, television news suffers from a variety of limitations and constraints. The process by which television producers, editors, and correspondents compile, summarize, and synthesize complicated issues often leads to misrepresentation or outright distortion of the news.

The unveiling of the B-2 demonstrated both the attraction of television news to the dramatic image and the weakness of television news once the image disappears from sight. Reviewing both print and network news coverage of the B-2 during its first year of visibility, November 1988 to November 1989, reveals a fixation by the networks on the cost of the airplane. By focusing almost solely on cost, the networks ignored critical, and oftentimes, controversial information.

THE "BATPLANE": NETWORK COVERAGE
VERSUS PRINT COVERAGE

The B-2 bomber was rolled out on a runway in Palmdale, California, on November 22, 1988. The image of the ominous-looking flying wing was picked up by all three networks, and each focused on the quarter- to half-a-billion-dollar price tag. But this blip on American television screens quickly disappeared.

It wasn't until Monday, July 10, 1989—nearly eight months later—that the network newscasts again picked up the stealthy bomber. This time, viewers were not only treated to another image of what the media had dubbed the "batplane"; they were also entertained by ABC's Diane Sawyer playing the role of the Riddler on ABC World News Tonight: "What's long overdue, way over budget, and proved today it can travel at least six miles on the ground?" Sawyer glibly asked. Answer: "The new B-2 Stealth bomber. It rolled up and down a runway in California today, the first time it's gone anywhere under its own power. The plane costs half a billion dollars, and may actually take to the air later this week."[170]

That was the extent of ABC's coverage of the B-2's taxiing tests, carried out in preparation for the bomber's maiden flight the following week. NBC Nightly News and CBS Evening News, though less glib, were only marginally better in their coverage, since each added that the B-2 was designed to evade enemy radar. All three, however, managed to emphasize the cost of the B-2. "The world's most expensive warplane revved up its engines for the first time today," Dan Rather began on July 10.

The B-2's price tag, of course, was a big part of the B-2 story, but it was not the only part, and it was far more complicated than the network anchors led their viewers to believe. But then again, television journalism tends to shy away from complicated events, focusing instead on simplicity . . . entertainment . . . images. The B-2 became network news on November 22, 1988, because it was the first time that television cameras were allowed to film the new stealth bomber, from 200 feet away, as it was towed out from its hanger at the Northrop Corporation facility in Palmdale, California.

Absent an image, television journalists do not seem interested in presenting in-depth news. And even with an image, broadcast journalism is becoming a field all its own, one that is less serious, and oftentimes less responsible, than its now far-removed cousin, print journalism. From November 22, 1988, to July 10, 1989, the B-2 barely existed, as far as the networks were concerned. Why? Because there were no interesting images to present and many correspondents simply did not understand the issues surrounding the controversial program.

Except for two brief stories in June,[171] the networks mentioned the B-2 only in passing during that period, usually in the context of what strategic weapons were winning out in the budget battles. Likewise, once the drama leading up to the B-2's maiden flight on July 17, 1989, had subsided, so did network news about the B-2.

In contrast, November 22, 1988, marked the starting point of increased coverage of the B-2 by print journalists. Intrepid editors at *Aviation Week & Space Technology*, a trade magazine, hired a small plane to take pictures of the B-2 from above.[172] But these and other pictures from the ground had a different effect on print journalists than they did on television correspondents: the pictures unleashed an avalanche of analysis of the plane's potential capabilities, its proposed mission, its cost, and its implications for arms control.

STEALTH GOES PUBLIC

November 1988 was the turning point in media coverage of stealth technology in general. On November 10, the Air Force finally admitted what had been widely reported: around 50 stealth fighters, designated the F-117A, were based at the Tonopah Test Range Airfield and assigned to the 4450th Tactical Group at Nellis Air Force Base, Nevada. The decision was apparently made because the Air Force wanted to begin flying the fighter planes during daytime so that the planes could become fully operational.[173] As was noted earlier, the networks and the public would not get their first close-up view of the F-117 until April 1990.

But less than two weeks after the F-117 disclosure in November 1988, the B-2 bomber was rolled out of its hangar. Its unveiling, originally scheduled for late 1987, had been delayed because of a major redesign of the wing that took place in 1984. In order to begin operational testing, the bomber had to leave the secrecy of the hangar and come into the daylight.

According to an article in Technology Review, "The newly revealed stealth bomber and stealth fighter are rewriting the rules to the game of aerial hide-and-seek that began half a century ago. Just before World War II, radar replaced the human eye as the surest way of spotting enemy aircraft. Since then, warplanes have avoided detection by flying above or below the range of their adversaries' radar or by electronically jamming, muffling, or distorting it."[174] Today, however, radars are becoming more and more sophisticated at the same time that weapons are increasing in accuracy and range. And so, concludes this same author, "modern warfare is approaching the equation 'first detection equals first kill.' For this reason, the new imperative in weapons design is stealth—an array of techniques for making a vehicle or weapon harder to detect."[175]

For their part, bombers have played a crucial role in strategic deterrence since the dropping of the first atomic bomb on Hiroshima in 1945. They form one leg of the nuclear triad of Intercontinental Ballistic Missiles (ICBMs), Submarine-launched Ballistic Missiles (SLBMs), and manned bombers. This triad is at the heart of US deterrent strategy. So when President Jimmy Carter announced in 1977 the cancellation of the B-1A bomber, which had been planned as a replacement for the B-52 bomber, there was an outcry from critics who believed that a follow-on to the B-52 was essential to maintain the strategic triad.[176]

Partly to answer these critics and partly to deflect then-presidential candidate Ronald Reagan's criticism that Carter was weak on defense, Defense Secretary Harold Brown made public the existence of the stealth bomber project in August 1980. Just before his announcement, a few reports about the existence of the top secret project had appeared in Aviation Week & Space Technology, Armed Forces Journal International, and the Washington Post.[177] However, Aviation Week had already published information on the Stealth bomber as early as January 29, 1979.[178] When Reagan became president, he reversed Carter's earlier decision on the B-1 bomber, placing it on a fast procurement track, while at the same time allowing the B-2 to proceed apace. Since the B-52's ability to penetrate Soviet airspace had steadily diminished, the 100 planned B-1Bs, which represented a modified version of the B-1A developed before the Carter administration, were designed to take up the role of penetrating bomber in the late eighties, eventually to be replaced in turn by the B-2.

After George Bush became president, and the world became kinder and gentler, lower defense budgets became a fact of life. When Dick Cheney finally walked into his Pentagon E-Ring office in mid-March 1989, the main debate over the defense budget was not whether to cut, but where to cut and how much to cut. Naturally, the B-2 program, with a projected price tag of $70 billion at the time, if all 132 planes were to be produced, attracted the new defense secretary's attention. Early on, Cheney publicly talked of taking a hard look at the B-2. But by the end of May 1989, after a trip to the Northrop plant, Cheney became a believer in the new technology and the capability it represented.[179] Meanwhile, Rep. Les Aspin (D-WI), then chairman of the House Armed Services Committee, and other critics began saying that Congress ought to consider terminating the costly B-2 bomber program.

THE NETWORKS' COVERAGE OF STEALTH

The B-2 bomber made news on November 22, 1988. All three networks covered its unveiling. ABC's Bob Zelnick likened the event to a debutante ball, since "cameras and guests were kept at a distance of nearly 200 feet." He then described the B-2's appearance and noted, "Unlike the smaller Stealth fighter, this so-called flying wing has yet to be flown. Each Stealth bomber will cost an estimated half a billion dollars, largely because it's made of expensive non-metallic materials designed to absorb, rather than reflect, radar."

Zelnick then let Secretary of the Air Force Edward Aldridge explain how the Soviet Union was beginning to make its targets harder and more mobile, and how the ability of the United States to hold them at risk enhanced deterrence. Zelnick immediately added, "But to maintain its Stealth design, the B-2 has sacrificed speed, defensive weapons, and some of its payload. And critics say it will have to rely on orbiting US satellites to find its targets." John Pike of the Federation of American Scientists presented more criticism before Zelnick chimed in again: "Now that research and development is complete, President-elect Bush and the Congress must decide how fast to press ahead with Stealth production. But with the B-1 bomber only recently deployed, many will say the country just got one bomber, why not wait on the other?"

NBC's Don Oliver started with a basic description, as had Zelnick. He then peppered his report with a bit of history, stating that Northrop designers had first conceived of the flying wing 40 years ago. Next, he made the point that "the Air Force says the aging fleet of B-52 bombers are no longer reliable and that the interim B-1B bomber doesn't have the Stealth characteristics necessary to be a long-term solution to America's defense needs."[180]

Oliver concluded by calling on critic John Pike, who said the United States cannot afford Stealth. To illustrate, Oliver noted that, at $500 million a plane, for five Stealth bombers, one aircraft carrier could be built. "And the plan is to build 132 of these ominous-looking weapons." Secretary Aldridge was then allowed to state that we cannot afford to be without this program.

CBS's David Martin was both fairer and more circumspect. He talked about how Stealth technology might change the rules of war, discussed the technology, and explained its rationale: "The effect is to reduce the range of Soviet radar, creating gaps in a system in which the Kremlin has invested tens of billions of dollars, allowing the B-2 to slip through to hit targets like underground command posts and mobile missiles."[181]

Martin also brought up the "state-of-the-art manufacturing procedures" involved in the B-2's production. Then after allowing Pike to call the weapon "gold-plated," Martin wrapped up by saying: "But now that the Stealth bomber has finally been unveiled, the public can at least begin to debate how much a plane like this is really worth."

A little over a week later, on December 1, 1988, Martin made a passing reference to the Stealth bomber in a report on nuclear weapons plants: "Department of Energy officials concede it is ironic that an Administration which spent eight years rearming America with sophisticated weapons, like the Stealth bomber, neglected the facilities which produce the nuclear explosives those weapons were built to carry."

On March 1, 1989, Tom Brokaw made another passing reference, this time in an NBC Nightly News story related to John Tower's failing nomination as secretary of defense. Brokaw cited a *Defense News* editorial that called for Tower's withdrawal because he was a consultant to companies that produce the B-1, the B-2, the MX missile and the proposed Midgetman missile.

On the weekend newscasts of April 22 and 23, 1989, all three networks included evening news segments on US strategic weapons. On the Saturday broadcasts, each network focused mainly on the MX and Midgetman missiles. On Sunday, CBS's Connie Chung and ABC's Sam Donaldson told viewers that Cheney was recommending cuts in the B-2 program and the Star Wars (SDI) missile defense program. By Monday, April 24, Bob Zelnick of ABC made another reference to the B-2 in a report on defense spending proposals. He said that production of the B-2, or Stealth Bomber, "will be slowed down without canceling the $68 billion program."

The last mention of the B-2 during the spring came on Wednesday, April 26, when CBS's David Martin provided an overview of the defense budget. In the context of Navy cuts to carrier groups and Air Force cuts in the total number of MX missiles, Martin said, "The Pentagon's most glamorous project, the B-2 Stealth bomber, is being delayed a year. And Cheney clearly has his doubts about the plane's future." Cheney then stated, "We've got problems with the B-2. I'm reluctant to reassure you that it's all under control and we know exactly what we're doing on the B-2 program, because I don't think we do yet."

Curiously, at the end of May and in early June, 1989, when reports appeared in the print media that Cheney and his deputy, Donald Atwood, had given

Northrop high marks for the quality control in the B-2 program and had both become supporters of the plane, the networks did not consider that newsworthy.

ONE STORY ON COST AND A NONSTORY

During congressional hearings in June 1989, Defense Department officials released the figure for how much money had already been invested in the B-2 program. Since the B-2 had been managed as a "black" program, only a handful of congressmen had been regularly briefed on the actual costs during the course of the B-2's development. That figure, $22.4 billion, was certainly newsworthy.

Of the three networks, only CBS did a story on the large investment already made in the B-2. David Martin noted that "much of the money has gone into a state-of-the-art production line, which so far has turned out just one completed aircraft, but which has about ten others in various stages of construction."[182] He then noted that a "carrier battle group, complete with escort ships and warplanes, costs about $19 billion." He concluded by pointing out that members of Congress will demand that more information about the B-2 be made public and that, in an era of declining defense budgets, the B-2 may fly through the air more easily than it might fly through Congress. Martin's story was relatively straightforward, but his comparison to a carrier battle group was essentially meaningless. NBC's Don Oliver, too, used the comparison to a carrier. This type of comparison is curious. For instance, the Pentagon could buy thousands and thousands of M-16 rifles for the price of a B-2, but unless the United States needs more rifles, or more carriers, the comparative price value is of little import.

The official announcement of total funds already invested in the B-2 was covered extensively in the print media since it figured into the debate about whether to cancel the bomber. Many stories in the print media also looked at the mission of the B-2 and the various strategic and budget considerations surrounding the question of whether it made sense to cancel outright a program into which over $22 billion had already been poured.

The second network story in June was more problematic. NBC decided to focus on the B-2's "deep trouble" on June 26. NBC's Henry Champ reported that the B-2 might be "shot down by exorbitant costs" and that legislators were concerned about the reputation of Northrop Corp.[183] Rep. John Dingell (D-MI), never one to miss a chance to make news, called Northrop "both incompetent and corrupt." Champ also referred to a suit filed by former Northrop employees who had charged that Northrop overcharged the government for part of its B-2 work. As a finale, Robert Costello, former undersecretary of defense for acquisition, said he had raised concerns with Secretary Cheney about the B-2. Champ made a quick reference to Northrop's internal investigation, which he said found no justification for the charges brought by the whistleblowers, then concluded: "Already, 22 ½ billion dollars has been spent, and the B-2 bomber has never flown. Some congressmen want work suspended until test flights are completed. A few others want it killed altogether."

Curiously, at this same time, no major newspaper or trade publication was focusing on the allegations of overcharging brought up by NBC. Why? Because there was no real story there. First of all, Costello had attempted to kill the B-2 program because of his worries about the alleged overall lack of quality at Northrop. The straw that broke the camel's back was the charge concerning the falsification of data related to guidance equipment for nuclear-armed cruise missiles, not the B-2 itself. Costello forced a management review of the B-2 program, but lost the battle to kill it when the B-2 passed the review.[184]

Northrop had been plagued with management and quality problems. The faulty MX missile guidance system was one case in point. The investigation of allegations of influence peddling in connection with the company's attempt to sell the South Koreans the F-20 fighter, which the American government did not buy, was another. Moreover, in July 1989, a Northrop unit, Precision Products Division, was suspended based on charges that the company knowingly supplied bad parts for the Air Force Air Launched Cruise Missile and the Marine Corps AV-8B Harrier aircraft and then falsely certified them.[185]

Wall Street Journal reporters Rick Wartzman and Andy Pasztor provided the overall context of these charges in a July 13 story: "The company [Northrop], which has been rocked in the past two years by allegations of overcharging and illegal foreign payoffs, views the B-2 as a way to polish its tarnished reputation. But just yesterday, the Pentagon suspended a Northrop unit [Precision Products Div.] from all new federal contracts for allegedly defrauding the government."[186]

As for the B-2 itself, it passed the review of the Defense Acquisition Board initiated by Costello, another review by the Defense Science Board, and numerous other reviews during its development. But NBC saw no reason to mention these or Cheney's and Atwood's firsthand review and endorsement of Northrop's management of this particular program. Instead, Champ misleadingly linked Costello to the B-2 whistleblower charges, which had not been regarded as a major story by any other respectable media organization.

There were plenty of possible stories about the B-2, including cost, mission, new manufacturing technologies, its technical capabilities, and the political wrangling on Capitol Hill over the defense budget. Why did NBC have to make up a story? What is quite clear is that during the eight months between the B-2's first and second appearances on the runway no substantive coverage by the three network evening news divisions occurred. Cost was by far the angle that attracted the most attention. Other issues, seldom touched by the television networks, included the change in design to enable the plane to fly low-level missions, the debate over the B-2's aerodynamics, and the way the new bomber was manufactured.

B-2 COVERAGE BY THE PRINT MEDIA

For their part, during the same period, the print media focused on the unveiling of some of the most revolutionary technology of the past several decades. In the January 23, 1989, issue of *Newsweek*, Gregg Easterbrook wrote that "the Air

Force recently revealed that . . . in 1983 the bomber was redesigned to enable it to fly near treetop level."[187] In February, Robert Ropelewski of *Armed Forces Journal International* explained this change in some detail: "The aircraft was conceived with the expectation that it would penetrate enemy airspace at medium altitudes in the 15,000 to 20,000-ft. range. Several years into the program, however, the Air Force concluded that survivability would be increased by penetrating at much lower altitudes—in the 200-500-ft. range—where terrain masking makes radar detection more unlikely."[188] According to industry sources cited by Ropelewski, it had been determined that the B-2 would not survive at medium-to-high altitudes even with its stealth features.

Between March and May 1989, a debate took place on the pages of *Defense News* over the flying wing's aerodynamics. Barbara Amouyal of *Defense News* cited critic Joseph Foa, an expert in propulsion at George Washington University in a March 20 report. "Foa claims that the flying wing configuration would have been ideal for a propeller-driven aircraft where the rate of fuel consumption is primarily a function of engine output. With jet propulsion, however, where the rate of consumption primarily involves jet thrust, the flying wing design poses the 'absolute worst possible configuration.' "[189]

Gen. Bernard Randolph, then commander of Air Force Systems Command, took on Foa and other critics by answering questions about performance. In the May 8 edition of *Defense News*, Amouyal wrote, "Randolph said the aircraft's rolling and banking movements are controlled through surfaces known as elevons on the back edge of the flying wing. Control of the aircraft's direction is provided through differential drag, he said, which produces a turning movement."[190]

As for the B-2's manufacture, Jane Callen of the trade newsletter *Inside the Pentagon* noted on June 9 that, according to Northrop, "the aircraft, to include the first vehicle, are being built on production hard tooling versus the standard method of prototyping early vehicles. The B-2 design and manufacturing program has made extensive use of Computer-Aided Design and Manufacturing (CAD/CAM)"; "The B-2 design can accommodate improvements in sensors and avionics, ensuring its effectiveness and adaptability throughout a 30-year operational life"; and "computerization of the B-2 extends to the flight line. B-2 mechanics will tap into a data base that has been generated from the aircraft's CAD/CAM system. A series of computer menus will aid the mechanic with troubleshooting."[191]

The computer-aided design and manufacture of the B-2 was one of the most revolutionary aspects of the program. Never before had a plane been built and tested by computer. There were 750,000 hours of system and subsystem testing by computer before the plane even got into the air, according to Northrop. The design was also subjected to 24,000 hours of testing in a wind tunnel.

All of these issues appeared in major newspapers and in trade publications. The closest the networks came to spotlighting any of these three areas was David Martin's brief mention on CBS of the "state-of-the-art production line," an ambiguous formulation at best about manufacturing technology that was revolutionizing the aerospace industry. While it is understood that television news can never cover issues and events with the detail of print reporters, it is the job of television news to at least highlight the major issues briefly. In the first eight months after the unveiling of the B-2, the networks failed to do even that, choosing instead the sensational costs and the prospects for cuts in the B-2 program alongside other defense budget cuts without any real context.

DRAMA TAKES PRECEDENCE

After the three networks' scant coverage of the July 10, 1989, taxiing tests, network camera crews must have begun to eagerly await the actual flight test of the B-2, originally scheduled for July 15. Tension was mounting during the humid days of July in the nation's capital. Hearings on July 12 on Capitol Hill were covered by ABC and CBS. Bob Zelnick of ABC noted that members of Congress found the B-2's price tag to be a big problem, in spite of its successful runway test. Two sound bites from two congressmen who appeared on the networks would resonate not only on the airwaves, but in the print media as well.

Zelnick cut to Rep. John Kasich, a conservative Republican from Ohio who opposed the B-2, and who made this now-famous comment: "You want to fly a $600 million airplane against a $1 million bridge. That doesn't make a lot of sense."[192]

Rep. Les Aspin (D-WI), another opponent of the B-2, also made a memorable and widely quoted remark: "There are only 12 countries in the world that have annual defense budgets that are greater than $8 billion a year. I mean, is this conceivable that we're going to do this? No chance. No chance."[193]

CBS's David Martin used Aspin's remark in his report, and both Zelnick and Martin had Rep. William Dickinson (R-AL) mention that the B-2 was in political trouble. In Martin's report, Dickinson said, "And when the Chairman [Aspin] tells you that, politically, you're not going to get six, seven, eight billion dollars a year for this one weapon system, you can put that in your pocket and take it to the bank."[194]

These troubles on Capitol Hill only added to the suspense surrounding the maiden flight of the B-2. Moreover, network coverage left viewers with this question in mind: Might the technological marvel of this flying wing taking to the air change some lawmakers' minds or was the B-2 doomed on Capitol Hill?

Well, the answer was not to come, at least not on July 15. When a gauge indicated that the B-2 had low fuel pressure, the test flight had to be delayed. But since the networks had obviously planned coverage of the event, B-2 stories appeared on each of their newscasts.

CBS's David Martin said that "delays in flight tests are normal. But there is nothing normal about the $70 billion project to build 132 of the radar-evading bombers. Even before today's delay, members of Congress had vowed they would never vote the $8 billion a year the Air Force wants for full-scale production. But any cut in the budget will only slow down production and drive the cost of each plane higher."[195]

Concluding, Martin said, "Each day's delay only adds to the controversy over whether the Stealth bomber is worth the price." Zelnick of ABC echoed Martin, stating, "Today's scrub was no indication of any fundamental problem with the B-2, which the Air Force says will soon be flying. But with the entire Stealth program in deep trouble on Capitol Hill, it was the sort of glitch the Air Force could well have lived without."[196]

NBC's Fred Francis devoted almost all of his segment to the cost of the B-2. After juxtaposing Gen. Larry Welch's statement that the B-2 is suitable for 60 percent of the total targets the US must cover, and is, therefore, cost efficient, with statements by three congressmen critical of the program, Francis summed up: "Congress is not happy about its choices. It can freeze the program and waste much of the $23 billion invested. It can fund the bomber for another $50 billion over several years. Or it can build fewer planes, raising the cost to as much as a billion dollars a plane."[197]

Francis then made a final point: "Many blame the Pentagon for the budget dilemma, for keeping the project too secret for too long. Those critics say that Pentagon planners naively thought that the 'gee whiz' factor of a plane that radar could not see would dazzle most congressmen." As he implied, it did not.

Two days later, on July 17, what might otherwise have been touted as a technological feat, similar to the first launch of the space shuttle, turned into more news reports focusing on the B-2's price tag. Martin of CBS began by discussing some of the B-2's features in less than glowing terms: "Today's first flight was not a test of the half-billion-dollar plane's ability to evade radar. In fact, it flew with its wheels down to make it easier to track. Max speed was only 180 knots, maximum altitude 10,000 feet. Today the pilots only wanted to know if the giant flying wing performed the way thousands of hours of wind tunnel tests and computer simulations said it would."[198] He also noted that the B-2's first flight "did not appear to change many minds in Congress, where members are reeling from the sticker shock of a program that costs $70 billion for 132 planes."

ABC's Bob Zelnick took a similar tack, describing the flight, noting that it was only designed to see whether the B-2 could actually fly, and ending with the point that the flight had failed to convert the B-2's critics on Capitol Hill. NBC's Francis, too, combined a brief description of the flight with a focus on the price tag. His opening said it all: "The bat-winged bomber, the costliest weapon system ever built, 18 months overdue, and already being trashed by Congress, lifted gracefully into the California dawn."[199]

Several reports on the B-2 followed before July came to a close. This coverage included a brief look at the arms control angle, a note on how defense companies were advertising their newest technology, and a wrap-up of the budget issue.

On July 21, Dan Rather began his CBS report by stating that "President Bush and his aides warned today that if Congress rejects the B-2 bomber, it will wreck the US bargaining position in arms control talks with Moscow." Correspondent Eric Engberg then explained: "The [Air Force] generals asserted the new bomber provides a deterrent the US will need if other strategic weapons are reduced in the current START talks. But some Democrats chided them for overselling the plane's importance." Sens. Edward Kennedy (D-MA) and Timothy Wirth (D-CO) objected to the Air Force's stand. Wirth called it "legislative blackmail."

On July 23, NBC's Maria Shriver, who was the anchor that night, brought up a related issue on the Nightly News: "The debate is growing over whether there really is a need for the Stealth in a time of tight money and warming relations with the Soviet Union." Correspondent Sandy Gilmore then pointed out, "The B-2 has become a tougher sale with the thaw in Soviet-American relations, with Soviet sailors permitted to take shore leave at Norfolk Naval Base, and the visit of top Soviet adviser General Sergei Akhromeyev to Congress."[200]

To combat this changing atmosphere, Shriver explained in her introduction to the next segment, defense companies were resorting to heavy advertising. NBC correspondent Henry Champ then pointed to a B-2 commercial by Northrop and added, "A few months ago the B-2 bomber was one of the country's most closely guarded secrets, and now it is in danger of media overexposure."

CBS's coverage was similar on July 23. Jacqueline Adams began a report by stating, "Northrop, the bomber's manufacturer, hit the airwaves this weekend to win support for the most expensive airplane ever built. Congress this week will vote to kill or severely limit the Stealth."[201]

On July 25, as part of a budget story, ABC's Bob Zelnick noted that the "Administration seemed to be having better luck with funding for the Stealth bomber. Vice President Quayle argued that without the B-2 as a backup, it would be more difficult for the US to reach an agreement with the Soviets cutting long-range missiles."[202] Zelnick then added that the Senate is expected to cut only $300 million from Stealth, but will require good test flights before buying more planes.

B-2 FLIES OUT OF SIGHT

With the summer phase of the budget process wrapped up, the networks found little that was "newsworthy" about the B-2 in the months that followed. A few brief notes about the successful test flights cropped up. But, generally, when weapons systems are successful, when they do meet their deadlines and, occasionally, even cost ceilings, when they do represent a technological success, that is not news in the networks' eyes.

For example, on August 12, 1989, ABC substitute anchor Carole Simpson only broke the silence when something went wrong. Her entire report went like this: "A second test flight of the controversial B-2 Stealth bomber was postponed today at Edwards Air Force Base in California because of technical problems. The flight will have to take place sometime after this weekend because the same base is being used tomorrow for the return of the shuttle Columbia."[203]

On August 16, Ted Koppel of ABC, sitting in for Peter Jennings, reported, "The new Stealth bomber took its second test flight today, but landed after only an hour when an oil pressure gauge flashed a warning signal. Officials say they don't know if it was really low pressure or just a faulty gauge."

NBC's Tom Brokaw, on the same night, said, "And for the United States plane with the $530 million price tag, a second test flight today. But there was a problem." Bob Schieffer of CBS noted that the flight was cut short and concluded with: "The plane, designed to be invisible to enemy radar, is already at the center of a funding dispute in Congress, where some say its half-billion dollar price tag is just too high."[204]

On August 25, Mary Alice Williams of NBC reported: "The Air Force today provided a footnote to last week's aborted test flight of the B-2 Stealth bomber. The flight was cut short because of a defective part which caused a drop in the plane's oil pressure. Air Force officials said today the defective part was provided by a defense contractor once fined for billing fraud, Sundstrand."[205]

Subtle, but still unfair: defective parts, corrupt contractors, aborted tests, these are the images the networks prefer to convey to the American public when it comes to their coverage of weapons systems.

CBS, on August 26, was the only network to make a brief report on a successful test. Susan Spencer said, "The Air Force says the B-2 Stealth bomber had its third and longest test flight today over California's Mojave Desert. A spokesman said the B-2 landed safely after a 4½ hour flight, one that was not announced in advance."[206] The tag on the end was meant to suggest that camera crews could not get there to provide viewers new images.

In September, the B-2 was beginning to fade from the short memory of the television news networks. But on September 26, Tom Brokaw of NBC broke the silence with this report: "And there were more problems for the B-2 stealth bomber today. The Pentagon says two test flights had to be cut short, one because of high winds; the other because of a drop in oil pressure. The stealth is the most expensive plane ever built. They cost $530 million a copy."

On November 1, Brokaw gave viewers another footnote on the B-2: "NBC's Andrea Mitchell reports tonight that congressional leaders have reached agreement on the defense budget, and it calls for a slowdown in the B-2 Stealth bomber program and deep cuts in SDI, Star Wars. It does provide money, however, for two aircraft that Defense Secretary Cheney wanted to kill [V-22 Osprey tilt-rotor aircraft and F-14D fighter]."

A year after the B-2 rolled out for the first time, what images had the evening news divisions left with the American public? The ominous-looking batplane. "Sticker shock" on Capitol Hill. Failed or delayed test flights. An Air Force ploy to use arms control arguments to save the most expensive plane ever built. Defective parts. And corrupt or incompetent defense companies. Given that the American public looks to television as a major source of news, to what extent was public opinion on the B-2—generally running in a negative direction—attributable to this distorted reporting?

Over the entire year, the B-2 only ranked among the top 30 network news stories for a given month in July 1989, when the B-2 took to the air for the first time, according to the *Tyndall Report*, a newsletter that tracks network news coverage. In that month, the B-2 Stealth Bomber program ranked 11th out of 30 stories.[207] For the whole month of July, one of the most sophisticated and complex weapons systems ever built was explained to the American public in 12 minutes or less on the evening news broadcasts (5 minutes on ABC, 12 minutes on CBS, and 8 minutes on NBC). For the three-month period, June–August 1989, the period leading up to the test flight and following it, total coverage by the three networks amounted to 32 minutes.

A DIFFERENT PICTURE ALTOGETHER

From June to November 1989, the print media painted a very different picture than did broadcast journalists. Aside from the greater detail, which would be expected, print journalists covered a number of aspects that were at the heart of the debate over whether the United States needed what was estimated at the time to be a $532 million bomber.

Before and after the test flight, the capabilities of the B-2 were treated extensively in trade and general interest publications. The mission of the B-2 was also frequently mentioned, almost as often as cost came up. For their part, television news teams completely ignored the bomber's mission, framing the whole debate in terms of dollars alone. The issue of countermeasures to stealth technology was another area print reporters covered. This, too, was an extremely important consideration when contemplating such high costs.

Arms control issues, scantily treated on the networks, were also a major news element in the print media. While cost also got more ink in newspapers, magazines, and newsletters than any other single aspect of the B-2 program, the discussion was more intelligent, balanced, and informative than on the evening newscasts, although there were occasional exceptions.

As for capabilities, well before the test flight in July, Gen. Bernard Randolph delivered a speech to aviation writers in Phoenix, Arizona, on April 29, 1989.[208] Many of the details and counterarguments aimed at critics then found their way into the trade press and the general press. Randolph stated that "while its low observability precludes external weapons carriage, its internal carriage capacity is up to 50,000 pounds of either nuclear or conventional ordinance. Its range of over 6000 nautical miles unrefueled at high altitude, and over 10,000 nautical miles at high altitude with one refueling, is greater than the B-52. . . . With one air refueling, operating from just four bases (two stateside and two overseas), the B-2 could cover any point on the world's land mass on a non-stop radius mission carrying a full conventional payload. Those possibilities could deter a great deal of adventurism."

The general also covered the production process: "A quantum leap in production accuracy. Compared to conventional methods, for example, the team achieved a 17 to 1 improvement in the quality of complex forming structures and a 6 to 1 reduction in typical first-part fit errors during assembly. A better than 90 percent success rate was achieved on the first installation of tubing, fluid systems and mechanical systems, compared with traditional rates near 60 percent. Similarly, the hydraulic tubing for the B-2 was precisely produced at better than 90 percent on the first try, a sixfold improvement over earlier methods."

The B-2, unlike any previous aircraft, including the B-1 bomber, was designed and developed simultaneously to produce an operationally configured aircraft, not a prototype, which would then have to be tested and modified. This did not escape George Wilson of the *Washington Post*, who included a number of long quotations from the Pentagon's testing director, John E. Krings alongside his discussion of the B-2's cost and political troubles.[209]

Around and during the test flight period, most articles that appeared in the general press avoided including just cost as their focus. Richard Halloran of the *New York Times* wrote a thorough and fair overview of the B-2 program on July 17. The headline read: "Stealth Bomber Suffers from Secrecy, High Cost and an Unclear Purpose."[210] All valid issues at the time.

On July 13, Molly Moore of the *Washington Post* outlined the Air Force's "counterattack in defense of B-2 'Stealth' " during a congressional hearing.[211] The following day, *Post* reporter Adela Gooch outlined Cheney's arguments for why the bomber should be funded.[212] On the day after the flight, July 18, the *New York Times* carried an article by Richard W. Stevenson under the headline, "US Stealth Bomber Makes Test Flight Without Mishap."[213] *Los Angeles Times* reporter Ralph Vartabedian's article appeared under the headline, "Stealth Bomber Makes 1st Flight: Air Force Pleased by 2-Hour Test, but Cost Doubts Are Not Erased."[214]

While not overly positive, these and other articles at least provided coverage of the different issues surrounding the B-2. Though negative coverage of weapons systems is a fact of life in the print media as well as on television, the context found in print often gave the reader a fighting chance to form his own opinion.[215]

Print also allowed more space for analysis and good news. On September 15, London's *Financial Times* carried a piece by Lynton McLain that explained in detail the CAD/CAM manufacturing process that Northrop used to produce the B-2.[216] And for their part, trade publications, like *Aviation Week* and *Flight International* devoted a lot of space in the months following the first test flight to the B-2's successful test performances.[217]

On October 2, the newsletter *Defense Daily* ran a story that revealed after five test flights that the B-2 handled better than expected. According to the newsletter, "the Air Force says it has performed 'better than expected in the areas of handling qualities, especially smooth aircraft control in the refueling position.' "[218] The article also explained that the low oil pressure readings continued during the third and fourth flights, but were corrected by the fifth flight.

A crack in the gear box, the Airframe Mounted Accessory Drive, had been discovered. But thanks to the automated production capability, the process was able to be changed quickly to eliminate a ridge that is molded in the case when the AMAD is manufactured. Network television news only told viewers that a corrupt contractor, Sundstrand, had produced the faulty part.

Another newsletter, *Aerospace Daily*, provided coverage on September 22 of a presentation that Northrop made during the Air Force Association convention in Washington, D.C. It, too, highlighted how well the test flights had proceeded. "A highlight of the B-2 program, [a veteran test pilot] said, is 'the tremendous amount' of high quality data that is generated by each flight. 'We combine a bunch of different tests on different subsystems all at the same time, so you can satisfy a whole roomful of engineers with one test maneuver.' "[219]

Aside from good news, the networks also missed a mini-controversy surrounding the B-2's range. On October 6, George Wilson of the *Washington Post* reported that a "secret part of the Defense Department budget" revealed that the B-2 had less cruising range than the cheaper B-1B. According to Wilson, the black budget included an estimate of a range of 6,400 miles for the B-1 and 6,000 for the B-2 without refueling.[220]

Ten days later, the Air Force released performance details for the B-2, which were outlined in an October 17 report in the *Washington Times* by Rowan Scarborough. "In a high-altitude mission, a B-2 carrying eight short-range attack missiles [SRAMs] and eight B61 gravity bombs has a range of 6,600 miles. A B-1B toting the same weapons could fly 5,600 miles, according to the Air Force."[221]

Where were the networks in October? They were in East Germany covering the East Germans going west, in Panama covering the failed coup attempt, and in San Francisco covering the earthquake. When they were home, news coverage focused on abortion.[222]

Meanwhile, *Popular Science* ran an October story covering the technical details learned from the first flight of the B-2,[223] and *Washington Post* reporter Rick Atkinson wrote an in-depth three-part series on the B-2's procurement history, the debate over its mission, and how the political consensus crumbled on Capitol Hill.[224]

Articles on the B-2's mission also appeared, sometimes linked to cost, sometimes not. Small and regional newspaper editors around the country realized that mission was important, why didn't television news producers and correspondents?

On July 25, for example, the *Hartford Courant*'s editorial read, "If the warplane is essential to global peace and credible national defense, money will be found to build it. The question of need has yet to be answered persuasively, however."[225]

The *Atlanta Constitution* on July 21 made a similar point. "Even if the B-2 passes [all its tests] with flying colors, though, there are questions to be answered about the program itself that are just as critical as whether the plane works."[226] After mentioning its "colossal cost," the editorial stated, "then there's the question of the B-2's mission. Mr. Cheney has yet to make a good case that it would knock out Soviet mobile strategic missiles more effectively than a 100-times less costly cruise missile fired from a B-52 or a B-1."

The *Arizona Republic* stated on July 23 that it was in favor of rethinking the triad. "The US should work for the eventual elimination of land-based ICBMs, which would mean going ahead with the Stealth bomber, cruise missiles and submarines. But even if the Soviets refused to go along, we still should rethink the makeup of the triad."[227] Opinion pieces across the country asked similar questions about the mission, many with a great deal of sophistication. As important, competing viewpoints were offered to readers. Syndicated columnist George Will argued for the B-2 in a July 23 column, stating, "The B-2 would vitiate more than $200 billion of Soviet investment in air defenses."[228] The same day, an opinion piece by Paul Walker argued against it in the *Boston Globe*. He said, "I vote to leave B-2 and its old, aggressive Cold War imagery to Batman and build Red Cross ships, grain barges and other images of positive and peaceful world leadership which bring real security to allies and friends."[229]

Another point of view came from David Broder of the *Washington Post*, who wrote on July 26, "The first principle is that weapons decisions must follow strategy, not drive it. The second is that dismantling the American strategic deterrent must be the last step, not the first, in the negotiated reduction of Cold War defense forces."[230]

In August and September, the editor and chairman of the board of *Armed Forces Journal International*, Benjamin Schemmer and John Tower, respectively, debated the case of the B-2's mission in successive editorials.[231] In news stories, too, mission was part and parcel of print coverage. The July 31 issue of *Time*, for instance, carried a piece by Bruce Van Voorst that included not only the debate over the B-2's cost, but also the debate over its mission.[232]

As far as the technology itself, and prospective countermeasures, a piece by Jay Mallin of the *Washington Times* on September 29 covered the ways the B-2 might be detected in a discussion about over-the-horizon/backscatter radar, bistatic radar and carrier-free radar.[233] *USA Today*'s Tom Squitieri also reported on an Australian advanced Jindalee over-the-horizon radar on October 13, noting it might be able to detect the B-2.[234] Then on November 2, Mark Thompson of the Knight-Ridder news service reported that "the Air Force, continuing to pare back its claims for the B-2 Stealth bomber, now says the enemy will be able to detect—but not destroy—the $532 million warplane."[235]

Were these developments not newsworthy? The lack of network coverage suggests that network news producers and correspondents thought not.

And what about arms control? The networks implied that the Air Force and Vice President Dan Quayle were using the arms control argument as a ploy to blackmail liberal congressmen into funding the B-2. In contrast to the broadcast impression left with viewers, *Washington Times* reporter Chris Harvey's article on July 24 quoted Sen. Sam Nunn (D-GA), chairman of the Senate Armed Services Committee, who said, "If we do not have a penetrating bomber, and the B-1 is not going to penetrate much beyond the mid-1990s, we're going to have to go back and re-examine our entire arms control position."[236] Though Nunn, like others, had "sticker shock" when he heard the price of the B-2, he suggested that the alternatives may be even more expensive.

Even in a period of warming US-Soviet relations, the Soviets still possessed a modern, highly sophisticated strategic arsenal. The Soviet capabilities, however, never seemed to come up on network news. A quick review of the 1989 edition of the Pentagon's *Soviet Military Power* publication, however, would have provided the networks with all the raw data needed to make comparisons.

Cost of the bomber, too, was presented without any context on the networks. In the print media, too, cost was sometimes presented as the sole reason for coming out against the B-2 in op-ed pieces or, in the case of some news stories, as the only angle of the story. But more often than not, context was provided.

Take, for instance, the famous remark by Rep. John Kasich (R-OH), who asked, Why use a $600 million bomber to take out a $1 million bridge? In the print media, columnist Charles Krauthammer answered him and others who used different variations of the same theme. "Congressional opponents argue that it is absurd to send a $500 million airplane to destroy a $5 million bridge. What about the F-111s that we sent to destroy Gadhafi's tent? Was it absurd to send a $36 million plane to destroy something that costs less than a Buick?"[237] Krauthammer cited their faulty reasoning as "an example of the silliness that passes for strategic thinking these days." Krauthammer also noted that "the cost of sending radar-vulnerable F-111s against Libya was, we tend to forget, one downed plane and two dead American flyers. The reason to have a very expensive but radar-evading plane like Stealth, which can fly 10,000 miles on a single refueling, is to be able to strike almost anywhere in the world with high confidence that the planes and the men will not be shot down. We either want that capability or we don't. If we do, we have to pay for it."

Another angle of the cost of B-2 is the pork barrel. According to a report in *USA Today* on July 26, Northrop released data that showed that 46 states, including 383 congressional districts, stood to gain if the bomber were funded.[238] Spreading out such contracts is an art that requires collusion between industry, the military services, and Congress. That would have been a juicy story for the networks.

While critics of weapons programs generally get more space and attention in the print media and on television, at least other views appeared in long enough form in print to allow for the presentation of a sophisticated argument for such a system. On the evening newscasts, that was virtually impossible. Usually, officials were given only 5 to 10 second sound bites out of obligation, then they were outgunned by critics.

In contrast, Deputy Defense Secretary Donald Atwood was given space on the *New York Times* op-ed page on July 27 to make a different point about cost: "Some people argue that, at $7 billion to $8 billion a year, the B-2 would eat up too much of the defense budget for one weapon system. But the B-52 accounted for 1.4 percent of the defense budget during its procurement period of 1952 to 1961. The B-1 consumed 1.6 percent of the defense budget from 1982 to 1986. The B-2 is projected to take only 1.3 percent of the budget between 1987 and 1996."[239]

Gen. John T. Chain Jr., then commander in chief of the Strategic Air Command, responded to critics by making points about the B-2's role in deterrence in the *Christian Science Monitor* the day before, concluding, "The United States can ill afford to turn its back on such technological advances if we are to remain committed to deterrence as a means to prevent war."[240]

Were any of these views juxtaposed fairly or given time equal to the critics on network news? The answer is an undeniable "no."

MISINFORMING THE PUBLIC

When the networks look only for the drama and the sensational and the simple, they distort, whether intentional or not. In the case of the B-2, network correspondents, producers, and anchors never provided enough time or attention to adequately explain the controversial bomber program—even on the most basic level. Any American who had the misfortune of getting all his news from the networks would have had no idea about how cost related to the B-2's mission, the technological advances made, the link to arms control, or even some of the controversies surrounding its technical capabilities, like range and aerodynamics.

As print coverage of the B-2 demonstrated, there were many newsworthy aspects of the stealth bomber program. The networks, however, tended to ignore the most complicated ones, choosing instead to focus on the simple, but incomplete, cost angle. In the end, this approach led to a distorted picture of the B-2, one that certainly failed to measure up to Reuven Frank's notion of "probity" and "responsibility."

Diane Sawyer may have enjoyed playing the role of the Riddler, but when it came right down to it, she and her colleagues were only fooling themselves and misinforming the American public.

Chapter 11

The Romanian Revolution . . . Beyond the Images

Toward the end of December 1989, it appeared that the last communist regime in Eastern Europe was about to go the way of Poland, Hungary, East Germany, Bulgaria, and Czechoslovakia.

The sudden demise of Romanian dictator Nicolae Ceausescu featured shocking and dramatic images—dead bodies of the victims of a government-orchestrated "massacre," outraged "reformers" putting the hated dictator on trial, the dictator and his wife lying dead after being executed, and scenes of the masses celebrating, waving the Romanian flag with a hole cut out of the middle where the Communist red-star emblem used to be.

The networks latched on to these images and told the story of a revolution that did not follow the same peaceful path as the other East European countries. But, to the networks, the script for change from communism to democracy needed only to be altered to incorporate the violence of this "revolution."

Unfortunately, that script did not tell the whole story. Romania's revolution was far more complicated; it involved duplicity on the part of the "reformers," ancient ethnic antagonisms, and communist disinformation being passed off as news. Making the situation all the more difficult, Romania's borders were initially closed to all foreign media.

The networks did tell this riveting story, however, with the help of modern technology—from wire services to satellite images. But in the end, the story of the Romanian revolution showed not the triumph of technology, but its limits in the hands of journalists lacking extensive knowledge of Romania's past and present.

Images and wire service reports drove television coverage of the Romanian revolution. The television story of the revolution spanned a little more than a two-week period beginning on December 18, 1989. According to ADT Research, which monitors the three networks' evening newscasts, the Romanian revolution had some tough competition on US airwaves in late December 1989. After all, the

United States had invaded Panama on December 20. In its *Tyndall Report*, ADT Research noted, "Partly because of the invasion's overriding national importance, partly because of the difficulty of separating fact from rumor and of obtaining news footage from Romania, the revolution was never the Number One story of the day."[241]

But, the *Tyndall Report* continued, "the stories ran in tandem. Each day, Ceausescu's atrocities dwarfed Noriega's mere crimes; the desperate heroism of the Romanian people exposed the fecklessness of Panamanian opposition to their dictator. Romania may have received second billing, but it was breathtakingly more vivid than anything from Panama."

The same report added that the Panama story received 240 minutes of coverage, while the Romanian revolution weighed in with 89 minutes, making it the number two story of the month of December. Among the networks, ABC devoted 34 minutes, CBS 27 minutes, and NBC 28 minutes. CNN is not among the networks tracked by this research service, but CNN certainly played an important role. Its images were similar to those of the networks, but they were played and replayed with even more frequency.

TIMISOARA: A REVOLUTION ERUPTS

On December 18, news of protests in the Romanian city of Timisoara began reaching the West. Among the largest cities in Romania, the commercial and industrial center of Timisoara is located in the region of Romania known as Transylvania, an area of geography that has been controlled historically by Hungary, the Ottoman Turks, the Prince of Savoy, and Austria, before being ceded to Romania in the Treaty of Trianon after World War I. Ethnic tensions with Hungary are deeply rooted, and the Hungarian minority in the region plays an important role in relations between Romania and Hungary.

The networks would make their first reports on December 18, after the story had ricocheted around Eastern Europe. In fact, the Timisoara protests first made television news on Hungarian television on December 17. On that day, Budapest Television Service broadcast a story by correspondent Anna Juranyi, stationed in Szeged, Hungary:

"A young person, who did not want to make his name public, and who came home to Szeged this evening from Timisoara, gave an account of dramatic events. Together with his hosts in Timisoara, he reportedly witnessed, at 0200 in the morning, that after an attempt to evict [Presbyterian minister] Laszlo Tokes from his house, all hell broke loose. A human chain turned into a several-thousand-strong crowd of demonstrators. People thronging the streets shouted: 'Liberty' and 'Down with Ceausescu.' Those who marched toward the Party Committee headquarters set fire to cars, smashed in shop windows, burned up Ceausescu books, and smashed Ceausescu pictures into bits. There were clashes with the police, who, with protective shields and truncheons, had curbed the passion of the crowds by 0400 in the morning. Our witness saw young people who had been beaten until they were covered with blood and heard of several who had been arrested."[242]

The world's news wire services also sprang into action. On December 17, *Reuters*, citing the Hungarian news agency *MTI*, reported on the demonstrations in Timisoara that broke out on Saturday, December 16, after the ethnic Hungarian priest Laszlo Tokes was evicted from his apartment by the police.[243] The *Associated Press* (*AP*) followed up the next day from its Washington bureau, basing its report on a US State Department briefing. It said that at least two people were killed, citing "a person traveling in the region," and added, "an unconfirmed report in the West German media said hundreds were killed."[244]

December 18 was the day that Romania closed its borders to Western correspondents. On that day, *AP* carried a report from its bureau in Vienna, Austria. It stated, "in West Germany, Radio Bremen quoted William Totok, an ethnic German author who emigrated from Romania to West Germany, as saying that eyewitnesses told him as many as 300 to 400 people were killed." It then added, "the report could not be independently confirmed."[245] This same report cited a Yugoslav traveling in Romania, who said Yugoslavian tourists saw more dead in Timisoara. And it cited both Budapest radio, which said that Romanian security troops had sealed off Timisoara, and the Hungarian news agency, *MTI*, which said it took police nearly two hours to regain control in the city.

Meanwhile, another *AP* correspondent in Vienna cited the Yugoslavian news agency, *Tanjug*, which said that Romanian security forces took full control Monday [December 18] of Timisoara.[246] For its part, *Reuters* out of Belgrade, Yugoslavia, reported on December 18 that a Yugoslav witness, Radislav Dencic, said Romanian security forces had killed dozens of people in Timisoara. Dencic said that security forces were firing on the protesters with rifles and from helicopters. " 'Hundreds of people were falling on the pavement in front of my eyes,' he told reporters."[247]

That same day, *Reuters* out of Budapest, Hungary, added, "Eyewitnesses arriving from Romania claimed several hundred people were killed in clashes Sunday between the army and demonstrators in the western city of Timisoara, the Yugoslav news agency *Tanjug* reported Monday."

US television networks picked up the story on December 18 and defined their respective approaches. ABC was the most cautious when it came to casualty figures, citing reports that two people had died in Timisoara during protests. Peter Jennings concluded by suggesting there were no prospects for change in Romania, despite the mass demonstrations. CBS was the most sensational. Dan Rather talked of a challenge to the regime, mentioning reports that dozens, if not hundreds, had died. NBC fell in between, speaking about a crackdown by the Ceausescu regime that may have left dozens dead. The images presented by the three networks over the course of the story were remarkably similar; only tone and some details distinguished one network from the other.[248]

On December 19, wire stories continued to flow. *AP*'s Washington bureau set to work writing a background piece on Ceausescu's Romania.[249] Meanwhile, more reports came out of its Vienna bureau. "Greek dental students" crossing into

Yugoslavia were quoted, saying they had seen soldiers "killing dozens." There was no direct attribution, but these same Greek students had also been mentioned in a *Tanjug* report.[250] Indeed, high up in the story, the *AP* writer noted that most reports have come "from travelers leaving Romania or from news agencies able to reach residents by telephone." In the same report, a "Western resident of Timisoara," who wished to remain anonymous, said, "Tiananmen is nothing compared to Timisoara." Budapest radio was also quoted: "The radio quoted a Hungarian who said he had several physician relatives working in Timisoara hospitals." They said, "between 300 and 400 people were killed in the city by troops, with 250 bodies taken to one hospital."[251]

A second *AP* report out of Vienna was the first to quote a death toll of 2,000 in Timisoara,[252] a figure that can also be traced to *Tanjug*.[253] By this point, the various sources began to pile up upon each other. This *AP* report also cited the Greek students, who said dozens were killed, and mentioned the previous estimates of 300 to 400 killed. Additionally, it added *Tanjug*'s line: "Witnesses claim that police are taking the arrested demonstrators to the central Timisoara Square, where they beat them and stab them with bayonets, before shoving them into lorries (trucks) and driving them away no one knows where."[254]

This line became a favorite among Western wire reporters. On December 19, *Reuters* out of Budapest also quoted it, as well as *Tanjug*'s figure of 2,000 killed. Another *Reuters* report out of Vienna on December 20 also repeated the line that demonstrators had been beaten and stabbed on the central square.[255]

On December 19, ABC and CBS each seem to have found a "Western diplomat" who said that "Tiananmen was nothing compared to Timisoara." ABC mentioned a Polish woman's secondhand report that hundreds may have been killed. Romanian exiles were also quoted; they said men, women and children were shot. In addition to the Tiananmen comparison, CBS mentioned bloody protests, tanks encircling the airport, and gunfire in Timisoara. CBS and NBC both mentioned a Yugoslavian report that 2,000 may have died. NBC, however, did not attribute it to the Yugoslavian media, stating simply that "one report said." But then NBC mentioned that students in Yugoslavia said they saw a massacre and that soldiers were firing all night. According to NBC, one of its camera crews was told that the blood was so thick in the streets that it had to be hosed down. For its part, CBS played it up as well, adding that many were shot and bayoneted. CBS also mentioned that the opposition to the regime was unorganized and leaderless.

On December 20, all the wire services added yet another set of numbers to their reports. East Germany's *ADN* put forth a death toll of 3,000 to 4,000—and it was eagerly repeated. *AP*'s Vienna bureau reported, "In a dispatch quoting Romanians working in East Germany, the official East German agency *ADN* said unrest had spread to at least eight other Romanian cities and the death toll in Timisoara could reach 3,000 or 4,000."[256]

UPI, quoting East German television, which was quoting *ADN*, gave the same figures, adding, "East German television said there were so many dead that security forces had to haul them away to mass graves."[257] In the same report, *UPI* also presented Athens' twist to the Greek medical students' line, stating, "50 Greek medical students returning from western Romania told the semi-official *Athens News Agency* that 600 to 1,000 people were killed in clashes Sunday between police and pro-democracy demonstrators in Timisoara." It continued, "A female medical student said the city's three hospitals overflowed with the dead and wounded."

For its part, *Reuters*, reporting out of East Berlin, quoted *ADN* directly on the 3,000 to 4,000 casualties, but then added a theme that first appeared in *Tanjug*. *ADN* either picked it up from *Tanjug* or released it on its own: "*ADN* quoted travelers from Romania as saying soldiers and police in Timisoara took surviving demonstrators to the main square and beat them brutally, sometimes jabbing them with bayonets. *ADN* said there were so many bodies in the town that they had to be buried in mass graves on the outskirts or cremated."[258]

In a second report out of Belgrade, *Reuters* played another *Tanjug* theme: "It quoted passengers arriving by train from Bucharest at the Yugoslav border town of Vrsac for the report. They spoke of a massacre before the cathedral in central Timisoara of 36 children, who carried candles in an appeal for bread, peace and human dignity, *Tanjug* said."[259]

For their part, on December 20, the three networks, in very brief reports, focused on the state of emergency that had been declared. ABC was still unwilling to pin itself to any of the numbers that were flying about. It said that 50,000 demonstrated and that some of the soldiers joined in, adding that there were many dead. It ended by stating that Romania was refusing to budge from communism. CBS, however, reported that the death toll may have reached 4,000 over the last few days. NBC, too, stated that the deaths might number in the thousands.

On the first day of the story, ABC had a man in Budapest and CBS a man in Brussels. By December 19, CBS and NBC had reports coming from London. By December 20, ABC had a report coming from Yugoslavia, while CBS and NBC left the story to the anchors.

THE REVOLUTION SPREADS

On December 21, the "revolution" seemed to be reaching a crescendo. The wire services relayed more East European wire reports that described how the violence was spreading to other Romanian cities, including the capital of Bucharest. *AP* reported, "Ceausescu sent tanks into the streets of Bucharest Thursday and security forces with submachine guns fired on young demonstrators protesting his iron rule, killing at least 13 people."[260] *AP* added that the State Department called it "a massacre of undetermined proportions." More information on Timisoara from Yugoslavian news reports was also part of the report: "Yugoslav media, quoting witnesses, reported that soldiers and police who refused to fire on anti-government protesters in Timisoara were executed." Another *AP* report from Vienna on the same day repeated this same line.[261]

Also on December 21, *UPI*'s Budapest bureau began its report this way:

"Troops fired automatic weapons at pro-democracy demonstrations protesting communist rule in three Romanian cities Thursday in a snowballing uprising that may have killed thousands of people during the past few days, official East European news reports said."[262]

Meanwhile, from London, *UPI* sent out an update on Timisoara. This time, it did not have to quote one of the East European news agencies. Instead, it reached a 27-year-old doctor, who requested anonymity, in Bucharest. According to the report, she had been in Timisoara until December 19. "The Army was shooting at ambulances. We saw hundreds of bodies loaded into great trucks and taken away no one knows where," she said. Four Bulgarians were also quoted by *UPI* off of the Bulgarian state news agency, *BTA*: "They spoke of a center city square [in Timisoara] being 'strewn with corpses' and said they had watched a soldier bayonet a woman standing with a child."[263]

As for the networks, on December 21, ABC tapped into its correspondent in Hungary and added a perspective from its correspondent in Moscow. Both CBS and NBC continued to receive reports from London.

In those critical first few days, ABC had correspondents right in Yugoslavia and Hungary, the sources of the most exaggerated information of all, yet ABC remained far more cautious than the other two networks. For their part, CBS and NBC seemed to be relying on wire reports, which, based on the numbers cited by each, were coming out of Yugoslavia and Hungary.

Lengthy reports by all three networks appeared on December 21. ABC noted that, if reports are true, then Tiananmen Square "would only be the second worst attack on civilians in a year." As ABC added, violence was spreading to Romania's capital, Bucharest, where Ceausescu's speech had been interrupted by jeering crowds, a scene that made all the networks. ABC also cited a British diplomat, who said he had seen eight or nine dead bodies, and "witnesses" in Timisoara who said that officers had executed some of their men for disobeying orders to fire into the crowds.

To its credit, ABC also made the point in this same newscast that it was difficult to get firsthand information and that the real reporting was coming from Romania's socialist allies, specifically the Soviet Union (where an ABC correspondent happened to be). On this day, ABC also joined the choir by stating that thousands may have been killed during the massacres.

For its part, CBS led off on December 21 by stating that 13 people had been killed that day and thousands may have been killed the previous weekend in Timisoara. The British embassy tally of 8 or 9 bodies seen was also reported, the rally in Bucharest was shown, along with the statement that a massacre followed it, and the number of 4,000 casualties was repeated. NBC stated that it appeared that a bloodbath was taking place, and there was nothing like it in Eastern Europe. The report added that death tolls were rising and that some Eastern European agencies were reporting thousands killed.

A day later, on December 22, the wires were reporting on the downfall of the Ceausescu regime. *UPI* announced, "The new leader of the East European nation is former Foreign Minister Corneliu Manescu, official reports from Belgrade, Yugoslavia, and Budapest said. It is likely the 73-year-old communist will be a caretaker leader until a new government can be formed."[264] Budapest and Belgrade were wrong again, however. The *UPI* report also included a reference to an announcement made by Ion Iliescu on Romanian television, which described a 23-point "radical plan" for change. It included "the release of all political prisoners, freedom to travel abroad, the dismantling of the internal secret police, trials for former party officials, free elections, a new constitution and such minor reforms as a more liberal abortion law and an end to gasoline rationing."

In the same report, *UPI* quoted the Hungarian news agency, *MTI*, which said there were 632 bodies in one of the mass graves "where dead protesters were dumped by police." An NBC cameraman who was also quoted by *UPI* said he saw at least 100 bodies. An *AP* reporter, who filed a December 22 dispatch from Timisoara, wrote, "Hundreds of people were digging up mass graves discovered in the forest district of Timisoara, trying to find the remains of their friends and relatives killed in last weekend's crackdown." He added, "Three such mass graves are believed to be holding as many as 4,500 corpses." Quoting an electrician, he added that the corpses had been transported by garbage trucks to the area and that the drivers were later shot so that there would be no witnesses.[265] No where in the article did the reporter say that he had checked out these assertions or seen any bodies himself.

The most significant media event on December 22, however, was the television broadcast of one of these "mass graves." *Reuters* out of Vienna wrote, "Romanian television broadcast late Friday grisly pictures of disfigured corpses it said were found dumped in mass graves in the western city of Timisoara, where security forces this week massacred thousands of anti-government protesters. Barbed wire bound some of the bodies of men, women and children. The body of one small child lay on top of an adult corpse."[266] *AP* also mentioned the broadcast.[267]

On December 22, both ABC and CBS reported the news that Ceausescu was on the run and they ran one of the two most striking images of the Romanian revolution—the mass graves. ABC carried scenes of fighting in Bucharest, the bloodied son of Ceausescu in custody, and mourners at the site of mass graves. ABC added that 26 children had been killed. ABC also stated, "Romanian television, from which we obtained all these pictures, has declared itself free after all these years of censorship." That declaration was enough for the American networks.

In its broadcast on December 22, ABC also carried a second report on Romania with the "latest" information, noting that Romanian television for the first time was now telling the world what had been going on. Reporting out of Belgrade, Yugoslavia, the ABC correspondent told how Romanian "dissidents" took over the television station and were now reporting everything. There were scenes of singing crowds, the famous Romanian flag with its center cut out, and celebrations in Timisoara over Ceausescu's downfall. Jennings closed by stating that these are "amazing times."

CBS's correspondent was in Bucharest on December 22. Dan Rather began his report by warning his viewers that the scenes to follow were bloody. Similar scenes of a night of fighting, the celebrations over Ceausescu's downfall, and the mass graves appeared. The CBS correspondent noted that of those alleged to have been murdered, more than 600 bodies are said to be buried here [the site of the mass graves]. Total deaths, the report added, could exceed 4,000.

NBC had scenes of pitched battles, the flag with its center cut out, and some scenes from Bucharest, but its correspondent was reporting from London, which may explain why the mass graves did not appear. NBC also concentrated part of its broadcast on Ceausescu's cult of personality, as had ABC.

By December 22, the "thousands of dead" were no longer simply figures quoted from East European news agencies: they had become accepted fact. Moreover, no wire reporter or network reporter seemed the least bit suspicious of the source of the television footage of the mass graves. After all, Romania's "dissidents" had seized the television station. It was now "free," as Jennings said.

The image of the mass graves was powerful. It was played and replayed throughout the West leaving one of the two principal images in the minds of Western television viewers; the other would be the dead body of Ceausescu.

For the next two days, the wire services had the story to themselves, as the networks were preoccupied with the Panama invasion.

In an ironic twist, *UPI* on December 23 quoted a Romanian banker, Wilhelm Vaslag, who "said one grave in the Transylvanian town of Timisoara contained at least two dozen bodies stripped of their clothing. All had been cut open down the chest, perhaps by bayonet, 'like a very clumsy autopsy,' he said."[268] Only later would it be learned that many of the bodies shown in the Romanian television footage had been transported from a local morgue and had indeed had autopsies.

More news on casualties came on December 23. *Reuters* out of Moscow quoted East German television, which "said pro-Ceausescu security forces had slain more than 12,000 people in the western city [Timisoara] since December 16—4,632 during anti-government demonstrations and 7,413 who were 'summarily executed' after capture."[269] From Belgrade that same day, *Reuters* stated, "Students told *Reuters* in Timisoara that at least 4,600 people were killed in five days of riots there and at least 50,000 were wounded."[270] For some reason, this high number of casualties in a city of 350,000 did not strike the *Reuters* correspondent as the least bit odd.

By December 24, *AP* out of Bucharest reported, "Supporters of Ceausescu penetrated the headquarters of Romania's revolutionary leaders, shooting and stabbing at random before they were subdued by armed forces." It then added, "The National Salvation Committee is trying to lead the chaotic country from inside the television station building, and the army said the building remained secure after the attack, which reportedly killed three people."[271]

Only two days earlier, *AP* had reported attacks on the radio and television station by "security forces." However, "rebel troops repulsed the attacks. Dissidents and those trying to form a new leadership had been broadcasting from the

TV center on Friday."[272] These "security forces," or Securitate troops, were the same ones that Western media organizations had previously painted in fearsome terms—sharpshooters, the elite guard of Ceausescu, large numbers, and so on.[273] Yet, no one thought it odd that these elite troops could not take out the television or radio antenna.

THE SUMMARY EXECUTION OF THE CEAUSESCUS

By Christmas Day, Western wire reporters dutifully relayed the charges leveled against Ceausescu by those leading the revolt, and they reported on his summary execution. "Bucharest Radio blamed the Ceausescus for the deaths of more than 60,000 Romanians and said they plundered the poor country of more than $1 billion that they deposited in foreign banks," *AP* wrote. It continued, recounting more exaggerated figures on total casualties during the revolution: "Hungarian radio named unspecified 'authoritative sources' as saying that between 70,000 and 80,000 people had died. Then it cited Victor Ciobanu, health minister under Ceausescu and now in opposition to him, as denying that such a large number of people had died." These claims by Hungarian radio would turn out to be grossly inflated.

The same report made one other notable statement on Ceausescu's execution: "The National Salvation Committee had announced over the weekend that it would put the Ceausescus on trial and impose severe punishment. It was not immediately clear why the committee pledging to restore democracy in Romania chose to put the Ceausescus on trial in secret and execute them immediately."

Also on December 25, *AP* profiled Ion Iliescu, the leader of the National Salvation Front, noting that he was "said to be a close friend of Mikhail S. Gorbachev." It added, "His reported friendly ties with Gorbachev saved him from a more dramatic fall, informed sources said." The report also stated that, after Iliescu was demoted from the Central Committee in 1971, he became regional party secretary in Timisoara. At one point earlier in his career, according to this article, Iliescu headed the Central Committee's Department of Propaganda.[274]

As was the case with other aspects of the revolution, *AP* and other news organizations did not follow up on the connection between Iliescu and the party apparatus in Timisoara or on his ties to Gorbachev.[275]

On Christmas day, CBS and NBC reported on the execution of Ceausescu after the secret trial, but CBS noted that it had no confirmation. CBS and NBC mentioned that Romanian television said that Ceausescu was accused of crimes against Romania and genocide. They also both carried scenes of fighting and sniper attacks. Additionally, there were scenes of Christmas masses. CBS showed Romanian television footage of Ceausescu's luxurious home as well, and CBS stated that the death toll had reached 60,000.

The second, and perhaps most powerful, image of the Romanian revolution was aired on December 26 by all three networks: the dead body of Nicolae Ceausescu. ABC and CBS regarded this image as proof that Ceausescu was dead.

An ABC correspondent in Bucharest noted that some of the people had demanded to be shown the bodies of the Ceausescus. NBC reported that the firing squad had to be chosen by lottery because there were too many volunteers.

Ion Iliescu was also included in all three broadcasts. ABC described him as "a man much admired" who lost his job as a communist party secretary. ABC also pointed out that there was a lack of democratic traditions in Romania, so the talk of organizing a democracy should be taken with a grain of salt. To conclude, the network showed people who were happy then cut to the image of the grieving families of those who had been killed.

CBS was even more skeptical of the new Romanian leaders, noting that Iliescu was a friend of Gorbachev and that too many of the new leaders had Stalinist stripes. CBS also stated that 3,000 new graves were needed for the victims of the revolution. For its part, NBC characterized the new provisional government as "organized anarchy." Firefights, mourners, and Iliescu were also part of NBC's report. All three networks noted that President George Bush recognized the new government, and CBS and NBC stated that the United States would offer the new government one-half of one million dollars in aid.

After the striking images of mass graves and Ceausescu's dead body on December 22 and 26, respectively, along with the many images of crowds, bloodied protesters, the Romanian flag without its center, and the many mourners, the television story would begin to taper off.

ABC's man in Bucharest stated on December 27 that some Romanians who wanted to be heard were locked out by the new leadership. He added that not all the people trusted the new leaders, either. Besides this and the announcement that Romania was no longer a communist state, ABC provided more coverage of "massacres" that had taken place in Sibiu, how hospitals had been overwhelmed, and a report that the Securitate had poisoned the water supply. This report ended with scenes of mourners.

CBS began its coverage of December 27 with news of an unsuccessful attack on the television station by the Securitate. It then turned to the "savagery" that had taken place in Sibiu, bodies shown in a hospital, and the poisoned water supply. CBS also replayed scenes from the "trial" and "execution" of Ceausescu on Romanian television.

NBC took a slightly different approach, focusing on the declaration that Romania was no longer a communist state. Then it contrasted the "calm" on the surface with the search for members of the Securitate, who, reportedly, had taken refuge in a complex of underground tunnels they had previously operated out of. NBC also briefly mentioned the provisional government, talked of laws being repealed, including the requirement to address each other as "comrade," and noted that rebuilding would take years. It closed, however, with the scene of mourners at a cemetery where "800 dead have been buried."

On December 28, ABC showed scenes of the elaborate system of tunnels used by Ceausescu and his security operatives. The focus of the report was on the pursuit of members of the Securitate that might be holed up in the tunnels. It was also stated that many of the members of the Securitate were "recruited when they were teen-aged orphans." The Securitate's chemical lab, and gadgets that might have been used for torture, were also shown. The other significant news was the suicide of Ceausescu's brother. CBS led off with the suicide, then cut to the funerals in Timisoara. It noted that no one knew how many were killed, but reports of tens of thousands now seemed exaggerated. It also noted that local committees were being set up and there was a search on for good leaders. CBS also included the tunnels, and the report about Romanian orphans being sold or joining the Securitate. NBC had a brief report on how the new government was still contending with loyalists and that Ceausescu's brother had been found hanged.

By December 29, a report on CBS demonstrated one element that became much more prominent on the broadcast medium than it was in print: the idea that the Securitate were on the loose everywhere and represented a serious threat to the new regime. All three stations had previously covered the tunnels and the snipers, who were assumed to be members of the Securitate. Now CBS would report that some of the secret police were being brought to trial, but that the provisional government said a few hundred were still at large. Hungarians were also quoted, who said the Securitate was still a coherent force. They came to this conclusion by reportedly monitoring the secret police's radio channels.

ABC reported on December 29 that it was still difficult for Romanians to separate truth from lies. It added that some Romanians were chanting against the new leaders, and the new leaders were calling them "terrorists." NBC talked of communist symbols being stripped away, the army declaring victory, and the plush private residence of Ceausescu.

After a brief New Year's respite, the three networks rejoined the Romania story on January 2, 1990. All three reported that 60 high officials from the old regime had been detained. ABC added that the death penalty had been banned, and that the government said all parties could participate in elections, including the Communist Party. Its correspondent in Bucharest talked of people grieving and of the lack of trust among the people, since one in four was reportedly working for the secret police.

CBS's correspondent reported from the Carpathian Mountains, showing scenes of homes that had been bulldozed as a result of Ceausescu's policies. Scenes of the Communist Party headquarters in Cluj being burned were also shown, along with a report that 36 had died. It ended by saying that it might be difficult for Romania to cope with democracy since confusion reigned.

NBC showed tanks in Bucharest before stating that some feared the National Salvation Front, since most of its members were communists. NSF members Petre Roman and Silviu Brucan were also shown preaching democracy before the segment ended with scenes of mourners.

On January 3, ABC reported on some of the changes taking place in Romania, including the legalization of abortion. On January 5, CBS reported on Soviet Foreign Minister Eduard Shevardnadze's upcoming visit to Bucharest, noting how most Romanians did not like the Soviet Union or the Communist Party. Its report also included scenes of people at a grave. On January 8, CBS and NBC carried brief reports on the start of the trials of the secret police. CBS mentioned the repeal of the death penalty, while NBC stated that one sentence of nine years had been imposed and that the government refused to give details of how many were arrested. It also noted that some feared that the NSF was trying to save the country for itself.

On January 10, ABC reported on the minutes of a Ceausescu meeting five days before he was overthrown. Ceausescu was reported to have raged at the army for not firing at the "hooligans." CBS and NBC picked this up a day later, adding that the government says 10,000 died during the revolution. CBS also did a short sketch of Elena Ceausescu. For its part, NBC noted that the army was firing blanks at one point.

January 12 pretty much marked the end of the television story of the Romanian revolution. ABC opened its report with mourners then cut to protesters who jeered both Petre Roman and Ion Iliescu. To try to mollify the crowds, the NSF announced that the Communist Party would be abolished and that the suspension of the death penalty would be put to a referendum. CBS had a similar report, which ended with the statement that some of the people thought the "revolution was being taken away." NBC had similar elements to its report, but also mentioned that 4,000 to 7,000 people had been killed during the revolution.

Maybe the networks had simply run out of steam, or maybe their correspondents were tiring of Romanian hotels, but the Romanian story was far from over. There was something to the reports of the crowds jeering Romania's new leaders and to statements like, "the revolution is being taken away." Nevertheless, the American viewing public would be left only with a series of powerful images and information garnered from East European sources suggesting thousands had died, genocide had been committed, and that the new leaders, though hampered by a communist past themselves, were moving toward democracy.

As for the scenes of the mass graves provided by Romanian television, as early as December 26, the *Washington Post* reported that the chief surgeon at one of Timisoara's hospitals stated, "In their sweep of the hospital morgue, [Peter] Radelscu said, the security men also collected bodies of people who died in the hospital of natural causes apparently explaining why some corpses unearthed here in the last week show signs of having been autopsied."[276]

Only on January 25, 1990, did Peter Jennings of ABC, who was the least guilty of all, have the professional courage to admit that the network made a mistake in airing the Romanian footage. In a footnote to the Romanian revolution, he said: "A television station in Luxembourg reports tonight that what we were seeing at one of the most incredible moments in the Romanian revolution may not have been real. You may remember the pictures of a mass grave in the city of Timisoara. We were told at the time that they were filled with thousands of victims killed by the Romanian secret police. A Romanian pathologist from Timisoara now says the bodies actually came from the city morgues and were laid out as part of some 'sinister theater' as she put it." End of story.

THE CASUALTY NUMBERS AND CHARGES
OF "GENOCIDE"

Michel Castex, who covered the Romanian revolution for *Agence France-Presse* (*AFP*), was one of the few journalists who went back and took a closer look at the trial of Ceausescu. He found it hard to believe that Western journalists simply repeated the charge of genocide leveled at Ceausescu by his accusers without giving it any more thought.[277]

In 1948, the United Nations adopted the Genocide Convention, which included the following definition of genocide: "Genocide means any of the following acts committed with intent to destroy, in whole or in part, a national, ethnical, racial or religious group, as such: (a) Killing members of the group; (b) Causing serious bodily or mental harm to members of the group; (c) Deliberately inflicting on the group conditions of life calculated to bring about its physical destruction in whole or in part; (d) Imposing measures intended to prevent births within the group; (e) Forcibly transferring children of the group to another group."[278] After examining this definition and many others put forth by a wide range of scholars, two authors suggested a more concise definition: "genocide is a form of one-sided mass killing in which a state or other authority intends to destroy a group, as that group and membership in it are defined by the perpetrator."[279]

Whether one of these definitions is used or one of the many others, there is usually a very distinct element that must be there for a killing spree to be defined as genocide: an *intent* to systematically annihilate a targeted group. Certainly, calling indiscriminate killings a massacre makes perfect sense, but to fail to question the charges of genocide against Ceausescu represents a major oversight in US media coverage of the Timisoara uprising.

At the most hyperbolic moment of the revolution, on December 24, 1989, Hungarian radio reported, "According to authoritative sources, so far there have been 70,000–80,000 deaths in the Romanian revolution. The number of injured reaches 300,000."[280] Even if that number had been true, Ceausescu's accusers would have still had to prove some intent to wipe out a group in order for the charge of genocide to be credible.

On Christmas day, the day of Ceausescu's execution, *Agence France-Presse* reported from Bucharest, "Around 500 people have been killed and 2,500 wounded here since street battles erupted on Friday, Health Minister Victor Ciobanu told a press conference here Monday. He said that 'several thousand' had died throughout the country, but described an earlier estimate of 70,000 dead as 'very exaggerated.' "[281]

A few days later, *Agence France-Presse* stated, "Reports in Timisoara said only about 100 victims have been buried by their families, with thousands of bodies apparently still unrecovered. Various sources said the victims of the mass shootings by Ceausescu troops in downtown Timisoara were carried off by secret police troops and not seen again."[282] Of course, these "thousands" never were going to materialize because they never existed in the first place. By late January 1990, even the colorful Yugoslavian news agency, *Tanjug*, had scaled back its original estimates. "About 100 people were killed in Timisoara in the bloody December clashes between Ceausescu's followers and the people, Army commander of the Timis District General George Popescu told *Tanjug* special correspondent today. This represents an official denial of the claims about 4,000 victims in Timisoara, launched by members of the leadership of today's National Salvation Front." Popescu then added that 79 victims had been identified so far and that of the 34 persons missing, 12 have been found.[283]

In February, an official casualty count for the Romanian army was released: among army "conscripts, cadres, and civilians participating in the December 1989 revolution," there were 270 dead and 673 wounded.[284] The next month, the Romanian air force released its figures for casualties suffered during the revolution: 22 dead and 37 wounded.[285]

During March 1990, the trial of former secret police and militia officers began, revealing the official death toll for Timisoara. "The chief judge in the military tribunal, Colonel Cornel Badoiu, said Friday that 98 people were killed, 300 wounded and 23 missing after troops opened fire on demonstrators in Timisoara," *Agence France-Presse* reported.[286] "Prosecutors also said that General Macri and a colonel in the militia, Nicolae Chircoias, were responsible for the 'theft' of 40 bodies from the morgue of a Timisoara hospital in an attempt to 'wipe out the traces of genocide,' " *AFP* continued. According to later testimony, the 40 corpses were stolen from the Timis County Hospital Mortuary and taken to the Bucharest Cenusa crematorium.[287]

The other incident related to bodies from a mortuary involved the television footage shown on December 22 of the "mass graves." It was later learned that the grave shown by Romanian television was actually located in a paupers' cemetery, which contained unknown vagrants, indigents, and infants. Twenty-seven of the bodies showed traces of bullet marks, while the others had died of natural causes and came from a morgue where they had been subjected to autopsies, as is the rule in Romania.[288]

Though the official figures of deaths during the revolution were eventually scaled back, even by the NSF, over the months that followed the December clashes in Timisoara, it was clearly in the Front's interest to create confusion and allow the exaggerated figures to stand as long as possible. By making Ceausescu look as bad as possible, the Front stood to gain in the eyes of the Romanian public.

RELIABLE SOURCES?

On December 23, 1989, a *Reuters* correspondent from London wrote: "The East European news agencies, noted in the past mainly for their faithful reporting of official statements, have brought the world fast, colorful coverage of the overthrow of Romanian President Nicolae Ceausescu. With most of the world's press barred from Romania after frontiers were closed as unrest broke out last weekend, East Bloc journalists stationed in Bucharest have had the story to themselves."[289] With undisguised admiration, the same correspondent recounted how these East

Bloc journalists "raced each other to report every twist of the often violent drama unfolding in Romania." He cited another Western correspondent who said that the East German news agency, *ADN*, "is a normal news agency." And he pointed out with satisfaction how "agency names unfamiliar to most outsiders like *ADN*, *Tanjug* (Yugoslavia) and *PAP* (Poland) have been regularly quoted this week on Western television news broadcasts."

These "unfamiliar" agencies were clearly what US and other Western wire reporters based their dispatches on, both during the few days, beginning on December 18, when Western journalists were barred from entering Romania and afterward. As a whole, most Western journalists failed miserably to take into account the fundamental nature and role of communist media organs, whose primary purpose was to spread propaganda or disinformation, depending on the intended audience.

In December 1989, *ADN* was still linked to a transitional communist government in East Germany. Yugoslavia's *Tanjug* was no more reliable, given its own communist origins and links and the state of disarray in the Yugoslavian government. And the other major source of firsthand information, Hungary's *MTI* news agency and its television network, had always been suspect when it came to reporting on Romania because of the ethnic tensions and historical animosity between the two countries. Yet American, and many other Western correspondents, gladly accepted the "colorful" reports coming from these media organizations.

As the Romanian revolution unfolded, it was remarkable that so few Western reporters applied any of the basic practices of the journalistic profession: assessing the credibility of sources; placing dramatic developments in the proper context by researching background material; and subjecting statements by politicians, tourists, disgruntled expatriots, and even other media outlets to the kind of scrutiny and healthy skepticism that are the staples of Western-style journalism.

In reality, the Romanian revolution had little in common with the images beamed into American living rooms—images that shocked the world but evoked almost no critical evaluation. The words reaching the West also sketched an inflated picture of the scope of violence that accompanied an admittedly bloody revolution. Given the relatively peaceful change in the other East European countries, namely Poland, Hungary, East Germany, Bulgaria, and Czechoslovakia—change prompted by mass protests, demonstrations, and some disturbances—the Romanian revolution represented a much more sensational story to the American and other Western media. After all, what other revolution featured bloody massacres by a feared and detested secret police, the mock trial of a paranoid dictator and his despised wife, and their subsequent demise?

In the end, the Romanian revolution made for great television. It also provided some colorful copy for newspapers and magazines. But many significant elements of the story were misreported or ignored entirely by the US media. For instance, at the most fundamental level, was this a true "revolution" or was it actually the seizure of power by a group of "reform" communists whose methods varied very little from the regime it replaced? American journalists never provided an answer. By contrast, Castex believed something was amiss almost from the start. His 1990 book was essentially a *mea culpa,* in which he equated the media story of the Romanian revolution to one of the biggest lies of the century.[290] His thesis was quite straightforward: Most Western journalists, intoxicated after covering the successive downfalls of the East European communist regimes, were duped. According to Castex, the American media, fueled by faithful and continuous wire service reports from several East European capitals (and from inside Romania at certain points), were perhaps the biggest stooges of all. Incomplete images—which led to false interpretations and conclusions—blanketed millions of television screens, while newspaper headlines screamed of massacres and genocide committed by a heinous dictator, the likes of which were without modern-day rival.

This portrait of Ceausescu, of course, was partly true: he was a brutal, neo-Stalinist dictator. But was he that different from other communist tyrants over the years? And why was this ogre and mass murderer recognized with a British knighthood, rewarded with US most-favored-nation status for relaxing his emigration policies and improving human rights, and visited by French and American presidents, among other influential heads of state? The answer is simple: on the one hand, Ceausescu exploited some genuine expressions of Romanian nationalism and won favor in the West by cultivating the image of being a maverick within the Warsaw Pact, the bad boy who often refused to do Moscow's bidding; on the other hand, Romanian deception and manipulation successfully diverted the West's attention from the repression and squalor that existed in Romania.

To varying degrees, Ceausescu and other Eastern bloc leaders managed to hide many aspects of their bankrupt and repressive communist regimes from the West. The abject poverty, rampant pollution, and racism of the Eastern European regimes are just a few examples of what was suddenly discovered as the Iron Curtain was ripped to shreds.[291] By accident or historical fate, the implosion of the communist system toward the end of 1989 destroyed the veil so carefully constructed by totalitarian regimes and shattered many of the illusions harbored in the West for decades. Who would have imagined that by the end of 1989—except for the few holdouts, including China, Albania, and Cuba—there would be near universal agreement on the bankrupt nature of communism, even among the leaders of the Soviet Union?

At the same time, when communism did begin to collapse, there seemed to be a pervasive belief among journalists that the Eastern European regimes had instantly converted to democracy. In painting the dramatic changes in the East in simplistic terms, the Western media missed many aspects of the painful and prolonged transitions required, the nature of the dissident movements in these countries and the emerging societies.[292]

One author wrote, "The theme of freedom's victory over totalitarianism pervaded the initial stories of captive peoples punching holes in the Iron Curtain. The conventional wisdom seemed to hold that the cold war was, indeed, over, with the United States, or at least the West, 'coming out on top.' . . . The idea that progress toward Western-style democracy was occurring with the inevitability and relent-lessness of the forces of nature permeated news stories."[293]

In the case of Romania, "the last communist holdout," the democratic forces would naturally triumph, according to the conventional wisdom and the expecta-tions that had been created. But democratic forces did not necessarily prevail. Overall, the media were ill equipped to recognize the complex and confusing developments that took place in Romania.

If there was one fatal flaw in the approach taken by US news organizations during their coverage of the Romanian revolution, it was their inclination to immediately apply the logic of the democratic victory over communism to former communist structures of government, especially the state media organs. Was it really possible in less than a few months to dismantle the entire propaganda appa-ratus of these communist regimes in transition? And were all former connections between these "news agencies" and Moscow suddenly severed overnight? Hardly.

The media story of the Romanian revolution contains a marvelous paradox: at a time when walls between East and West were being torn down and decades of lies being exposed, many of the West's leaders and journalists, possessing more information and having more access than ever before, allowed themselves to be manipulated and deceived.

Indeed, the very technology that has been so indispensable to the advancement of the Western way of life and to change throughout the world does not always lead to a clearer and more realistic view of the world in which we live. In some cases, advanced communications technology has even contributed to a diminished understanding by fostering a laziness among journalists (who previously dug much deeper and took great pains to place pictures and images in context) and a false sense of superiority among those who produce and transmit dramatic but incomplete words and images. The end result: a distorted view of reality among those who receive them.

If the American media, and many of their compatriots, were susceptible to being misled because of their intoxication with the events taking place in Eastern Europe, as Castex suggests, the French media, by and large, did not fall into the same trap. Though Castex, who was working for *Agence France-Presse*, suc-cumbed to the same fate as American and British wire reporters in the days lead-ing up to Ceausescu's ouster and death, *AFP* soon recovered, and a surprising number of French publications began almost immediately to question what was coming over the wires and to pursue the real story long after American journalists had packed their bags and moved on.

Le Nouvel Observateur, Le Monde, Le Monde Diplomatique, Libération, and especially *Le Point*, which had very solid coverage, did not take the Romanian revolution at face value. They scrutinized, analyzed, and eventually were able to offer an explanation of what was actually going on, not what appeared to be going on based on false television broadcasts and communist wire service reports.

For their part, most American media tended to exaggerate and distort images of a revolution that was partly real and partly staged. Casualty figures in the thou-

sands were dutifully relayed, rumors about mass murders were played and replayed, and charges of genocide were repeated as if systematic murder were
commonplace—all without American journalists once asking themselves the most
fundamental question: Is any of this credible or even possible?

Which American journalist actually saw blood flowing in the streets, as some
reports described? What credible source tripped over dozens or hundreds of bodies? And didn't it even seem the least bit odd that the widely acclaimed Ceausescu
was suddenly the most hideous tyrant to ever walk on the face of the Earth, a
vampire, and a mass murderer responsible for the genocide of his own people?
Why hadn't there been any previous indications?

Of course, successful disinformation often contains a kernel of truth, and that
is what makes it believable. Ceausescu's successors, aided by communist media
organs, succeeded at discrediting the "Genius of the Carpathians" in the most
exaggerated terms by mixing tidbits of truth with sheer fantasy, thus paving the
way for their own accession to power.

Behind these new leaders was the helping hand of Soviet President Mikhail
S. Gorbachev, whom Castex dubs the "conductor of the orchestra."[294] Gorbachev
may have decided to stand by and watch the regimes of his former communist
allies in Eastern Europe collapse, but all of his mechanisms of influence did not
disappear overnight. In his original grand plan, an economic recovery of a "transformed" socialist Eastern Europe, and the open door to the West it would have
represented, was considered essential to an eventual Soviet economic recovery.

WHAT WENT WRONG ON TELEVISION

Le Monde Diplomatique called the false carnage at Timisoara "without doubt
the most important deception since the invention of the television."[295] That may
be overstating the case, but the French media, at least, went after the whole story
taking it to its natural conclusion with the rigged election of Ion Iliescu in May
1990. In this same report, *Le Monde Diplomatique* added that many of the false
images were possible because of journalists' inclination to explain the Romanian
revolution in the context of yet another of the twentieth century's evils meeting its
historic demise. Nazism was a favorite analogy, according to the report. Journalists, therefore, required strong images to represent another evil's dramatic end.
The images of Ceausescu the monster, the super-powerful Securitate holding on,
the involvement of Arab terrorists, the poisoned water supplies, and the mass
graves, all demonstrated the evil nature of communism—but all were false.

Le Monde Diplomatique pointed out that there was absolutely no skepticism
or critical sense on the part of the media. In the context of the end of the Cold War
and the condemnation of communism forever, the little lies and their images were
truly logical. "They also served to ratify the function of television in a world where
one tends to replace reality with a staged production."

Only six months before the Romanian revolution, the Western broadcast
media managed a similar feat. The broadcast coverage of Tiananmen Square,

which was so regularly cited as a comparison by both the print and broadcast media covering the Romanian revolution, contained similar distortions and misrepresentations of reality, all because journalists lacked the sophistication to understand the complex nature of Chinese society and government.

In a revealing account in *Asiaweek*, one reporter wrote that "a paroxysm of killing took place that night." And there was no doubt "that civilians as well as troops were killed." But "what has never been clear was how many died." He continued: "On June 4, the Chinese Red Cross allegedly issued an estimate of 2,600 dead. The figure was soon disavowed, but the June 5 edition of Hongkong's *South China Morning Post*, citing diplomatic sources, reckoned a death toll of 1,400. Next day, it rose to 4,000. Two days later 7,000."[296] Later estimates put the toll at somewhere between 200 to 300, 36 of whom were students.

It was eerily similar to the rumors that circulated in Romania. *Asiaweek* pointed out that "news reports feasted on rumours: troops were drugged before being sent into Tiananmen; bodies were burned in the square; Deng was dead; someone shot Premier Li Peng." Later, a Chinese student at Harvard admitted creating that rumor to find out what happened to Li Peng, *Asiaweek* added. It also noted that *Newsweek* ignored the rumors. Its Asia Regional editor, Melinda Liu, stated, "Since it was a struggle between democratic ideals and a totalitarian system, many people were simplifying the situation and didn't understand the reality of China."

The problem with the Tiananmen Square and Romanian revolution television stories is very significant in an age of instantaneous communications: first, images are not properly evaluated before being transmitted; and second, after the distortion is created, there is never a sensational correction of the "reality."

The centrally linked network of wire services was another aspect of the problem. The great disadvantage of such a centrally linked network occurs when several bureaus of a wire service are all reporting the wrong information. When that happens, the bad information is transmitted and multiplied with lightning speed. For such a chain of events to take place, certain conditions must exist. First and foremost, the sources of information must be tightly controlled and coordinated. Secondly, access to information that would refute or corroborate the original sources also must be limited. And finally, normally savvy reporters must be fooled because of an air of credibility that exists, a lack of background information on their part, or a lack of linguistic and cultural knowledge.

In Timisoara, on December 17, 1989, this combination of conditions existed. What it proved was that manipulation was still possible in an age of instantaneous communications, and that when such a manipulation is executed in the high-tech age it is more efficient and has more immediate impact than ever before.

In the case of television coverage of the Romanian revolution, the image of the false mass graves wasn't ever corrected in most Americans' minds. Why? Because journalists do not like to be wrong or admit their errors and, secondly, because another image a few days later, Ceausescu's dead body, diverted attention from the mass graves.

At best, images can concisely and accurately reflect reality in brief. At worst, they can completely distort reality by overemphasizing a picture that is not representative of what actually happened. Coverage of the Romanian revolution included some dramatic and shocking images, but few of them had anything to do with what was actually taking place in Romania.

POSTSCRIPT TO A REVOLUTION

Was the Romanian revolution a true expression of the people's will or was it a classic power struggle between communist factions? In the end, the faces changed, but had the system been truly reformed?

After the "revolution," Iliescu was initially able to argue that there was no organized democratic alternative to the National Salvation Front. But even as alternative parties began to organize, the communist-dominated National Salvation Front still held all the reins of power, including control of the media. Challengers to the NSF were essentially denied any real means of reaching the public.

At the start, of course, democratic participants in the revolution were coopted by the National Salvation Front, which changed its name in January 1990 to the Provisional National Unity Council, but they soon resigned in disgust or were forced out. The signs of what the French called the "confiscation of the revolution" seemed to be everywhere.[297] Securitate officers either kept their jobs in the new government under the Ministry of National Defense, which had incorporated the Interior Ministry, or were reassigned with new titles.[298] For instance, one "leading intelligence officer" popped up as a diplomat in Austria near the end of January 1990.[299]

What opposition to the NSF that existed was openly roughed up and attacked and more subtly prevented from effectively campaigning through NSF control of the media.[300] In response to the NSF's heavy-handed treatment of the alternative parties, the United States said it was "deeply troubled."[301] In February, the European Commission's vice president added another weak voice of protest from Europe, describing evidence that Iliescu had blocked the creation of a free television and radio station as "very disquieting."[302]

When Iliescu called for the formation of an antifascist movement to fend off extremist violence, the West yawned. According to one report, Iliescu said: "All responsible and conscious democratic forces must form a common front to bar the road to new fascist movements."[303] Was this not a familiar refrain?

In March, a document entitled the "Timisoara Proclamation" was issued, stating that "the revolution was categorically anticommunist" and requesting "the immediate abolition of this totalitarian and bankrupt system," according to Bucharest radio.[304] The appeal was ignored, as was another section of the proclamation that proposed amending the electoral law to prohibit former communists and former Securitate officers from serving in the first three consecutive legislatures.[305]

By controlling all the mechanisms of power and the media, the National Salvation Front's candidate, Ion Iliescu, was elected president by an overwhelming margin in May 1990. Less than a month later, when dissatisfied crowds chanted "Iliescu equals Ceausescu" and the "NSF equals the KGB," the newly installed Romanian government showed its true colors, violently suppressing the demonstrators using the police and vigilante miners who "spontaneously" appeared to defend the government. During the fracas, the leader of the student movement, Marian Muteanu, was seriously injured and taken into custody.[306] He was later released, but he got the message. Even the US media took note of these heavy-handed measures.[307]

As for the Western media's role in the Romanian revolution itself, inflated and inaccurate news reports clearly aided the National Salvation Front in its accession to power. Unwittingly, the western media amplified and reinforced the false stories emanating from the East European media organs.

By discrediting Ceausescu in the most exaggerated terms, Iliescu and company appeared as the great reformers and opponents of the old communist regime. They were neither. In the end, modern technology made the job of the NSF's propagandists easier than it might have been. The Western wire services spread the story with lightning speed, and the broadcast journalists sensed the drama and chased after the shocking images made available by Romania's newly "liberated" television station. Many of these images were dramatic, but they were also supplied by Romania's new leaders for a specific purpose: to make the world believe that Ceausescu was the personification of evil. The NSF succeeded brilliantly.

France's *Le Nouvel Observateur* pointed out that communications technology, including satellites and lightweight cameras, has advanced at such a dizzying pace that few reporters have even begun to understand how it has changed their profession. The magazine added that strong images are instantly available and have an enormously powerful impact. But too often reporters are tempted to use them before they fully make sense of them.[308] A French reporter cited in *Le Nouvel Observateur* went on to suggest that it is the media's responsibility to redefine their work and their responsibilities, given these technological changes. The book by Castex and the many analytical pieces that appeared in the French media in the wake of Timisoara indicated that such introspection already had begun in France.

In the US media, however, there never was even a basic admission that a problem existed, that they were duped, that they were wrong. While ABC admitted, and some of the major newspapers ran stories that included the evidence, that a manipulation surrounding the mass graves took place, few, if any, delved into the other aspects of the disinformation issued by the NSF. No US network ever admitted that the charge of genocide was ludicrous on the face of it. And no network doggedly pursued the story behind Iliescu's rise to power.

As far as the network news divisions were concerned, the story ended when the dramatic images faded away. Scenes of protesters had been played and replayed during the revolution, so when new crowds appeared to protest the accession to power by the NSF, it was old hat. The camera crews stayed home. Moreover, there was no hint of the kind of bloody violence that accompanied the Timisoara riots.

By June 1990, long after the seizure of power by Iliescu, scenes of miners beating up student protesters once again captured the attention of America's broadcast journalists. But it was too late, and television journalists were as ill prepared to make sense of Iliescu's repressive tactics then as they were months before.

The Romanian revolution was not a simple story. Quite the contrary, it was complicated and demanded context. Neither the quick-scribbling (or typing) wire reporters nor the image-driven television reporters were prepared to pause for a minute and analyze what was really going on.

In April 1990, while campaigning, Iliescu was questioned about his view of democracy. He responded, "There may be democracy in a totalitarian regime, too, but with a wise despot! Our despot was completely lacking in wisdom!"[309]

In May 1990, after an interview with Iliescu, a French reporter with *Le Monde* wrote: "Ion Iliescu is visibly still a prisoner of the communist way of thinking. . . . [He] is also a prisoner of the old regime's structures which he has not managed to replace. Most of the opposition intellectuals value his 'willingness to listen' and do not deny his sincerity, but see in him a man who has not managed to make a fundamental break with his education and his career. 'He is clever,' George Seban, one of the Timisoara leaders said, 'but he still thinks like a Communist.' "[310] A month later, when the miners appeared with their clubs, the US media and US government discovered he still acted like a communist, too.

One year after Timisoara, the *New York Times* quoted Traian Orban, who was part of an organization representing the victims of Timisoara. He put it succinctly during a demonstration against the Iliescu regime: "Timisoara knows the truth. That is why we are on the streets. A coup d'état was affixed to the body of the revolution."[311]

Chapter 12

A Few Notes on Network Coverage of the Gulf War

Unlike the case of the Romanian revolution, where technology and lack of expertise conspired against the networks, the Gulf War represented a case where the networks took advantage of experts, at least on the Washington–New York axis, and allotted enough time to try to make sense of the "news." In the narrow slice of network war coverage that was presented each night on the evening newscasts, Pentagon correspondents and outside experts were at center stage. They were able to take what information was available and provide the public with informed analysis.

That, of course, is not the same as saying that the information available provided a clear and accurate picture of what was taking place in the Gulf. Given the lack of direct access to the battlefield, the very nature of a war conducted primarily with airpower, and the lack of knowledge among many of the journalists in theater, the information beamed directly from the theater often fell short and was heavily influenced by the military.[312]

Back in the United States, however, seasoned Pentagon correspondents were able to work their sources unfettered, and outside experts added a valuable perspective to the normally nearsighted anchor desks. Each night, the evening newscasts were focused almost entirely on the war. This gave the networks the unusual opportunity to devote almost all of their 22-minute format to military matters. Many angles of war coverage were reflected, including the operational side, the foreign policy dimensions, issues related to military personnel, the weapons being employed, and even the policy and strategy aspects of the war. But, by far, national security news was dominated by coverage of the military operations and foreign policy at the center of the Gulf War (see Figure 12.1).

As for the use of experts, Pentagon correspondents and foreign correspondents accounted for 61.9 percent of all national security coverage during the Gulf War, and the rate of problematic coverage from these beats was the lowest among all the

Figure 12.1

Gulf War Coverage by Topic and Number of Reports for Jan.–Feb. 1991

coverage sampled, with rates of 8 percent and 8.7 percent, respectively (see Table 12.1). Anchor reporting was distinguished by a similarly low problematic rate of 8.1 percent, compared to an overall anchor problematic rate of 36 percent, and there was a much lower share of anchor-only reports, at 13.4 percent of total Gulf War coverage compared with a 29 percent slice of the coverage pie during the other periods.

At least part of the low problematic rate can be explained by the presence of outside experts during the anchor-only reports on the Gulf War, especially in the case of ABC, which relied heavily on Anthony Cordesman, an expert on the Middle East and military capabilities. ABC featured Cordesman in 14 out of its 15 anchor-only reports beginning on January 13, just three days before the start of the war, along with the occasional appearances of retired Marine Lt. Gen. Bernard Trainor. On another occasion, anchor Peter Jennings turned to military expert Trevor Dupuy and two others for their perspectives.

The bottom line for ABC: balanced and informative coverage from the anchor desk on the evening news virtually all the time during the Gulf War. The one report determined to be problematic involved Cordesman revealing actual US military dispositions on the map, one of the few times sensitive information was passed out to the world.

CBS also relied on experts at the anchor desk. Leading up to the war, it was Fouad Ajami, a Middle East expert. During the war, retired Marine Gen. George Crist and retired Air Force Gen. Michael Dugan were on hand. However, instead of turning to one set of experts, in half of the anchor-only reports, Dan Rather chose to interview administration officials or military commanders, like Secretary

Table 12.1

Gulf War Coverage by Beat, Number, and Percentage for Jan.–Feb. 1991

Beat	Total Reports	Problem Reports	Total Coverage	Problematic Coverage
Pentagon	124	10	33.8%	8.0%
Foreign	103	9	28.1%	8.7%
Wash/Gen	50	16	13.6%	32.0%
Anchor	49	4	13.4%	8.1%
White House	28	4	7.6%	14.2%
State	12	0	3.3%	0.0%
Total	366	43	99.8%	11.7%

Source: Author's Database. See appendix 1.

of Defense Dick Cheney and Gen. Norman Schwarzkopf, and to seek other perspectives, like the Iranian ambassador to the United Nations and Sen. Sam Nunn (D-GA), an approach that also proved to be more informative than the traditionally short anchor reports aired in noncrisis periods. The one problematic report out of 14 anchor-only reports by CBS occurred as the war started on January 16 and Dan Rather stumbled along on pure speculation before the network recovered and began feeding Rather up-to-date information on the beginning of the air campaign.

For its part, NBC hired retired Army Col. Harry Summers and military expert James Dunnigan, who appeared a little less than one-third of the time during the evening newscast. NBC's two problematic anchor reports came before the war began. The first occurred when anchor Faith Daniels reported on "a chemical engineer" who "told a London scientific conference that smoke from oil fires could disrupt Asia's monsoon rains, and that could cause crop failures, and that, he said, could mean starvation for one billion people." Daniels provided no context or expert opinion on the likelihood of this "chemical engineer" being right. The second problematic report occurred when Tom Brokaw reported on a non–Gulf War story, the cancellation of the A-12 aircraft, without providing adequate background.

THE NETWORKS' OWN EXPERTS

War and crisis are the obvious times when the networks turn heavily toward their national security experts on the specialized beats. The Gulf War showcased the knowledge and analytical ability of the seasoned Pentagon correspondents,

Bob Zelnick of ABC, Fred Francis of NBC, and David Martin of CBS, not to mention the producers who worked the halls of the Pentagon and helped research and report the many complex areas of the war.

The Pentagon correspondents not only provided solid summaries of what the networks' knew of the day's main action, but also broke a number of the major stories during the war. Fred Francis of NBC has pointed out that CBS's David Martin reported the first troop movements and the start of the conflict. Francis also credits the networks with the first reports on the November 1990 decision to double the US forces in the Gulf, the first news of the Kuwaiti resistance, and the intelligence that thousands of Iraqis were expected to surrender in the first few days of the ground war. Moreover, it was a network Pentagon correspondent who forecast that it would be a very short war with very few casualties.[313]

Francis also detailed the advantage that a network of affiliates provided him. He cited the case of NBC affiliates in Savannah, Georgia, and Jacksonville, Florida, which provided videotape of the 24th Division loading its tanks and armored personnel carriers for its trip to the Gulf. What struck Francis was the inclusion of bridging equipment. Since he knew there were no rivers in Saudi Arabia and Kuwait, it was clear to him even before the war started that there was a plan to go into Iraq if necessary.[314]

The networks' foreign correspondents also shined, especially during the period before Desert Storm began, when they covered the frantic diplomatic activity from capitals in Europe, the Soviet Union, and the Middle East. The advantage (and potential pitfall) the networks had in their foreign correspondents, several of whom covered the war from Saudi Arabia and Israel, was the ability to blend perspectives from around the globe instantaneously.

WHAT DID THE NETWORKS ACTUALLY COVER?

In labeling Gulf War coverage as relatively free of problems, it is also important to mention briefly the limitations on the networks' ability to cover the war.

Contrary to the popular view that the Gulf War was the first "live war," it actually was the first war "briefed" in real time. Apart from the few dramatic images of bombs going down elevator shafts and through windows, supplied by the US military, most of the live coverage was from Riyadh and Dhahran in Saudi Arabia. Only infrequently, particularly in the last 100 hours of the war, did the networks come anywhere close to the actual battle front.

While network correspondents can claim a number of dramatic moments, from the first days' warnings of Scud missiles inbound for Saudi Arabia and the short battle of Khafji at the end of January to the shocking footage of the damage a Scud missile did to the American barracks near Dhahran toward the end of the war, much of the reporting in front of, or on top of, hotels was based on the daily briefings and backgrounders conducted by military public affairs officers and on interviews with top officers in the operational chain of command.

Because the US military, along with its coalition partners, was the only real source of information aside from CNN's Peter Arnett, who was reporting under another set of restrictions from Baghdad, some have painted a picture of a grand conspiracy to control the media, a conspiracy carefully thought out ahead of time and flawlessly executed.[315] Although the military did succeed at controlling in-theater coverage to a large degree, the conspiracy theory tends to give the military far more credit than it deserves. Much of the military's "control" amounted to ineptitude and the lack of resources required to move print and broadcast pool reports in a timely manner.[316]

In reality, the nature of the air war precluded actual battlefield coverage for most of the war. For that reason, evaluation of the information provided by the military was more important than ever, which put a premium on inside and outside expertise. Apart from the inevitable flaws in early after-action reports, the wartime assessments of damage to the enemy and the effectiveness of US weapons systems, the information provided by the military and filtered through the networks' inside and outside experts, many of whom worked their sources in Washington, gave the public a good understanding of what its government was doing, regardless of whether every detail was available.

Since the Gulf War, there certainly has been a legitimate debate about what level of detail the American public should be exposed to during the course of a war. In the Gulf, the "video-game" images were clearly not an accurate reflection of many of the gruesome realities of war. The "clinical" and "blood-free" images, aside from a few exceptions, like the destruction of the Iraqi command center that had been turned into a bomb shelter for civilians, did play a role in the Gulf War, and they overwhelming played to the advantage of the coalition.[317]

Of course, there was an obvious effort by the military and the administration to put the best face possible on the war. On the other hand, reporters did try to break through the veneer. Unfortunately, many covering the war from the Gulf were ill prepared in terms of knowledge to punch through it.

Why the military had the advantage in this duel also can be partly explained by two aspects of the Gulf War that may not be present in a future war: control of access to the front lines and the fact that the war went well from start to finish.

TECHNOLOGY AND THE BATTLEFIELD

The ability to provide multiple images in real time is certainly one of the marvels of network news operations, but one that raises concerns among the government and the military in wartime and during crises, when the protection of operational information is at a premium.

While most of the knowledgeable network correspondents are usually careful not to report operational information, it is quite possible that some of it will slip through. As has already been pointed out, each of the networks did discuss in varying degrees of detail the coalition's plan for a left hook attack into Iraq. Among the avalanche of other information being put out over the networks, this detail was likely overlooked by Saddam Hussein or not believed—but it was there.

During the Desert Shield buildup, it was clear that at least one network president had a complete lack of understanding of military information. In an opinion piece in the *Wall Street Journal* on August 30, 1990, only a few weeks after the deployment of US troops to the region, NBC News President Michael Gartner charged that the "war" was being "censored." He could not understand why the military would establish ground rules that prohibited reporting the exact number of troops, the number and types of equipment they have, their locations, and information regarding future operations. In Gartner's view, this was all fair game. Fortunately, he seemed to be in the minority among journalists, and he is no longer president of NBC News.

Despite all the care taken by seasoned network correspondents, and the trust built up during peacetime reporting, the military is always going to try to control the flow of battlefield information. The problem for the military, of course, is that the circumstances of the Gulf War were not typical. Bosnia, Haiti, Somalia, and even Panama, where reporters were already on the ground even as the national media pool deployment was botched,[318] are more the norm. In those cases, reporters were able to roam rather freely, calculating their own personal security needs and the extent to which they would seek US military assistance.

As for the networks, they will likely try to cover a war "live" in the future. Technology and geographic circumstance may possibly converge to allow unfettered access to the battlefield. Even in the Gulf War, the networks had a fully equipped mobile van that could have relayed television signals back to the United States from anywhere on the battlefield. Only geography and logistics controlled by the military prevented that from happening.

The real question, here, is whether the networks understand that technology has transformed their role from observer to active participant in war or during crises. What gets reported and beamed around the world in wartime will continue to be the concern not just of the US military, but also of any potential future enemy. As Maj. Gen. Perry Smith, USAF (Ret.), has pointed out, in his capacity as CNN's on-air expert, he was able to float policy ideas that might have influenced US leadership. He also explained how he tried to send signals to the Iraqi leadership.[319] While most reporters would not necessarily subscribe to an activist approach like Smith's during a war, they should realize that, just by doing their jobs, they are part of the conduct of the war, like it or not.

THE GULF WAR MODEL

Though issues related to media access to the battlefield will remain dynamic, depending on each geographic circumstance, one of the lessons of the Gulf War should be taken into account in the future: the networks' reliance on a wide range of experts to help interpret and explain wartime developments to the American public. While all elements of the media would have liked to have had more information (and more firsthand access) during the Gulf War, the networks' evening newscasts made the most out of what information was available. The foreign correspondents, who were familiar with the region, were able to provide insight into the diplomatic maneuvering before and after the war from capitals around the region. Back in Washington, the networks' Pentagon correspondents and producers sifted through information coming from briefings in Saudi Arabia and in Washington and took advantage of sources they had cultivated over many years. Add to these resources the outside experts hired for the duration of the war, and it becomes pretty clear that the networks were well equipped to report on the information that was trickling out of the war zone.

In reviewing the 366 network reports from the evening newscasts alone, it became obvious that network coverage was informative and full of context and background information. Just from these broadcasts alone, which did not include the many extended hours of coverage the networks devoted to the war, the American public had more information available at a faster pace than ever before.

Chapter 13

Policy-makers Still Read All About It

At the beginning of this book, it was pointed out that there is a relationship between policy-makers and the public, with the media often in the middle. As was already suggested, the public must depend on the media, especially television, for much of the information it receives related to national security. For their part, policy-makers are concerned about gaining public and congressional support for their policies and must attempt to convey complex policies to these groups in part through the media.

The nature of the interaction among policy-makers, the media, and the public has been treated elsewhere.[320] But those who have studied it recognize the key role of the media, policy-makers, and the experts in helping move the public from raw opinion to informed judgment.[321] A pattern of distorted coverage, then, can mislead the public and make it difficult, if not impossible, for some policy views to be adequately conveyed and well understood.

There also is a growing body of work on the influence the media may or may not have on policy-makers' perceptions and actions, especially during wars and crises.[322] But what about the policy-makers themselves? Where do they turn for their national security news and how might they be influenced by the network newscasts? The answer: they do not turn to television.

The focus of this chapter is the news habits of policy-makers. Above all, national security policy-makers rely on the written word for news, even when it comes to digesting what has been aired on television newscasts and other public affairs programs. Since they do not turn to television for their news, it appears that policy-makers would not be exposed to the pattern of distorted defense coverage to the same degree that the public would be.

For years, policy-makers in the Pentagon, the State Department, the CIA, and the White House have been fed a steady diet of national-security news articles and radio and TV transcripts via the Pentagon's *Current News* publications—all in print. While TV news, especially CNN, is regularly cited by policy-makers during crises or fast-breaking developments, on a day-to-day basis, TV news plays a relatively small part in the overall flow of information within the national security establishment. Robert Sims, who served as assistant secretary of defense for Public Affairs under Secretary of Defense Caspar Weinberger from 1985–1987, had no doubt that print was the dominant medium during his tenure at the Pentagon.[323]

Clues as to why television, which has become the dominant news medium for many Americans, still takes a back seat to print in the top national security policy circles can be found in the Pentagon's own information-gathering techniques and the institutional structures that have evolved to feed a rather voracious appetite for news, not to mention the lack of time policy-makers have to watch television news.

PAPER, PAPER, EVERYWHERE

The Current News Analysis and Research Service is still tucked away in the C-Ring between the eighth and ninth corridors of the Pentagon's fourth floor. Even though entry is blocked off on one side, insiders of all stripes know exactly where this office is. When former Secretary of Defense Les Aspin was introduced to Herbert J. Coleman, then chief of the Current News Analysis and Research Service, he said, "Well, I've finally met the most important man in the Pentagon."[324] Coleman's predecessor, Harry Zubkoff, who held the same position for 36 years, was an institution. Known as the Pentagon's "information czar," he brought good news and bad news alike to the key policy-makers.

The reason for the notoriety of Coleman, Zubkoff, and to a lesser extent their successors has to do with the well-known product they oversaw—the Pentagon's "Early Bird," a daily compilation of newspaper and wire stories. On a daily basis, the *Current News* staff reprints full-text articles from national and regional newspapers, wire services, and myriad general interest and specialized periodicals. These articles currently appear in two daily publications, the Early Bird, which runs about 16 to 20 pages a day (8½ x 11"), and the "Supplement," which can run 60 to 70 pages, including short and longer articles, along with transcripts of news conferences and speeches from the various wire services (*Reuters* in particular).[325] The Supplement was instituted in the mid-1980s, having replaced another series of publications called "Special Editions."[326] Special Editions included a collection of clips on a single topic like arms control, chemical weapons, terrorism, the Strategic Defense Initiative, and technology security, among others, or a single longer journal or magazine article on a strategic or foreign policy topic.[327]

Radio and television news reports are distributed in a daily 6 to 8 page "Radio-TV Defense Dialog," which contains verbatim transcripts of any segments of the previous evening's network newscasts that dealt with national security topics. The Dialog also contains a list of other defense-related transcripts available, including Sunday talk shows, evening news magazines, and special programs on defense topics.[328]

Another publication, which disappeared in the early 1990s, was a weekly "Friday Review of Defense Literature." It contained reviews of books, studies, or symposium proceedings dealing with military/strategic or foreign policy issues.[329]

Over the years, specific *Current News* publications have come and gone depending on the interest of policy-makers. One example was a publication devoted to clips about energy issues during the 1970s. In 1988, however, the *Current News* operation was transferred from the Office of the Secretary of the Air Force, which had been running it for the Department of Defense since the early 1960s, to the Office of the Assistant Secretary of Defense for Public Affairs.[330] Since then, there have been a number of cutbacks in staff and services.

The Early Bird has always enjoyed the greatest attention and had the largest circulation among the *Current News* publications. In the 1990s, circulation was around 6,000 copies, compared to 1,500 for the Radio-TV Defense Dialog and 800 for the Supplement, numbers that are small by even local newspaper standards.[331] Yet what the Early Bird circulation lacks in numbers, it more than makes up for in influence. The Early Bird reaches the most powerful people in government, from the president to the National Security Council, the secretary of defense, the secretary of state, the director of central intelligence, to all of their supporting policy-makers and aides. It travels to every military commander in chief (CINC) around the world via fax each morning. And it is now available from the Internet, which further extends its reach in the government and military.

Since Robert S. McNamara held the office of secretary of defense, every secretary has found the Early Bird waiting for him in the limousine that comes to collect the secretary in the early hours of the morning.

As Coleman pointed out, the Early Bird also has a way of "cloning" itself. "For example, one Navy office runs off 1,000 copies on its own," Coleman said. "And one Air Force command has set up its own fax exchange service for 60 of its offices."[332] While it is difficult to determine the exact number of Early Bird readers, the kind of anecdotal information cited by Coleman was borne out in a 1991 survey that determined that there were actually over 15,000 readers of the Early Bird, which had a circulation of over 8,000 when the survey was conducted.[333]

Under Zubkoff and Coleman, the Current News Analysis and Research Service typically screened around 60 daily newspapers and about 500 periodicals. Circulation of the Early Bird grew steadily until the early 1990s, when budget cuts forced a paring down of the mailing and printing numbers.

TRACKING THE TUBE

Within this newsclipping empire, television news did not even become a factor until the early 1960s. The Pentagon's Radio-TV Defense Dialog was started in 1963 by the Office of the Assistant Secretary of Defense for Public Affairs. At that time, it was noted that broadcast news programs were reaching "as large an audience as were newspapers."[334] As it tracked media treatment of defense affairs, the Office of Public Affairs felt it had to begin taking broadcasts into account, particularly since the impact of a single broadcast could dwarf the influence of any single newspaper.[335] The responsibility for monitoring broadcasts was turned over to the *Current News* in 1964. Unlike the print side of the news clipping service, the Dialog has been contracted out since its inception. The contract is bid out each year. During the past 30 years, the contract was held for one year by a firm called V.R. Birmingham Company, for two years by the Radio-TV Monitoring Service, and for the rest of the time by Radio-TV Reports, Inc., with a home office in New York and branch offices around the country.[336]

From an aesthetic perspective, it is interesting to note that the Early Bird contains actual headlines and copy from newspapers, rearranged and pasted down. However, newspaper articles are stripped of pictures and most graphics. For its part, the Radio-TV Defense Dialog represents only what was said on television newscasts, without images and sound.

Besides the daily verbatim transcripts of network news reports contained in the Dialog, the contract provides the *Current News* office with access to several hundred other transcripts of defense-related public affairs programming each month. By the early 1980s, according to Zubkoff, the demand for the Dialog had reached 3,500, compared to 5,500 for the Early Bird at the same time.[337]

Interest in television transcripts can be traced to McNamara's tenure and the emergence of television as a major source of news. According to Zubkoff, McNamara was especially interested in the Sunday talk shows, "Meet the Press" and "Face the Nation."[338] McNamara wanted the transcripts right away, so that he could be prepared for any questions related to defense matters raised on these programs. However, as Zubkoff explained, the networks did not release the unedited transcripts right away. Zubkoff found it curious that the networks would release the unedited transcripts to the major newspapers, but not to the government, upon which many of them depended for their guests. Eventually, Zubkoff prevailed upon the networks to leave edited transcripts for pick-up on Sunday afternoon. The secretary of defense received them on Sunday evening, a practice that continued after McNamara left office.

CONGRESS ASKS, "WHY MONITOR TELEVISION NEWS?"

When an obscure invitation to bids was announced in the *Commerce Business Daily* on May 20, 1971, Sen. William Proxmire (D-WI) wondered what the Pentagon was up to this time. Proxmire made a career of ferreting out government waste and became best-known for his "Golden Fleece Award," which was given to government agencies that wasted taxpayers' dollars. In this case, the announcement involved the annual bids for the radio and television monitoring services administered by the *Current News* office.

Proxmire dashed off a letter to Secretary of Defense Melvin Laird. "Why does the Department of Defense feel it is necessary to spend taxpayers' money to get word-for-word recordings of all radio and television broadcasts in the Washington,

D.C. area?" he wrote.[339] "While it is interesting that the Pentagon is seeking to involve the free-enterprise system in its snooping activities, it is truly alarming that the Defense establishment is getting ready to stretch out another surveillance tentacle." Proxmire posed 12 questions, to which he expected answers. They included why the Defense Department has a need for such transcripts, how that activity squared "with the expressed desires of President Nixon and yourself to reduce public relations expenditures," what costs were involved, who authorized the activity, what happened to the recordings, whether the Department of Defense (DoD) did its own recordings, and what precedents there were for this monitoring, among other more trivial questions.

Since this activity was the responsibility of the *Current News* office, Zubkoff was enlisted to help draft the response, which was eventually sent under the signature of Daniel Z. Henkin, then assistant secretary of defense for Public Affairs.[340]

The answer to the first question posed by Proxmire, the "why," reveals the very practical and mundane reason for such monitoring: "When an important official appears on a television or radio interview show and comments about Department of Defense programs and activities, queries often are received promptly both from the Congress, the press and the public, who have a need and a right to know as much about these activities as can be told, consistent with national security requirements. To respond intelligently and in timely fashion to such queries, we must know what was said."

Zubkoff explained that one radio or television broadcast could generate hundreds of letters to the Pentagon or other parts of the government. He estimated that each year some 10,000 to 12,000 queries directed to the White House, Congress, and the Pentagon required research assistance from the *Current News* office involving transcripts. The Pentagon's various legislative liaison offices had to frequently prepare responses to such queries, and *Current News* had the transcripts they needed. He noted that the transcript files "were worth their weight in gold."[341] Not surprisingly, in the 1970s, researchers had to make appointments to gain access to these files.

Henkin also made the point in his letter that monitoring radio and television "enables us to inform Defense officials of the views of those both inside and outside the Government as reported in the news media." He then added, "We feel the content of news broadcasts is fully as significant and relevant as the content of printed media. In short, this contract represents an electronic 'clipping service,' similar in nature to a newspaper clipping service such as that contracted for by many Congressional offices."

Henkin stated that the transcripts were used by "those officials directly concerned with policy formulation on the specific subject of the news broadcast." The daily summaries, he wrote, also were made available to all key officials and were regularly used by "newsmen covering Defense affairs."

Proxmire also asked what type of monitoring DoD does on its own. Henkin replied that DoD "videotapes the morning and evening network news programs to permit a review of those items of interest to DoD. Occasionally, documentary programs of unusual interest are also recorded by DoD, but these are isolated instances."

The Proxmire flap received wide coverage. "News Taped for Pentagon" blared the headline of the *Washington Star*.[342] "News monitoring: 'Snooping' or not?" asked a headline in *Long Island Newsday*.[343] Zubkoff, who had been interviewed in the *Star* piece, noted that the Fiscal Year 1972 contract required the monitoring service to track radio stations WMAL, WRC, WTOP, WOL, WAVA, and WWDC, and television channels WRC-NBC, WTTG-Metromedia, WMAL-ABC, and WTOP-CBS, along with four UHF frequencies, one of which carried the PBS broadcast. With a few changes, like the addition of CNN and Fox, the contract varies little today, and its purpose is exactly what it was in 1971.

Looking back on Proxmire's charges of "snooping," the whole episode seems like much ado about nothing. Nevertheless, it illustrates that television was in 1971, and still is today, an evolving medium. In relative terms, newspapers have changed little in the way they present the news (except for color), while television has been regularly affected by new technologies, commercial imperatives, and by changing government regulations.

DOES ANYONE IN THE PENTAGON
ACTUALLY WATCH TV?

While policy-makers tend to monitor TV news and public affairs programming via transcripts, there are a number of key people in the Pentagon who actually watch the tube. Outside of the Pentagon's intelligence and command and control centers, it is the Directorate for Defense Information, which reports to the assistant secretary of defense for public affairs, that monitors the television networks and serves as an early warning network for Pentagon policy-makers.

The DDI is actually a central clearing house for media queries. It is staffed by military representatives from all services and by civilians. The DDI traces its history back to the first secretary of defense, James Forrestal, whose initial, decentralized approach to public affairs contact with the media resulted in "bitter and extensive conflicts over roles and missions and limited resources" among the military services, which were taking their individual arguments to the media. Before resigning in 1949, Forrestal consolidated the service media sections into a single Office of Public Information within the Office of the Secretary of Defense.[344]

Media queries serve as one warning device for DoD and each of the individual services, which maintain separate media relations offices. Queries tip off public affairs officers as to what stories journalists have set their sights on, and sometimes the DDI has advance knowledge of reports that will air on the television networks.[345]

According to Miguel Monteverde, who served as director for defense information from 1988–1991, it was Assistant Secretary of Defense for Public Affairs Pete Williams who really brought the television era to DDI. Williams, who served under Secretary of Defense Dick Cheney, set up monitors and VCRs in his own office to track all four networks, ABC, CBS, NBC, and CNN. The sets would run throughout the day into the early evening when the newscasts came on, a practice that has been carried on by his successors, except for a brief period when Vernon Guidry temporarily occupied the office during the first few months of Secretary of Defense Les Aspin's short tenure.[346]

Williams also supported the renovation of DDI office space and the addition of television, VCR, and updated computer equipment. Before the renovation, DDI had four TVs and could monitor all four networks. Now, however, a TV set adorns the desk of every action officer in DDI, and every network is running on one television or another, according to David H. Burpee, who served as director for defense information from 1991 to 1993.[347] The services' individual public affairs offices also have TV sets of their own, which further enhances DDI's early warning network.

Though many TV news stories can pass quickly, Burpee noted that for the accident, or breaking news event, TV news plays a very significant role. "Even if it's 1½ minutes on TV, if a story's a big deal, it's a big deal—and that can lead to a media feeding frenzy," Burpee said. So television is closely monitored, even if it's not the coin of the realm in a Pentagon geared toward the printed word.

Another recent director for defense information, Navy Capt. Michael Doubleday, agreed that TV serves as an early warning network, but he said, "This building still goes by print." In the Clinton administration, he explained, there is particular interest in the more extensive coverage that appears in major newspapers, like the *Wall Street Journal*, the *Washington Post*, *New York Times*, and *Los Angeles Times*.[348]

Monteverde added that policy-makers are more print-oriented for a number of reasons. Print goes into greater depth. Paper can be easily put aside and returned to in contrast to the technical limitations involved in watching a TV at the given moment or having to tape a program. Many times, he notes, senior officials miss TV, but they have the Early Bird delivered directly to them. In Monteverde's experience, public affairs officers had to draw senior policy-makers' attention to television, whether it was running down the hallway and telling them to turn the set on in their offices or bringing a video clip to them.[349]

On a day-to-day basis, the Army's audiovisual agency has the mission of videotaping the evening news. DDI also tapes the evening newscasts and the morning news programs. Burpee explained that the taping is done as a back-up mechanism. Doubleday also pointed out that since the Gulf War, DDI began videotaping CNN 24 hours a day. The tapes are used for quick reference and retrieval.[350]

Should a policy-maker who is responsible for a particular area see something in the Radio-TV Defense Dialog or hear about a report that aired pertaining to his area, there might be a request for the actual videotape of the news segment, so having quick access to the previous evening's newscasts and CNN is important. Williams would often request video news clips, Burpee said. They would be used either directly by Williams for his own preparation and research, or Williams might be getting a video clip for Cheney or another policy-maker. A similar situation existed with Assistant to the Secretary of Defense for Public Affairs Kathleen deLaski, according to Doubleday.

Another critical node in the Pentagon that monitors television newscasts, according to Burpee, is the National Military Command Center (NMCC). The NMCC oversees a worldwide intelligence and information network that serves as an early warning system for military command and control. It is a highly classified and sensitive area. And TV and print wire output is just one of many things the NMCC monitors. In fact, before DDI had the capability to tape all the networks continuously, DDI would on occasion borrow tapes from the NMCC to fulfill requests by policy-makers, Monteverde explained.

As was obvious during the Gulf War, CNN has become a universal early warning system, a video news service on demand. Monteverde noted that CNN was available in the Pentagon before much of Washington, D.C., had been wired for cable. Somehow, Ted Turner, the founder of CNN, learned that the Pentagon was not able to receive it, given the lack of local cable. So, at the time of Weinberger's tenure, Turner funded the installation of a satellite dish on the Pentagon to receive CNN.[351]

Curiously, while the public affairs establishment has been monitoring CNN for some time, transcripts of CNN news segments, particularly the evening "World Today" broadcast, were not available in the Radio-TV Defense Dialog until sometime after the Gulf War. The reason, according to Coleman, was the lack of cable in sections of the nation's capital until very recently, which affected the TV monitoring service.

Since the Gulf War, CNN has taken on greater importance across the board. In fact, its immediacy affects the whole governmental policy structure, because once an important story is aired, White House and Pentagon public affairs offices are besieged with calls from reporters. They must respond instantly, and this circumstance means that there is much less deliberation than there used to be.

In the introduction to a monograph titled *Presidents, Television, and Foreign Crises*, Michael Beschloss provided this perspective: "Asked to participate in a conference on television and the Cuban Missile Crisis, John F. Kennedy's Secretary of Defense, Robert McNamara, first said, 'I'm afraid I can't help you. I don't think I turned on a television set during the whole two weeks of that crisis.' Secretary of Defense Dick Cheney would not have been likely to make a similar comment about the Persian Gulf War."[352]

PRINT BETTER POSITIONED TO INFLUENCE POLICY

On a day-to-day basis, print articles still figure more prominently in the Pentagon's policy process than television news. In fact, for many years now, articles that appear in the Early Bird have made their way into discussions during the secretary of defense's morning staff meeting.

In his book, *The Power Game: How Washington Works*, journalist Hedrick Smith called the Early Bird "one of Washington's best-read and most-influential daily newspapers." Describing the Early Bird's immediate impact, Smith wrote, "In the Reagan era, people at the pinnacle of the Pentagon learned it was perilous to show up at [Secretary of Defense Caspar W.] Weinberger's morning staff meeting without having scoured the Early Bird and prepared their rebuttals."[353]

Robert Sims, a former Pentagon spokesman who attended these meetings, recalled that Weinberger used the Early Bird as a management tool in the morning staff meeting. It gave him the opportunity to raise issues he wanted answers to, Sims said.[354] Weinberger himself explained that the Early Bird was "one of the first and best ways" of finding out what issues were before the public.[355]

Similarly, while explaining the role of the Early Bird to a military-media conference at the Naval War College in 1978, Daniel Z. Henkin, then deputy assistant secretary of defense for public affairs during the Carter administration, stated that the "0830 meetings have as one major purpose the opportunity for the Secretary [Harold Brown] and his immediate staff to become knowledgeable about what the press, in all its aspects, is reporting about national defense issues. And I remind you, to underscore its importance to you future top commanders, that this is one of the first items on the Secretary's busy daily agenda. It's not something he leaves for when he might be able to get around to it."[356]

The Early Bird, according to Henkin, augments other information provided to senior government officials in and out of the Pentagon. "And what they read in Zubkoff's pages will influence policy decisions." Henkin added, "Secretary Brown realizes fully, and so must you, that effective national defense policies and programs in the United States must have public understanding and support, or else they will fail. That is one reason why Zubkoff's work is so crucially important, for his compilations are a daily barometer of public attitudes and opinion as reflected in the press."

Weinberger, too, emphasized the role of public opinion. "We did react to public opinion as expressed in the media, both print and television," Weinberger said. "I felt that supportive public opinion was extremely necessary and that anything that interfered with that needed to be breached very quickly."[357]

On another level, the Early Bird is somewhat of a circular vehicle for exchanges between the media and the Pentagon's public affairs establishment. Each morning, the military services' public affairs shops dissect the Early Bird and develop responses to likely questions by reporters, who also read the Early Bird.

The services will feed responses to the Directorate for Defense Information, which is charged with preparing the Pentagon spokesperson to face the Pentagon press corps as a whole every Tuesday and Thursday and individually on a day-to-day basis. When the spokesperson answers questions, those answers may figure in a future article that appears in the Early Bird. And so, the cycle continues.

The main purpose of the *Current News* operation, however, continues to be to expose policy-makers to numerous sources of news and information. The approach taken by the *Current News* staff does of course produce consequences, some

intended and some unintended. For instance, there is the sometimes disproportion-
ate influence a regional newspaper article or trade article might exert within the
Pentagon's policy process. Under normal circumstances, few policy-makers would
see a piece in the *Omaha World-Herald*, or the *St. Louis Post-Dispatch*, or the
Kansas City Star. But if an article from these or other regional papers makes the
front page of the Early Bird, it might be the topic of the day at the secretary of
defense's morning staff meeting.

From his vantage point, this did not overly concern then Secretary of Defense
Weinberger. He believed that views from around the country were very important,
mainly because they provided him with a fuller understanding of public opinion.

In terms of the policy process itself, author Hedrick Smith argued that the
"Early Bird plays into the hands of the rank-and-file against the top brass. It is a
central element in the 'dissident triangle'—the triangular power network formed
among the Pentagon's internal critics, their allies in Congress, and the press,
which harvests news leaks from both."[358]

Smith added, "The Early Bird acts as a proxy for the Washington press in the
Pentagon's inner circle, magnifying press influence by prodding policy-makers to
react to what is in print." His theory: "The Early Bird is an institutional channel
for rebels and whistle blowers within the military establishment, giving these
dissenters a voice—albeit an anonymous one—in the supreme councils of the
Pentagon." The internal battles waged by dissidents inside the Pentagon then wind
their way over to the "open battleground of Congress."[359]

Smith is right when he describes the various power plays in Washington;
however, Early Bird or not, these "dissidents" would still use the media for their
own ends, just as Congress does and the Executive Branch attempts to do. What
the Early Bird does that is significant is to efficiently collect defense-related articles and to place them next to one another, providing the policy-maker a unique
perspective on the range of material out there, or, in some cases, a sense of the
pack journalism that often takes over during big stories.

As for television news, the Radio-TV Defense Dialog is, in many respects, a
quick reference tool used to monitor what has appeared on television news programs. Actual video is viewed only when there is a keen interest in a particular
story. Weinberger said he rarely watched television, and he didn't usually see the
Dialog until later in the day or later in the week. But he did participate in television a great deal because he felt it was one of the best ways of reaching the public
with his overarching message: the need to rearm the United States in the face of
Soviet military power. Through television, especially the talk shows, he explained,
the policy-maker's views will come through, "no matter how much they try to
harass you."[360]

Weinberger contrasted live television with the filtering process that exists in
most Pentagon press conferences, which were seldom covered live and in full
during his tenure. In press conferences, print reporters selected what to concentrate on and they characterized it, from the simple form—Weinberger "admitted"
versus Weinberger "said"—to the substantive focus of their articles. If TV cameras

were present, their greatest power was in the selection—the few seconds or minute that might make it into what Weinberger called "the 6 minutes of hard news" that coexisted with the commercials and entertainment during a 30-minute newscast.[361]

Given this system for gathering news and bringing it to the attention of policy-makers, policy-makers are not as likely to be influenced by the contextual, emotional, or sensational shortcomings of the national security content of the evening newscasts as members of the public might be, since the public relies more heavily on television for its news. On the other hand, policy-makers must certainly react to the public and Congress when network news coverage prompts intense interest or calls for action from one or both, especially in the case of a crisis. Leaving those instances aside, policy-makers are not among regular viewers of network news.

Conclusion

Expertise and Standards Matter

In speaking specifically of television news, former Secretary of Defense Caspar Weinberger said, "I think there are more people who are interested in watching it today, and that is why it is so important that the information be accurate, and that the public be properly informed."[362] In terms of numbers of viewers, the three networks still deliver the largest audience of any medium, despite the shrinking size of that audience.

Just the same, the nature of network news is one of brevity and often visual drama. When done with precision and care, the networks can provide a compelling way to convey information instantaneously. On the other hand, the danger of the medium is that, by reducing complexity to manageable lengths, the networks risk distorting complex issues, neglecting key background material, or masking the overall context.

In the course of an interview with one of the network producers in New York, the question came up about what my research was revealing. It was pointed out that much of national security reporting passes the test when measured against good journalistic standards; in fact, some 70 percent of coverage does. Yet, as with anything else, what is right about the news is not often the subject of books like this. "Oh," he said, "sounds like what we do."

Context is just as important when drawing conclusions from a study of the content of network news as it is each day when the networks churn out a 22-minute picture of our world. It is important to acknowledge that many areas of national security are superbly reported upon given the inherent limitations of the network news format, from general foreign policy stories to military operations, to human interest stories. Moreover, the networks have excelled during periods of crisis and war, where immediacy is one of the most valuable currencies.

On the other hand, certain aspects of national security reporting during the 1980s and 1990s seemed to miss the mark. It appeared that the networks were emphasizing certain "news" and points of view while neglecting others. In general, it seemed as if many of the so-called "hard-line" policies surrounding Reagan's defense buildup were being reported out of context or heavily tilted toward critics of the administration. Horror stories about waste and abuse in weapons procurement seemed to foster stereotypes of a "corrupt" defense industry. Moreover, network reporting on complex areas of national security, like arms control, seemed to rely heavily on the establishment view.

DEFENSE AS THE BIG STORY

While this book focuses on very limited periods of time in the 1980s and 1990s, it should be noted that during the 1980s defense was a big story. The Reagan administration launched the largest defense buildup ever seen in peacetime. That was news, as was the level of defense spending, particularly at a time of major tax cuts. Likewise, the Reagan administration's radical approach to arms control marked a dramatic shift in thinking from previous Democratic and Republican administrations. This, too, was significant and deserved coverage.

In short, the network news divisions and the print media had a clear role to play in scrutinizing the policies and decisions that were at the heart of Reagan's modernization program, and in explaining them to the American public.

As former Assistant Secretary of Defense for Public Affairs Robert Sims noted in his 1983 book on Pentagon reporters, the networks had paid little attention to the Department of Defense during the 1970s. That all changed after the 1980 election. "As the eighties began," Sims wrote, "the question changed from why television was not covering defense enough, to why television was covering defense the way it was. Paradoxically, having gained public support for a stronger America, many defense leaders would then have been happy with a return to television's benign neglect of defense that characterized much of the seventies. They failed to realize that without continued public awareness of the need for a strong national defense, no government could will such strength. Television is the key to that broad public awareness."[363] It may have been the key, as Sims suggested, but in the area of defense, it was a mixed blessing when it came to informing the public.

The networks did beef up their Pentagon operations in the early 1980s. Correspondents, like NBC's Fred Francis, who succeeded Richard Valeriani, CBS's David Martin, who shared the beat for a time with Bill Lynch and then took it over, and ABC's John McWethy and Bob Zelnick, all made names for themselves covering this corner of Washington's "golden triangle."

The Pentagon correspondents, however, were not the real problem, though they did at times succumb to the conventional wisdom and the proclivities of the networks for sensational touches. Focusing on weapons costs without providing broader context is one example of how they occasionally missed the mark during the periods analyzed. For the most part, the big story of defense was distorted not by the specialists, but by the generalists. For example, White House correspond-

ents and correspondents from other beats, like Capitol Hill and general assignment, covered the defense budget twice as often as the Pentagon correspondent,
with a story ratio of 64 to 27. Anchors, too, accounted for 37 stories, 10 more over
these periods than the Pentagon correspondents covered.

In the area of arms control, the State Department correspondent was in the
minority with 22 stories, compared with 29 for the White House correspondent,
22 for other Washington or general beats, and 79 from the anchor. Fortunately,
foreign correspondents with more knowledge than generalists and more time than
anchors accounted for 41. The concentration of industry and procurement coverage was also in the hands of the anchors, who had 33 stories, and general beat
correspondents, who had 22. The Pentagon correspondent hardly touched the
subject, with a mere 8 stories.

ATTITUDES BEHIND THE REPORTING

A number of messages were conveyed to the public during the 1980s, and to
some extent the 1990s, that tended to reinforce particular sides of issues and reflect
particular attitudes. The conventional wisdom of network anchors, producers, and
correspondents was evident in the heavy reliance on certain sources, especially
liberal Democrats and members of the arms control establishment. The unifying
bond among these groups: opposition to the Reagan-Weinberger defense buildup
and their hard-line approach to arms control. The pattern of coverage reflected a
number of themes that dominated during this period:

▸   On the defense budget, the liberal view in Congress was that too much money was
being directed at defense at a time when tax and spending cuts were threatening social
programs. To be fair, some conservative Republicans, too, who were concerned about
the deficit, were also looking for defense cuts. The networks covered both, but echoed
most often the liberal view.
▸   New weapons purchases ran into trouble with both liberal Democrats and the conservative deficit hawks as they diverted resources away from already squeezed social
programs, in the one case, and deficit reduction in the other. Again, the first view was
a regular refrain on the networks.
▸   On arms control, the establishment view was that negotiation, rather than confronta-
tion, was the best way to manage relations with the Soviet Union. That, too, came
across loud and clear on the networks.
▸   Because the Strategic Defense Initiative threatened the prevailing views of the arms
control establishment, it was portrayed by the networks as being "destabilizing,"
technically infeasible, and too costly.
▸   Industry coverage was the most distorted, thanks to little tidbits spooned out by the
anchors involving scandals and corruption, all of which amounted to less than 1 percent of the day-to-day business industry conducted with the Defense Department.
Again, the liberal view tends to ascribe greed and corruption to business at large.
▸   Perhaps most revealing in ideological terms was coverage of Central America. Here
the liberal-conservative lines were obvious. In the case of El Salvador, the liberal view
was that the government was right-wing and bad, while the left-wing guerrillas were

noble and fighting for a good cause. Conservatives saw it just the opposite, i.e., that
the United States could influence the government to move toward democracy and help
reform the country's economic system; the guerrillas, by contrast, threatened a democratic transformation with their Marxist dogma.

▸ Nicaragua was the mirror image. Conservatives viewed the government as repressive
and Marxist, while liberals thought the Sandinistas should be left alone to find their
own way. The contras, on the other hand, were viewed as right-wing villains by liberals and as "freedom fighters" (and a way to destabilize the Marxist government) by
the conservatives. In both cases, the networks tilted toward the liberal view.

There is nothing sinister about these tendencies. As Robert Lichter and his
colleagues noted in their 1986 work on the media elite, journalists as a whole tend
to be more liberal than the public at large, and they tend to favor liberal
sources—people who think like they do, and people with whom they associate.[364]
In Washington, that tendency is even stronger. In a 1996 poll conducted by the
Freedom Forum and the Roper Center, 89 percent of the 139 Washington reporters
surveyed said they voted for Bill Clinton, and 91 percent described themselves as
liberal or moderate.[365] When Stephen Hess conducted his surveys at the end of the
1970s, 51 percent of Washington reporters agreed there was a bias in the Washington news corps. Of that 51 percent who agreed, 96 percent characterized the
bias as liberal.[366]

As a group, over the years journalists have steadily described themselves as
around 42 to 55 percent liberal and 17 to 21 percent conservative.[367] Journalists at
the national level who work at the networks and the major newspapers are also
better educated than the average citizen and better paid,[368] leading to regular
charges of elitism.

Besides the basic tendencies and attitudes of the media, in the early 1980s the
nation as a whole still had fresh memories of the Vietnam war. Reagan's election
was seen as the first step in overcoming what was dubbed the "Vietnam syn-
drome," a state of disrespect for the military at home and unwillingness to intervene abroad.[369] Reagan's military buildup, coupled with his early involvement in
El Salvador, did not sit well with a House of Representatives with a strong liberal
wing or with the media, with their own strong liberal inclinations.

Even if the media strove for objectivity, which they did most of the time, their
own attitudes and biases were bound to come through on occasion, and in some
cases even more often.

WHAT TO DO?

The liberal nature of the media, and the networks, is not about to change
overnight, and the tendency toward interpretation and explanation seems here to
stay, given the competitive pressure on the network newscasts from 24-hour television, radio and wire headline services, and the World Wide Web.

But will the longer, interpretive pieces swing toward the magazine-style
"infotainment" or toward more hard-news background and balanced analysis?

Initial indicators are not good. When it comes to national security, the view at the networks is that, after the Cold War, there is not as much interest in this subject. The absence of any defense budget stories during the Clinton administration period sampled is certainly evidence on one major level of this lack of interest.

On the other hand, except for the first Reagan period reviewed, the Clinton period had more stories on military operations than in either the Bush period or the second Reagan period. This is not surprising considering the increase in peacekeeping operations. Moreover, instability around the world promises to keep the foreign beats busy at a time when some foreign bureaus have been closed as part of downsizing and cost-cutting.

One writer who researched the cutbacks in the networks' Washington news operations cited a producer who saw the Pentagon story as "trying very hard to write its own ending."[370] But another was more upbeat: "There will always be stories from the Pentagon beat. The producers in New York recognize the reach of military stories. There are a lot of people out there who are involved with Reserve units or the National Guard."[371]

With a budget of about $250 billion, the Defense Department should certainly be the focus of regular coverage. Moreover, military operations around the world will always attract coverage, and they show no signs of letting up. In other areas, Russia still commands a vast nuclear arsenal. And a consolidated defense industry continues to build fewer, but still the most technologically advanced, weapons in the world. In the late 1990s, missile defense was still a hot topic and stated priority of the Republican-controlled Congress, a position that was at odds with the Clinton administration, which was opposed to any missile defense that would threaten the 1972 ABM Treaty. Defense increases above the Clinton administration's request had also started under the Republican-controlled 104th Congress, though, in real terms, the defense budget was still in decline. By 1998, there were calls for significant defense budget increases coming from congressional members of the Senate Armed Services Committee and the House National Security Committee, not to mention the Speaker of the House and the Senate Majority Leader. The terms of the next defense debate were clearly taking shape.

How the networks cover these developments and future ones will have an effect on public understanding and, to some extent, public support of the nation's defense and foreign policies. Any resurgence of the pattern of coverage that emerged in the 1980s, in this author's view, would be a great disservice to the American public. Whether sharp policy turns in defense or foreign policy take place remains to be seen. Nevertheless, the networks can take a number of steps to ensure that their batting average is better the next time they venture out into politically charged areas of defense policy:

▸   First of all, the networks should give much greater attention to their specialists when it comes to national security reporting. This seems so obvious that it is scary it has not been standard practice.
▸   In that same vein, the role of the White House beat should be scaled back to the one area it is suited to cover: the politics of the presidency.

- ▸ Anchor tells are probably the most challenging area for the networks, one fraught with dangers of distortion, oversimplification, lack of context, and outright bias. Serious consideration should be given to increasing the collaboration between anchor and the specialist as these tells are crafted. The choice of what to present in the anchor tell format also should be considered carefully. In cases where subjects lose all sense of coherence and context after being boiled down, the report should be abandoned entirely. Not all issues can be explained in less than a minute.
- ▸ Generalists should not be assigned to the longer, investigative pieces on national security topics. When it is necessary to use general assignment reporters, producers, and correspondents, they should be working for, and with, the Pentagon or State Department correspondents and producers, whatever the case may be.
- ▸ Developments on Capitol Hill related to defense, namely defense budget stories, which are usually covered by generalists or Capitol Hill correspondents, should be turned over entirely to the Pentagon correspondents and producers or, at very least, there should be collaboration.
- ▸ Industry stories, when they pertain to defense, should be joint efforts of the networks' business correspondents and producers and Pentagon correspondents and producers, not the so-called "investigative" correspondents.
- ▸ Long-form segments on defense or foreign policy, which are often produced by general beats, should be coordinated with specialists, whether that means State, the Pentagon, or a foreign beat.
- ▸ In areas of foreign policy and arms control, the networks should turn more frequently to the underemployed State Department correspondents and producers instead of going to the White House.
- ▸ Instead of cutting back on foreign bureaus, the networks should focus on maintaining and further developing the expertise of foreign correspondents, who tend to be most knowledgeable of the areas they regularly cover. This, however, will not eliminate the problem posed by "parachute journalism," where foreign correspondents venture into unknown terrain or where stringers provide video footage, which is sometimes narrated by a foreign correspondent sitting at a desk in a bureau far from the action.
- ▸ The networks should also avoid the temptation to fly anchors in to cover major international stories. Foreign correspondents are better informed and better positioned to cover the complex issues usually involved.
- ▸ Finally, at each network, the two senior producers in New York responsible for domestic and foreign news and their Washington counterparts should seek a civic leader tour sponsored by the Pentagon and make a similar visit to the State Department for briefings. The military, in particular, would welcome the opportunity to give key producers an orientation to the four services through base visits, equipment demonstrations, and briefings. This would provide a valuable perspective to the networks in terms of their own decision-making processes.

National security, and defense in particular, consumes a substantial amount of the nation's resources. The networks have proven that when they devote adequate resources, including time on the air, and turn to those best equipped to explain these complicated areas, they can make a valuable contribution to public understanding of these issues.

In the 1980s and early 1990s, the networks were one part of the problem. In the late 1990s and beyond, they should strive to be part of the solution.

Appendix 1

Notes on Methodology

The main tool for the findings and analytical conclusions in the introduction and chapters 3 through and 12 was a database compiled by the author from an analysis of daily transcripts of the network evening newscasts covering the periods January–April 1983, January–April 1985, January–April 1990, January–February 1991, and January–April 1994.

Chapter 10 was based on the author's analysis of all evening newscast daily transcripts where coverage of the B-2 occurred in the November 1988 to November 1989 time frame. Network coverage was then compared to print coverage over the same period.

Chapter 11, on the Romanian revolution, was based on the author's analysis of the actual video clips of the three networks' evening newscasts during the December 1989 and January 1990 time frames. East European print media sources were analyzed using Foreign Broadcast Information Service transcripts, and Western wire services were analyzed using the Lexis-Nexis® full-text database service.

Chapter 2 was based on a combination of the author's interviews with New York and Washington producers and correspondents from the three network newscasts, as well as general research of books and articles.

Chapter 13 was based on the author's interviews with past and present Pentagon officials as well as records and documents in the Pentagon's Current News Analysis and Research Service archives.

THE DATABASE METHODOLOGY

While a number of issues related to the database methodology were covered in chapter 3, what follows here covers each aspect of the overall methodology in greater detail.

The purpose of the database was to be able to evaluate the nature of routine, rather than war or crisis, coverage of national security affairs by the three network evening newscasts: ABC World News Tonight; CBS Evening News; and NBC Nightly News.

National security coverage was defined by what appeared in the daily Department of Defense's "Radio-TV Defense Dialog." This publication included full transcripts of segments of the evening newscasts that had national security content. Guidelines for what was and was not "national security" content were spelled out in guidance provided by the Defense Department to an outside contractor in the 1960s, and one contractor has had the contract for every year except for three of the early years.[372] Chapter 13 and appendix 2 provide additional historical and contextual detail about the Pentagon's use of this service. Typically, the Radio-TV Defense Dialog contained a broad range of national security material, from coverage of the military and the diverse operations of the Defense Department, to foreign affairs, coverage of intelligence matters, and military-related space developments, among other areas related to national security policy, like arms control.

For purposes of comparison, periods were selected from all four presidential administrations. In order to create a manageable set of data, the first four months of the year were selected as a baseline. In this period, budgets are prepared and major policy documents are developed, some of which are made public, including the Department of Defense Annual Report to Congress, which includes policy, strategy, and budget information required by Congress. The Gulf War period, from January–February 1991, was analyzed as a means of comparing network war coverage with more routine coverage.

As for the specific years from the four administrations, 1983, 1985, 1990, and 1994, the main goal was again to pick relatively routine periods, since there are almost no times when some military operation is not taking place. The real intent was to avoid major crises or wars so that the coverage analyzed might provide clues as to the range of national security material the networks normally cover.

"Routine" coverage, however, is not devoid of military operations. On the other hand, during the four administration periods analyzed, there were only 212 reports out of 2,581 that were coded as military operations, a mere 8 percent.

Those military operations that were in the news included everything from peacekeeping in the Sinai and Lebanon during the Reagan administrations, along with exercises in Honduras, military involvement in El Salvador, and the movement of military forces as tensions mounted with Libya, to the launching of the shuttle Discovery on a military mission. In the Bush period, there was coverage of troops occupying Panama during the post-invasion period, coverage of the drug war, and of exercises like Reforger. Operations at overseas bases also were featured in some coverage. The Clinton period included peacekeeping and peace enforcement, from the withdrawal from Somalia to the enforcement of the no-fly zone over Iraq. Issues related to the Team Spirit exercise in Korea also came up in the Clinton period. And in all four administrations, military crashes and accidents, which were routinely covered by the networks, were coded under the category of military operations.

On a more general note, during the first four months of 1983, the first Reagan administration was well into its defense buildup, and the battleground in the areas of budgets, arms control, and foreign policy was established. With Reagan's re-election, the first four months of 1985 provided an opportunity for the media to zero in on any changes in previous policies.

The Bush administration period was the first four months of 1990. This was the first chance for the administration to put its own mark on the defense budget and the nation's national security strategy. The only anomaly was some postwar reporting on the Panama invasion of 1989, with a heavy dose of reporting on the legal issues facing Manuel Noriega. Otherwise, it, too, reflected a range of national security coverage.

As for the Clinton administration, the first four months of 1994 seemed a logical choice, given the bottom-up review of military strategy that had taken place in 1993, along with major changes in the focus of US foreign policy. By 1994, the administration had laid down its overall approach to national security.

The Gulf War period, analyzed from January–February 1991, provided only a glimpse of overall network news war coverage, since the networks regularly extended their daily coverage of the war. Nevertheless, the evening newscast provided a good mechanism for sampling what the networks considered the highlights of a given day.

As was explained in chapter 3, national security coverage was analyzed in terms of specific "reports." A "report" was defined in three ways: a segment delivered by the anchor alone—the anchor tell; a segment where the anchor introduced just one correspondent; or a segment where the anchor introduced more than one correspondent up front, followed by their back-to-back reporting.

The anchor was essentially the dividing line between reports. So when an anchor introduced one correspondent discussing the Pentagon's view of a Soviet arms control initiative and then separately introduced another correspondent who provided the State Department's view, these were analyzed separately as two reports. If, however, the anchor linked the two up front, and then the correspondents reported back to back, this was treated as a single report for purposes of analysis.

One issue that occasionally arose in this area was related to determining whether a report was balanced or not. Obviously, in a linked report that included two correspondents, all angles of the two correspondents were considered and weighed.

On another matter, if an individual report was slanted one way, say against an administration budget proposal, and a separate second report seemed to slant the other way, heavily in favor of the administration, they were both tagged as problematic. This allowed for a second level of analysis by topics, in which a group of reports could be reviewed in terms of what sources came through most often and what points of view were most heavily emphasized in reporting on particular topics.

THE ANALYTICAL PROCESS USED IN
COMPILING THE DATABASE

Each report was analyzed and specific information entered into a database. Basic information on each report was filled in a formatted database record (see Format for Database Record, which follows). The date, the network, and the anchor entries are self-explanatory. Length was a function of the format of the Radio-TV Defense Dialog transcripts, which were in two single-spaced columns on 8½ by 11" sheets. *Short* was noted for reports up to ½ column, *medium* for ½ to 1½ columns, and *long* for a report over 1 ½ columns. The bulk of reports were medium in length.

Short	746	25.3%
Medium	1339	45.4%
Long	862	29.2%
Total	2947	99.9%

For *type*, a report was labeled as either a *news report*, *interview*, *investigative/series*, *commentary*, or *analysis*.

News Report	2745
Interview	65
Investigative/Series	64
Commentary	40
Analysis	33
Total	2947

The news report dominated the *type* category. Among the other types of reports, NBC used John Chancellor for commentary pieces during part of the periods analyzed, and ABC used George Will on a much less frequent basis. Anchors occasionally did interviews, and the occasional long-form defense story sometimes fell under the category investigative/series. Analysis also was an infrequent category, but this was the best description for reports by military experts hired by the networks during the Gulf War. Only 8 of the 33 analysis reports occurred in periods other than the Gulf War, and these reports were usually done by a State or Pentagon correspondent with the expertise needed to interpret events into an overall analytical framework.

Format for Database Record

Date   Network   Length   Anchor
_____ _____ _____ _____

Topic1   Type
_____ _____

Topic2   Effect
_____ _____

Topic3
_____

Topic4
_____

Correspondent1   Beat1
_____ _____

Correspondent2   Beat2
_____ _____

Correspondent3   Beat3
_____ _____

Correspondent4   Beat4
_____ _____

Sources
_____

Comments
_____

_____

_____

_____

Problems
_____

_____

_____

As for the category *topic*, a report could be assigned up to four topics, but rarely was. Topics were selected from a list of broad categories developed in advance with the aim of representing various dimensions of national security in as comprehensive, but manageable, a manner as was possible. Before settling on a set number of topics, about 500 news reports were sampled to get a sense of the range of material. The following list was established and worked well for the most part:

- Arms Control
- Defense Budget
- Foreign Policy
- Industry
- Military Operations
- Personnel
- Policy/Strategy
- Procurement
- Strategic Defense Initiative (SDI)
- Soviet Union/Russia
- Threats
- Weapons/Capabilities

SDI was purposely broken out as a result of its high profile during the 1980s and beyond. For purposes of broader analysis, it was grouped with weapons/capabilities. Soviet Union/Russia was treated as a separate category apart from foreign policy, with secondary categories being used to highlight various dimensions of the US-Soviet, and, later, US-Russian, relationship. Procurement, industry, and weapons/capabilities were all broken out as different aspects of the weapons development process that was so controversial in the 1980s. As might be expected, the more complex aspects of procurement were hardly covered. When appropriate, industry and procurement were grouped into a single category.

Most often, a single topic sufficed to capture the content of a particular report. Of the 2,947 reports, 1,813 were focused on single topics. Another 963 had just two topics assigned to describe the content, and 162 had three topics. Only 9 reports touched upon four topics.

The *correspondent* category contained the name or names of the correspondent(s) associated with an individual report. Here, too, there was room for up to four correspondents, the most found in any given report. But to put that in perspective, 856 reports were anchor *tells* where no correspondent appeared. Another 1,968 were reports featuring an anchor introduction and one correspondent. Only 114 reports had two correspondents reporting back to back; 8 reports had three, and 1 report had four.

The *beat* of each correspondent also was annotated in the record. The beats included the Pentagon, State Department, foreign correspondents, the White House, and Washington-based bureau or other beats (usually generalists covering Capitol Hill or investigative correspondents), and general assignment correspondents (whose home base was not always clear).

The *sources* category was used to annotate information about specific sources cited by correspondents or carried in sound bites. Many times, however, the *sources* entry was left blank because the content summary sufficiently covered the various sources.

The *comments* section of the record was used to describe the basic thrust of the report in terms of its content. There were four lines devoted to the process of taking notes on each report.

The *effect* category was created in order to flag any problematic coverage found. Each report carried a notation of *neutral* or *problematic*. Problematic coverage was determined by analyzing each report's overall content in terms of the journalistic standards of fairness, objectivity, and accuracy.[373] These key standards are elaborated upon in the 1993 Society of Professional Journalists' Code of Ethics:

IV. ACCURACY AND OBJECTIVITY:
Good faith with the public is the foundation of all worthy journalism.
1.   Truth is our ultimate goal.
2.   Objectivity in reporting the news is another goal that serves as the mark of an experienced professional. It is a standard of performance toward which we strive. We honor those who achieve it.
3.   There is no excuse for inaccuracies or lack of thoroughness.
4.   Newspaper headlines should be fully warranted by the contents of the articles they accompany. Photographs and telecasts should give an accurate picture of an event and not highlight an incident out of context.
5.   Sound practice makes clear distinction between news reports and expressions of opinion. News reports should be free of opinion or bias and represent all sides of an issue.
6.   Partisanship in editorial comment that knowingly departs from the truth violates the spirit of American journalism.
7.   Journalists recognize their responsibility for offering informed analysis, comment, and editorial opinion on public events and issues. They accept the obligation to present such material by individuals whose competence, experience, and judgment qualify them for it.
8.   Special articles or presentations devoted to advocacy or the writer's own conclusions and interpretations should be labeled as such.
V. FAIR PLAY:
Journalists at all times will show respect for the dignity, privacy, rights, and well-being of people encountered in the course of gathering and presenting the news.
1.   The news media should not communicate unofficial charges affecting reputation or moral character without giving the accused a chance to reply.
2.   The news media must guard against invading a person's right to privacy.
3.   The media should not pander to morbid curiosity about details of vice and crime.
4.   It is the duty of news media to make prompt and complete correction of their errors.
5.   Journalists should be accountable to the public for their reports and the public should be encouraged to voice its grievances against the media. Open dialogue with our readers, viewers, and listeners should be fostered.[374]

In reviewing each report, a checklist derived from the Code of Ethics' standards was used to make an evaluation:

1. Was the anchor or correspondent striving for objectivity?
2. Was the report thorough enough to provide the most basic context?
3. Was the report free of opinion and bias?
4. Was the report properly framed in terms of the one or several sides of an issue being presented?
5. Was the anchor or correspondent providing accurate information?
6. Did the anchor or correspondent reveal any information that could jeopardize an ongoing military operation or reveal highly sensitive information?
7. Did the report raise any fairness issues?

If the answer to the first five of these questions was "yes" and the answer to number 6 and 7 was "no," the *effect* of the report was *neutral*. If the answer to any one of the first five was "no" or to either number 6 or 7 was "yes," the report was labeled *problematic*. Despite the methodical approach, this category did require subjective judgment. This author had to rely on more than 15 years of experience in the national security field, with nearly half of them devoted to media analysis.

In assessing adherence to journalistic standards, the reports in which anchors introduced one or more correspondents provided an opportunity to evaluate context and approach, from the sources selected to the main points summarized by the correspondent. For example, was the correspondent aiming to describe different sides of an issue? If so, was the report balanced and fair? In other cases in which presenting a particular aspect of an issue was the goal, was the overall context established? In other words, was the report properly framed? And overall, when a complex topic was the subject of a report, was there enough context and background provided?

In terms of *effect*, the anchor reports presented a special case. Unlike the longer reports, anchor reports were judged mainly in terms of the basic context and the points and sources highlighted over time. Reports were flagged problematic when the topic was too complex to be framed in two or three sentences, when an issue was politically charged and difficult to describe in brief terms, or when the anchor report left unanswered questions that might have confused a viewer. The issue of balance was then treated separately; it could not be determined without looking at the whole collection of problematic anchor reports. So the analysis of anchor reports took place in two phases. First, anchor reports containing problems of context were identified. Second, the collection of problematic anchor reports was broken into specific topic areas and analyzed in terms of source selection and points of view expressed. This resulted in a content analysis that helped determine both the attitudes and viewpoints that were most prevalent.

For all problematic reports, anchor and correspondent reports, a three-line description of the nature of the problem was noted in the database record under the category *problems*. Ultimately, all problematic coverage was analyzed as a set and broken down into the most obvious areas. After carefully reviewing all 886 problematic reports, six problem areas were defined and further analyzed: general lack of balance or context; lack of context as a result of brevity; lack of knowledge on the part of the correspondent; overemphasis on drama or bad news at the expense of substance and context; loaded labeling or advocacy; and bad news judgment. While there is some overlap in these areas, this framework provided a way to analyze the coverage that complemented the breakdown and analysis by topics.

Each problematic report was coded by the problem area that best described it. Problematic reporting was also broken down by topics and looked at across the periods analyzed during the four administrations and the Gulf War.

Once all 2,947 reports had been analyzed and entered into the database, the data were further analyzed in numerous ways, some of which have been noted in the main chapters of this book. For example, data could be sorted by topics, correspondents, beats, effect, date periods, and by specific problems as coded. This database provided a powerful tool in helping determine the extent of problems, the way coverage was divided among topics, the way coverage was divided among beats, and so on.

When using specific examples of coverage to illustrate key points, the original transcripts, maintained chronologically, were consulted to ensure the greatest degree of accuracy when quoting from or characterizing specific coverage.

OVERVIEW OF FINDINGS RELATED TO TOPICS NOT ALREADY TREATED

The following sections provide a brief overview of areas of national security reporting that were not treated extensively in the main chapters of the book. Though they are not meant to be comprehensive, they do provide some additional insight into other areas of coverage.

Military Operations

When US military forces are involved in operations around the world, the networks pay attention. For all of the periods analyzed, problematic military coverage occurred only 19.3 percent of the time. However, the Gulf War period, which accounts for half of the military operations reports analyzed, tends to skew the level of problematic coverage. Looking at the coverage during the sample periods from the four administrations without the Gulf War period shows that problematic coverage is actually 32 percent, close to the 30 percent average.

Moreover, each sample period also varied widely when it came to problematic coverage. In the first Reagan administration, it was only 15.2 percent. In the second, it increased significantly to 50 percent, thanks in part to a chunk of bizarre network coverage of the shuttle Discovery flying a military mission, whose secrecy the networks found baffling.

Problematic coverage of military operations in the Bush administration was 24.3 percent, and it was 43.4 percent during the Clinton period analyzed, due in part to manipulative coverage of aircraft crashes using families of victims to tug the heartstrings at the expense of substantive reporting.

Military operations during the periods sampled varied, from the advisory role troops played in El Salvador in the early Reagan years, to the military standoff near the Libyan coast and peacekeeping in Lebanon. Bush administration coverage included deployments of ships in support of drug interdiction to the military intervention in Panama. Military interventions also were covered widely in the Clinton administration, from the Somalia pullout to the NATO bombing in Bosnia.

Other coverage from the four administrations included military exercises, missions of the National Guard and Corps of Engineers at home, and constant coverage of any crash or accident during routine military operations. The most dramatic of crash and accident stories occurred during the Clinton administration with the collision of an F-16 and C-130 at Pope Air Force Base in March 1994 and the shoot down of two US Blackhawk helicopters mistaken for Iraqi Hind helicopters in April 1994.

Personnel

While most of the categories are fairly straightforward, the personnel category was used to capture a range of diverse topics, from nominations to high office, CIA agents gone wrong, students not registering for the draft, and POW/MIA stories, to stories about American hostages abroad, the deaths of US servicemen, and pay raises for the troops, among others. These collective reports represent 11.8 percent of the coverage sampled, considerably more than the 4.3 percent devoted to the defense budget or the 6.4 percent devoted to weapons/capabilities.

Network news loves a human interest story, especially when it is the little guy against the government. A case in point was CBS's hoopla over a few students protesting draft registration during January 1983. In reality, these few were the exception to the multitudes who were complying with the law. The focus of the report, however, suggested just the opposite.

During the periods sampled, the Ames spy case received considerable coverage, given the seriousness of the espionage committed by Aldrich Ames and the dramatic nature of that story, with his extravagant lifestyle, the wife and child caught up in a web of deceit, and the lives lost because of the information Ames sold for large sums of money.

Indictments of officials always make the news, as does the occasional case of a deserter or the case of a military man perpetrating a violent crime. Similar to other areas, the corrupt, the bad, and the ugly are considered news while those who get the job done in a professional way are not.

For all of the periods analyzed, the quality of coverage of personnel issues was average, with 33.3 percent rated as problematic coverage. If there was an overarching question here, it was not so much with the journalistic nuts and bolts as it was with the news judgment.

Policy/Strategy

While not terribly surprising from a medium that relies on pictures, coverage of the central rationale for conducting foreign policy and for training, equipping, manning, deploying, and employing US armed forces is almost nonexistent. As a percentage of coverage of all the periods sampled, policy/strategy garnered a mere .61 percent. Of the 18 reports out of 2,947 that covered this complex area, 9 were aired during the Gulf War, which means that day-to-day coverage was actually .34 percent. Of that, 77.7 percent was problematic.

Network reports on the prospect of nuclear war, how the Anti-Ballistic Missile Treaty fits into national strategy, topics like Carl Sagan's view of nuclear winter, and an out-of-context gem about a West German armed forces chief's views on using a nuclear weapon to send a political signal if the Soviets were to attack first, were so simplistic and uninformed that it is probably better that the public not see any more of this kind of reporting than it already does.

Notably, there was not one network report on policy/strategy during the period sampled in the Clinton administration. At the same time, a debate was raging between the Pentagon and State Department over the shape of the National Security Strategy of the United States. Drafts of the administration's strategy paper were placing new emphasis on nontraditional national security concerns, like economic prosperity, population growth, mass migration of refugees, global climate change and the spread of AIDS, areas Pentagon officials did not believe deserved such prominence. Anyone who relied on network news to stay informed would have missed this debate entirely, with its implications for defense spending, foreign aid, and the potential shift in budget resources.

The inability of network news to deal with this particular topic is emblematic of the larger problem of the networks' lack of willingness to tackle complex material and then to convey it in a way that is balanced and in the proper context. Too often the networks simply shy away from complexity.

Soviet Union/Russia

Coverage of the Soviet Union and its successor state, Russia, cuts across a range of foreign policy and defense issues. As the principal adversary of the United States during the Cold War and as the only country whose nuclear posture continues to rival that of the United States, the Soviet Union and, later, Russia have been of special interest when it comes to US national security. Next to general coverage of foreign policy, the Soviet Union/Russia gained the most attention from the networks in the periods analyzed.

Of all coverage analyzed, foreign policy was the primary topic 34.6 percent of the time and the Soviet Union/Russia came in at 15.7 percent. Military operations followed with a 14.3 percent piece of the coverage pie. Also of note, about 10 percent of the primary foreign policy coverage identified in the sample periods analyzed was related to the Soviet Union or Russia (in these cases, "Soviet Union/Russia" would have been coded in the second, third, or fourth *topic* category). Looking at problematic coverage, the topic Soviet Union/Russia ranks among the lowest with problems only 13.7 percent of the time.

Threats

Coverage of threats to US security, apart from the heavy emphasis the networks placed on developments in the Soviet Union or Russia, is rather thin. Of the 2,947 network reports analyzed, only 69, or 2.3 percent, fell into this broad category of threats. During the periods sampled, the 1994 standoff between North Korea and the International Atomic Energy Agency on the question of nuclear inspections, along with the Clinton administration's response, accounted for 25 of the 69 threat reports. General terrorism, including bomb attacks on US personnel and installations and potential activity among terrorist groups, accounted for 17.

Other coverage ranged from threats like Iraq's germ warfare program and its efforts to obtain more powerful weapons to the possibility of countries like Iran, Iraq, Syria, and Libya using weapons of mass destruction. A few reports dealt with break-ins to Defense Department computers by hackers, the threat of nuclear war as determined by the Doomsday Clock, Chinese nuclear might, and efforts to remove nuclear weapons from the former republics of the Soviet Union.

With such scant coverage of the actual military threat posed by the Soviet Union during the Reagan years, and nonexistent coverage of potential regional threats in the post–Cold War era, it is no surprise that Americans who rely on network news might question why defense spending would have to be increased or maintained at levels necessary to modernize and to keep quality personnel.

On the positive side, there aren't too many ways to slant a story about terrorism or a country trying to acquire weapons of mass destruction, so only 10.1 percent of this coverage was problematic, the lowest in any category. Where problems did exist, they were related to the politics surrounding the Clinton administration's decision to send Patriot missiles to South Korea in the face of a standoff over the inspection of nuclear facilities in the North. Most of those reports did not adequately cover the administration's rationale, and a few others recycled old and inaccurate material on the Patriot missile.

STATISTICAL TABLES AND FIGURE

Table A.1

Breakdown of All National Security Coverage

Primary Topics	# Reports	# Prob. Reports	% Prob. Reports
Arms Control	201	88	43.7%
Defense Budget	128	92	71.8%
Foreign Policy	1022	257	25.1%
Industry	51	47	92.1%
Military Operations	423	82	19.3%
Personnel	348	116	33.3%
Policy/Strategy	18	8	44.4%
Procurement	12	10	83.3%
SDI	20	13	65.0%
Soviet Union/Russia	465	64	13.7%
Threats	69	7	10.1%
Weapons/Capabilities	190	102	53.6%
Total	2947	886	30.0%

Sample periods: Jan.–Apr. 1983, Jan.–Apr. 1985, Jan.–Apr. 1990, Jan.–Apr. 1994, and Jan.–Feb. 1991. Breakdown is by topic, total number of reports, total number of problematic reports, and percentage of total reports that were problematic for each topic.

Table A.2

Breakdown of Coverage by Period—Reagan 1

Primary Topics	# Reports	# Prob. Reports	% Prob. Reports
Arms Control	128	60	46.8%
Defense Budget	63	45	71.4%
Foreign Policy	215	77	35.8%
Industry	4	3	75.0%
Military Operations	72	11	15.2%
Personnel	66	16	24.2%
Policy/Strategy	6	6	100.0%
Procurement	1	1	100.0%
SDI	3	3	100.0%
Soviet Union	93	14	15.0%
Threats	0	0	n/a
Weapons/Capabilities	62	32	51.6%
Total	713	268	37.5%

Sample period: Jan.–Apr. 1983. Breakdown is by topic, total number of reports, total number of problematic reports, and percentage of total reports that were problematic for each topic.

Table A.3

Breakdown of Coverage by Period—Reagan 2

Primary Topics	# Reports	# Prob. Reports	% Prob. Reports
Arms Control	56	21	37.5%
Defense Budget	29	22	75.8%
Foreign Policy	173	83	47.9%
Industry	31	31	100.0%
Military Operations	50	25	50.0%
Personnel	75	20	26.6%
Policy/Strategy	2	1	50.0%
Procurement	5	4	80.0%
SDI	13	8	61.5%
Soviet Union	108	28	25.9%
Threats	10	0	n/a
Weapons/Capabilities	67	32	47.7%
Total	619	271	43.7%

Sample period: Jan.–Apr. 1985. Breakdown is by topic, total number of reports, total number of problematic reports, and percentage of total reports that were problematic for each topic.

Table A.4

Breakdown of Coverage by Period—Bush

Primary Topics	# Reports	# Prob. Reports	% Prob. Reports
Arms Control	17	7	41.1%
Defense Budget	26	21	80.7%
Foreign Policy	192	45	23.4%
Industry	8	8	100.0%
Military Operations	37	9	24.3%
Personnel	77	30	38.9%
Policy/Strategy	1	0	0.0%
Procurement	4	3	75.0%
SDI	4	2	50.0%
Soviet Union	232	18	7.7%
Threats	21	1	4.7%
Weapons/Capabilities	29	22	75.8%
Total	648	166	25.6%

Sample period: Jan.–Apr. 1990. Breakdown is by topic, total number of reports, total number of problematic reports, and percentage of total reports that were problematic for each topic.

Table A.5

Breakdown of Coverage by Period—Clinton

Primary Topics	# Reports	# Prob. Reports	% Prob. Reports
Arms Control	0	n/a	n/a
Defense Budget	0	n/a	n/a
Foreign Policy	359	41	11.4%
Industry	6	4	66.6%
Military Operations	53	23	43.4%
Personnel	108	46	42.5%
Policy/Strategy	0	n/a	n/a
Procurement	2	2	100.0%
SDI	0	n/a	n/a
Russia	30	4	13.3%
Threats	32	6	18.7%
Weapons/Capabilities	11	8	72.7%
Total	601	134	22.3%

Sample period: Jan.–Apr. 1994. Breakdown is by topic, total number of reports, total number of problematic reports, and percentage of total reports that were problematic for each topic.

Table A.6
Breakdown of Coverage by Period—Gulf War

Primary Topics	# Reports	# Prob. Reports	% Prob. Reports
Arms Control	0	n/a	n/a
Defense Budget	10	4	40.0%
Foreign Policy	83	11	13.2%
Industry	2	1	50.0%
Military Operations	211	14	6.6%
Personnel	22	4	18.1%
Policy/Strategy	9	1	11.0%
Procurement	0	n/a	n/a
SDI	0	n/a	n/a
Russia	2	0	0.0%
Threats	6	0	0.0%
Weapons/Capabilities	21	8	38.0%
Total	366	37	10.1%

Sample period: Jan.–Feb. 1991. Breakdown is by topic, total number of reports, total number of problematic reports, and percentage of total reports that were problematic for each topic.

Table A.7

Breakdown of Coverage (minus Gulf War Sample)

Primary Topics	# Reports	# Prob. Reports	% Prob. Reports
Arms Control	201	88	43.7%
Defense Budget	118	88	74.5%
Foreign Policy	939	246	26.2%
Industry	49	46	93.8%
Military Operations	212	68	32.0%
Personnel	326	112	34.3%
Policy/Strategy	9	7	77.7%
Procurement	12	10	83.3%
SDI	20	13	65.0%
Soviet Union/Russia	463	64	13.8%
Threats	63	7	11.1%
Weapons/Capabilities	169	94	55.6%
Total	2581	843	32.6%

Sample periods: Jan.–Apr. 1983, Jan.–Apr. 1985, Jan.–Apr. 1990, and Jan.–Apr. 1994. Breakdown is by topic, total number of reports, total number of problematic reports, and percentage of total reports that were problematic for each topic.

Table A.8

Breakdown of Number of Reports by Sample Period

Period	Dates	# Reports	# Prob. Reports	% Prob. Reports
Reagan 1	Jan–Apr 83	713	268	37.5%
Reagan 2	Jan–Apr 85	619	275	44.4%
Bush	Jan–Apr 90	648	166	25.6%
Clinton	Jan–Apr 94	601	134	22.3%
Gulf War	Jan–Feb 91	366	43	11.7%
All	All	2947	886	30.0%

Table A.9

Breakdown of Total Reports by Beat and Topic for Jan.–Apr. 1983, Jan.–Apr. 1985, Jan.–Apr. 1990, Jan.–Feb. 1991, and Jan.–Apr. 1994

Topic	Total	Wash-/Gen	WH	State	Pent	For	ANC
Arms Control	201	22	29	22	8	41	79
Defense Budget	128	32	32	0	27	0	37
Foreign Policy	1022	100	150	83	81	355	253
Industry	51	19	0	0	5	0	27
Military Operations	423	48	11	14	126	118	106
Personnel	348	119	16	9	52	37	115
Policy/Strategy	18	4	2	1	4	2	5
Procurement	12	3	0	0	3	0	6
SDI	20	3	3	1	1	3	9
Soviet Union/Russia	465	29	46	44	33	193	120
Threats	69	4	4	4	15	14	28
Weapons/Capabilities	190	36	15	0	59	9	71
Total	2947	419	308	178	414	772	856

Wash/Gen=Washington bureau and other beats; WH=White House; State=State Department; Pent=Pentagon; For=foreign beat; ANC=anchor.

Table A.10
Breakdown of Total Problematic Reports by Beat and Topic for Jan.–Apr. 1983, Jan.–Apr. 1985, Jan.–Apr. 1990, Jan.–Feb. 1991, and Jan.–Apr. 1994

Topics	Total Prob.	Wash-/Gen	WH	State	Pent	For	ANC
Arms Control	88	14	16	14	3	12	29
Defense Budget	92	25	24	0	19	0	24
Foreign Policy	257	39	45	14	18	60	81
Industry	47	17	0	0	5	0	25
Military Operations	82	19	1	2	16	10	34
Personnel	116	39	11	3	20	4	39
Policy/Strategy	8	2	0	0	1	1	4
Procurement	10	3	0	0	1	0	6
SDI	13	1	1	1	1	2	7
Soviet Union/Russia	64	3	14	5	3	8	31
Threats	7	0	1	0	4	1	1
Weapons/Capabilities	102	26	5	0	27	5	39
Total	886	188	118	39	118	103	320

Wash/Gen=Washington bureau and other beats; WH=White House; State=State Department; Pent=Pentagon; For=foreign beat; ANC=anchor.

Table A.11

Types of Problems Broken Down by Beats and Number of Reports for Jan.–Apr. 1983, Jan.–Apr. 1985, Jan.–Apr. 1990, Jan.–Feb. 1991, and Jan.–Apr. 1994

Types of Problems	Total	Wash-/Gen	WH	State	Pent	For	ANC
Lack of Balance or Context	248	57	46	20	59	49	17
Brevity and Context	180	0	0	0	0	0	180
Lack of Knowledge	112	38	30	0	16	14	14
Overemphasis on Drama, Bad News	185	51	20	3	29	22	60
Loaded Labeling or Advocacy	98	34	19	13	6	6	20
Bad News Judgment	63	8	3	3	8	12	29
Total	886	188	118	39	118	103	320

Wash/Gen=Washington bureau and other general beats; WH=White House; State=State Department; Pent=Pentagon; For=foreign beat; ANC=anchor.

Figure A.1

Number of Problematic Reports by Beat for Jan.–Apr. 1983, Jan.–Apr. 1985, Jan.–Apr. 1990, Jan.–Apr. 1994, and Jan.–Feb. 1991.

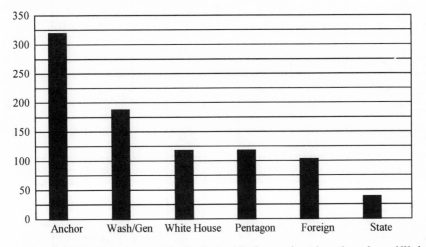

Out of a total of 886 problematic reports, the distribution falls disproportionately on the anchor and Washington bureau and other general beats.

Table A.12

Breakdown of Topics by Types of Problems and Number of Reports for Jan.–Apr. 1983, Jan.–Apr. 1985, Jan.-Apr. 1990, Jan.–Apr. 1994, and Jan.–Feb. 1991.

Topic	Total Reports	# Prob. Reports	Bal	Brev	Kn	Dra-ma	La-bel	Judg
Arms Control	201	88	34	15	4	7	25	3
Defense Budget	128	92	39	19	5	19	10	0
Foreign Policy	1022	257	95	59	29	32	28	14
Industry	51	47	2	8	7	28	2	0
Military Operations	423	82	11	5	18	30	3	15
Personnel	348	116	21	19	16	44	7	9
Policy/ Strategy	18	8	2	3	0	1	1	1
Procurement	12	10	0	4	4	1	0	1
SDI	20	13	4	4	1	0	3	1
Soviet Union /Russia	465	64	7	14	11	6	11	15
Threats	69	7	4	0	1	0	0	2
Weapons/ Capabilities	190	102	29	30	16	17	8	2
Total	2947	886	201	167	112	185	98	63

Bal=Lack of Balance or Context; Brev=Brevity and Context; Kn=Lack of Knowledge; Drama=Overemphasis on Drama, Bad News; Label=Loaded Labeling or Advocacy; Judg=Bad News Judgment.

Table A.13

Distribution of Total Reports and Problematic Reports by Beat for Jan.–Apr. 1983, Jan.–Apr. 1985, Jan.–Apr. 1990, Jan.–Apr. 1994, and Jan.–Feb. 1991.

Beat	# Reports	% Total Coverage	# Prob. Reports	% Total Prob. Coverage
Wash/Gen	419	14.2%	188	21.2%
White House	308	10.4%	118	13.3%
Pentagon	414	14.0%	118	13.3%
State	178	6.0%	39	4.4%
Foreign	772	26.2%	103	11.6%
Anchor	856	29.0%	320	36.1%
Total	2947	99.8%	886	99.9%

Breakdown is by number of reports from a beat, the percentage of total coverage those reports represent, the number of problematic reports from a beat, and the percentage of all problematic coverage those reports represent.

Appendix 2

The Pentagon's News-Gathering Operation

Since much of the content analysis relied on materials from the Pentagon's Current News Analysis and Research Service, a short history of the scope and function of that operation follows.

The origin of the Pentagon's news-gathering operation dates back to the establishment of the Department of Defense. According to Harry Zubkoff, who joined the staff of the administrative assistant to the secretary of the Air Force in 1950, it was the first Air Force secretary, Stuart Symington, who planted the seeds of the *Current News* by creating a Special Projects Office (SPO) in 1947 to track current events and write speeches and testimony.[375] With the Berlin Airlift of 1948, the SPO began providing the Secretary with significant articles out of the press each day. The SPO continued to perform this service, especially at times when important Air Force issues were making headlines. The B-36 hearings of 1949 are one example of the type of issues the SPO began tracking for the secretary of the Air Force.[376]

Newsclipping was not, however, limited to the SPO. According to an Air Force memorandum, as far back as April 1949, the Air Information Division Directorate of Public Relations, which reported to the secretary of the Air Force, was compiling articles for Air Force officials from a half dozen New York and Washington newspapers.[377] A little over a year later, around July 1950, the Office of the Secretary of Defense (OSD) Public Information Division began to produce a photostated booklet of "fairly complete" coverage of newspaper articles and what the Air Force memorandum described as "less complete" magazine coverage.

In May 1950, the Air Force Directorate of Public Relations was transferred to the Office of the Air Force Chief of Staff. Its Research and Analysis Branch was charged with internal information functions, including the compilation of "Current News." Meanwhile, the secretary's Special Projects Office was drawing material from both the Air Force compilation and the OSD compilation, as well as from other newspapers.[378] The Special Projects Office was expanded in 1950, as the Korean War broke out. Zubkoff was hired in October to follow press comments on the war. Employing a photostat machine that architects used to reproduce blueprints, Zubkoff began distributing copies of a half dozen significant articles each day to the secretary. The output was primitive, similar to a photographic negative, but the *Current News* was born that November.[379]

Then Air Force Secretary Thomas K. Finletter used to wave around his little compilation of articles at staff meetings, Zubkoff recalled, which led to more demand for it. Graduating to a mimeograph machine, the SPO staff began running 20 copies, but soon had to increase the number to around 30, which reached the defense secretary, the other service secretaries, and a number of senior policymakers.

In February 1952, the Air Force Directorate of Public Relations was transferred back to the Office of the Secretary of the Air Force. And, in August 1952, OSD ceased publishing its news compilation, "depriving the Air Force 'Current News' of a major source of supply of articles."[380]

"A decision was made at that time that the Air Force would continue to compile a daily news publication. Inasmuch as the Special Projects Office, OSAF [Office of the Secretary of the Air Force], was already screening many newspapers, the consolidated responsibility for publishing 'Current News' was transferred to that office, which in February 1952 had been assigned to the Administrative Assistant to the SAF."[381]

Throughout the 1950s, the size, the circulation, and the number of sources drawn upon all increased. By 1953, the SPO staff was screening 12 daily newspapers and 30 national periodicals. By 1958, the staff was screening 26 newspapers and 50 magazines. In the same period, circulation rose from 36 to over 200.[382]

By the end of the 1950s, circulation of this Air Force–produced news compilation had reached several hundred, and the other services had also created their own clipping operations. By the time Secretary of Defense Robert S. McNamara took the helm of the Pentagon in 1961, Zubkoff notes, about 500 copies of what had become known informally as the "Early Bird" were being distributed to the top echelons of the Pentagon across the services. Its format was 6 pages, and it typically included about a dozen articles from the leading newspapers of the day, including the *Washington Post*, *New York Times*, *Washington Star*, *Washington Times-Herald*, and the *Washington Daily News*.

There was always more than enough material on defense and foreign policy to fill the Early Bird, according to Zubkoff. During McNamara's tenure, a "Main Edition" was added to supplement the Early Bird, which was available by 8:00 a.m. The Main Edition started appearing between 11:00 a.m. and noon, adding articles that were not included in the Early Bird, as well as op-eds, editorials, and selected feature pieces.

What had evolved into the Research and Analysis Division, under the administrative assistant for research, Office of the Secretary of the Air Force, also produced other publications, like a "Foreign Media Edition," which began in 1978 and was eventually incorporated into the Early Bird, once the Foreign Broadcast Information Service went on-line. Over the years, there were also special compilations on international incidents and wars, like the Mayaguez, the Iranian Hostage Crisis, Grenada, and the Gulf War, to name a few.

From the start, journalists who covered the Pentagon were interested in what appeared in these various *Current News* compilations, especially the daily publications. Naturally, articles that were brought to the attention of the top policy-makers in the Early Bird or Main Edition took on added significance. They not only made their way into policy discussions, but also served to stimulate the interest of other journalists who had originally missed a story or particular angle.

These clips, and others that never made their way into one of the *Current News* publications, were filed in a morgue divided into meticulously organized categories and subcategories. By the 1980s, when most of these paper files had been converted to microfilm, and later overtaken by a computerized system of cross-referencing, the morgue had grown to some four million clips.[383] This morgue provided a gold mine of material that government and private researchers could use to track media trends and coverage of defense and foreign affairs policies.

As for the publications mined for articles and information, besides a fixed number of newspaper and periodical subscriptions, the *Current News* office created a web of exchange agreements over the years. This gave the staff access to hundreds of general interest and trade newsletters, think tank studies and reports, general interest and trade magazines, and professional journals. Even lengthier material, like journal articles, was often filed and/or reprinted in Special Editions and, later, the Supplement.

One result of this wealth of material was that the policy-makers benefited from being exposed to a wide range of both critical and supportive points of view. In fact, it was under Secretary of Defense James Schlesinger that Zubkoff started the Special Editions, which were usually reprints of think pieces from various journals. Zubkoff says Schlesinger wanted views from across the spectrum. He took this directive seriously and launched the Special Editions with several articles that were highly critical of the Ford administration's defense policies.[384]

CURRENT NEWS COMES OF AGE

Like many other parts of the Pentagon, the Current News Branch did not escape McNamara's proclivity for organizational tinkering and centralized control. By the early 1960s, the *Current News* was being distributed well beyond the Air Force to the three other services, the Office of the Secretary of Defense, the Office of the Joint Chiefs of Staff, as well as to departments, agencies, and private entities outside of the building. Nevertheless, that did not stop the Army, Navy, other defense agencies, and the Office of the Assistant Secretary of Defense for Public Affairs from assembling their own news compilations each day.

According to Zubkoff, none of these other compilations covered the range of subjects or had the circulation of the *Current News*. When talk of consolidation began, Zubkoff recalls that then Air Force Secretary Eugene Zuckert did not want to let Zubkoff or his boss, Murray Green, become a part of a centralized operation in the Office of the Secretary of Defense or the Joint Chiefs of Staff (JCS).[385] Besides overseeing the *Current News*, Zubkoff, Green, and the other members of the Research and Analysis Division performed research, wrote speeches and testimony, and compiled historical material for the secretary of the Air Force.

In the end, Zuckert agreed to take on the added responsibility of producing a department-wide news compilation as the executive agent for the Department of Defense.[386] So, in December 1963, then Deputy Secretary of Defense Roswell Gilpatric directed that the *Current News* put out clips for the entire department. Gilpatric wrote that consolidation of the three services' news analysis and clipping services "into one will promote economy and efficiency by eliminating administrative overhead and by providing the use of a common facility, thus reducing personnel requirements. It will foster effectiveness by providing one common service to which the Office of the Secretary of Defense, the Organization of the Joint Chiefs of Staff, the headquarters of the military departments, and the headquarters of Defense agencies (hereinafter called DoD headquarters) will have access."[387]

Gilpatric's memorandum directed that the news clipping service would compile "news material on matters of interest to the several DoD headquarters" on a daily basis; maintain a news clipping morgue or reference library; and maintain the capability of translating and analyzing articles of selected foreign language media. It also made provision for "a news analysis service which can provide a scientific measure of expressed opinion in the media." Overall policy guidance for the service was provided by the assistant secretary of defense for public affairs in coordination with the secretaries of the military departments.

According to Zubkoff, the Air Force began producing the department-wide news compilation right away, but it took over a year before the Department of Defense implementing directive could be issued, so strenuous were the objections of the other services. Ultimately, in March 1965, a number of positions were transferred from the other services to the Air Force.[388] For more than 20 years, the Air Force served the Department of Defense in this role. As Zubkoff explained, he had to defend the function many times during the 36 years he ran it.[389] But, from the standpoint of resources, he added, the office did not receive nearly the scrutiny it would have, had it been part of the Office of the Secretary of Defense or had it been under the supervision of the assistant secretary of defense for public affairs, both of which were reviewed by Congress annually.[390]

In 1988, two years after Zubkoff's retirement, *Current News* was transferred to the American Forces Information Service, directly under the assistant secretary of defense for public affairs. That change prompted a few articles by Pentagon press regulars that raised the specter of "news management" by public affairs officials.[391] Zubkoff had always maintained that there was a real conflict of interest between the public relations function of Public Affairs and the journalistic approach of the *Current News* staff. Zubkoff's view won the day each time serious studies were undertaken to consider consolidating *Current News* under Public Affairs.

Herbert Coleman, who succeeded Zubkoff and soon found himself working for Public Affairs, was strong enough to fight off some of the pressure to print certain stories over other stories. He was, however, subjected to a steady erosion of resources, which continued after he retired. Today the staff is smaller than it ever was, and it is fighting for its very existence. Though the Early Bird and electronic versions of the Supplement and Radio-TV Dialog are still available, the research function has virtually disappeared. And *Current News* no longer serves the function of bringing a steady stream journal articles, studies, and books before the policy-maker, something Zubkoff prided himself on.

Under Zubkoff's regime, the Air Force positions assigned to his office were actually on the personnel books at Randolph Air Force Base. Now on OSD's books, the *Current News* operation must deal with constant pressures to save money and downsize. Additionally, though now officially under OSD, the chief of *Current News* has virtually no access to top policy-makers. In Zubkoff's day, he would have regular contact with the secretary of defense and other key officials.

Coleman and his successors have found innovative ways to keep the main products alive through the use of new technologies, first with fax access through a 3M FaxXchange facsimile computer and, most recently, through a system for accessing *Current News* via the Internet.[392]

The Current News Analysis and Research Service now falls under the American Forces Information Service, which also oversees a wide range of internal information programs for the Department of Defense. AFIS reports to the assistant secretary of defense for public affairs. For its part, the *Current News* now resides in the AFIS Armed Forces Press and Publications Directorate.

After the transfer, the first thing Coleman said he had to deal with was new levels of bureaucracy and much more paperwork.[393] There was also much stricter enforcement of what the military terms "the chain of command." Coleman was not allowed direct contact with senior officials. In fact, Coleman recounted the stir caused by an impromptu visit one day by then Assistant Secretary of Defense for Public Affairs Pete Williams. Williams wandered into the *Current News* office and began looking for some material, recalled Coleman, who offered to help. Williams declined and found what he needed. When AFIS officials learned of the visit, colonels and top civilians were buzzing; they were anxious and wondered what "action" they should take. None, was Coleman's curt response.

Likewise, if the assistant secretary of defense for public affairs[394] wants something, the request travels through one or two civilians and three or four colonels before it reaches the chief of the Current News Analysis and Research Service.

More troublesome than the bureaucratic red tape faced by the head of the Pentagon's clipping service today is the lack of a champion in the policy structure. Zubkoff could rely on the administrative assistant to the secretary of the Air Force or the Air Force secretary himself. Controversies could also be elevated quickly to the level of the deputy secretary of defense or the secretary of defense, so important was the notion of an independent *Current News* operation during Zubkoff's tenure.[395]

Today the media themselves are a partial check on the occasional temptation of the public affairs establishment to interfere with *Current News* editorial policy. For example, in 1994, a colonel who oversaw the directorate to which the *Current News* reports invoked the name of a superior in the Office of the Assistant to the Secretary of Defense for Public Affairs and issued a directive to Coleman instructing him to cut the size of the Early Bird by a few pages and to concentrate more on the East Coast papers, like the *Washington Post*, *New York Times*, and *Wall Street Journal*.[396] Apparently, the directive resulted from what the top public affairs deputy interpreted as the needs of Secretary of Defense William Perry.[397]

When the story broke in the trade publication *Defense Week*, which just happened to be reprinted in the Early Bird, the backtracking was immediate. Pentagon spokeswoman Kathleen deLaski invalidated the colonel's directive, stating, "This is someone at the lower level trying to put into words his understanding of what we asked for. Unfortunately, he got it wrong."[398]

Since Coleman's retirement at the end of 1994, there have been several caretakers, none of whom could exert the kind of independent editorial judgment that was part of Zubkoff's and, to some extent, Coleman's jobs. A combination of budget pressures and public affairs interference has already affected the quality of the *Current News* product and could one day spell the end of the *Current News* operation.

Bringing news to the policy-makers will always be a requirement, but how that is accomplished affects the quality and quantity of material presented. On an intellectual level, the quality has gone down markedly since 1988. In late 1997, there was talk of possibly eliminating the Supplement, the only remaining vehicle for in-depth background articles. At the beginning of 1998, the staff had managed to create an electronic version available on the Internet, but the Supplement's future is still uncertain—as is the very future of the *Current News*.

Notes

1. See, for example, Liz Trotta, *Fighting for Air: In the Trenches with Television News* (New York: Simon & Schuster, 1991) and Terry Eastland, "Confessions of a Newsman," *American Spectator*, August 1990, pp. 29–31.

2. Mitchell Bard, "Strategic Thoughts about SDI," *Public Opinion*, March–April 1987, p. 18.

3. George Lardner, Jr., "Most Polled Disapprove of SDI," *Washington Post*, August 14, 1985, p. 10.

4. "American Attitudes on SDI, Arms Control and Defense," *American Sentinel*, June 8, 1987, p. 6.

5. "SDI Poll/Nuclear Arms," *Reuters*, March 17, 1988.

6. Luntz Research Companies, "Missile Defense Survey," January 2–3, 1995.

7. Richard R. Burt, "The News Media and National Security," in *The Media and Foreign Policy,* ed. Simon Serfaty (New York: St. Martin's Press, 1991), p. 137.

8. See, for instance, National Commission on Excellence in Education, "A Nation at Risk: The Imperative for Educational Reform" (Washington, D.C.: GPO, April 1983); The Business Roundtable, "The Role of Business in Education Reform: Blueprint for Action" (Washington, D.C.: The Business Roundtable, April 1988); and Aerospace Education Foundation, "America's Next Crisis: The Shortfall in Technical Manpower" (Washington, D.C.: Aerospace Education Foundation, September 1989).

9. See C. Joseph Bernardo and Eugene H. Bacon, *American Military Policy: Its Development Since 1775* (Harrisburg, Pa.: Stackpole Co., 1961).

10. Bernardo and Bacon, *American Military Policy*, p. 118 (see n. 9).

11. See James MacGregor Burns, *The Vineyard of Liberty* (New York: Vintage Books, 1982), pp. 195–196.

12. Times Mirror Database on Public Attentiveness to Major News Stories (1986–1995), Times Mirror Center for the People & the Press, 1995. In this example, 80 percent said they followed the space shuttle Challenger disaster closely; 73 percent said they followed the San Francisco earthquake closely; and 66 percent said they followed hurricane Andrew closely. By comparison, 66 percent followed closely Iraq's invasion of

Kuwait in August 1990, and 60 percent followed the US Panama invasion in December 1989 closely. (Note: In 1996, in a cost-cutting measure, Times Mirror ceased funding for the Center for the People & the Press. The Pew Charitable Trust stepped in and provided funding, insisting only that the name be changed to the Pew Research Center.)

13. Secretary of Defense William J. Perry, interview with Marvin Kalb, "The Pentagon and the Press," *Press Politics*, issue 1, 1996, p. 121.

14. Interview with Caspar W. Weinberger, conducted May 4, 1994.

15. See, for example, Francis P. Hoeber and William Schneider, Jr., eds., *Arms, Men, and Military Budgets* (New York: Crane, Russak & Company, 1977), pp. 1–3.

16. See, for example, Burns, *The Vineyard of Liberty*, pp. 215–217 (see n. 11); see also Bernardo and Bacon, *American Military Policy* (see n. 9); and Russell F. Weigley, *The American Way of War: A History of United States Military Strategy and Policy* (Bloomington: Indiana University Press, 1973).

17. See Steven L. Rearden, *History of the Office of the Secretary of Defense: The Formative Years: 1947–1950*, vol. 1 (Washington, D.C.: GPO, 1984), pp. 23–27.

18. "TV News Viewership Declines" (Washington, D.C.: Pew Research Center for the People & the Press), May 13, 1996.

19. "America's Watching: Public Attitudes Toward Television" (New York: The Roper Organization, 1993, 1994).

20. See, for example, Lawrence W. Lichty, "News from Everywhere," in *American Media: The Wilson Quarterly Reader*, eds. Philip S. Cook, Douglas Gomery, and Lawrence W. Lichty (Washington, D.C.: Woodrow Wilson Center Press, 1989), pp. 212–213; and W. Russell Neuman, Marion R. Just, and Ann N. Crigler, *Common Knowledge: News and the Construction of Political Meaning* (Chicago: University of Chicago Press, 1992), pp. 93, 122.

21. "Network Early Evening News (Sept.–April) 1970–1995," Nielsen Media Research, 1995.

22. See note 21.

23. See Penn Kimball, *Downsizing the News: Network Cutbacks in the Nation's Capital* (Washington, D.C.: Woodrow Wilson Center Press, 1994), p. 1.

24. Newspaper Association of America, "Highlights: The Year in Review" (NAA Worldwide Web Page, http://www.naa.org, 1995).

25. *Gale Directory of Publications and Broadcast Media* (Detroit, Mich.: Gale Research, 1996).

26. For a critique of the television rating system, see, for example, Ien Ang, *Desperately Seeking the Audience* (New York: Routledge, Chapman and Hall, 1991).

27. For a general discussion of media effects research, see Everett M. Rogers and James W. Dearing, "Agenda-Setting Research: Where Has It Been, Where Is It Going?" in Doris A. Graber, ed., *Media Power in Politics* (Washington, D.C.: Congressional Quarterly Press, 1994), pp. 77–95.

28. See R. McLure and T. Patterson, *The Unseeing Eye: The Myth of Television Power in National Elections* (New York: G.P. Putnam, 1976), p. 90.

29. Shanto Iyengar and Donald R. Kinder, *News That Matters: Television and American Opinion* (Chicago: University of Chicago Press, 1987), p. 2.

30. Doris A. Graber, *Mass Media and American Politics* (Washington, D.C.: Congressional Quarterly Press, 1989), p. 20.

31. For a brief discussion of the various phases of media research, see Dennis McQuail, "The Influence and Effects of Mass Media," in Doris A. Graber, ed., *Media Power in Politics* (Washington, D.C.: Congressional Quarterly Press, 1994), pp. 7–24.

32. W. Russell Neuman, Marion R. Just, and Ann N. Crigler, *Common Knowledge: News and the Construction of Political Meaning* (Chicago: University of Chicago Press, 1992).

33. For a discussion on the media's ability to influence policy-makers, see, for example, Patrick O'Heffernan, *Mass Media and American Foreign Policy* (Norwood, N.J.: Ablex Publishing, 1991); Simon Serfaty, ed., *The Media and Foreign Policy* (New York: St. Martin's Press, 1991); and Michael R. Beschloss, *Presidents, Television and Foreign Crises* (Washington, D.C.: Annenberg Washington Program, 1993). For aspects of the "CNN effect" or "CNN Curve," see Nick Gowing, "Real-time Television Coverage of Armed Conflicts and Diplomatic Crises: Does It Pressure or Distort Foreign Policy Decisions," (unpublished working paper 94-1, Cambridge, Mass.: Joan Shorenstein Barone Center on the Press, Politics and Public Policy, June 1994); Nick Gowing, "Behind the CNN Factor," *Washington Post*, July 31, 1994, p. C1; Perry M. Smith, *How CNN Fought the War: A View from the Inside* (New York: Carol Publishing Group, 1991); Johanna Neuman, *Lights, Camera, War: Is Media Technology Driving International Politics?* (New York: St. Martin's Press, 1996); and Tom Rosenstiel, "The Myth of CNN," *New Republic*, August 22–29, 1994, p. 27. For a discussion of the media's role in terrorism, see Dr. Rudolf Levy, "Terrorism and the Mass Media," *Military Intelligence*, October–December 1985, pp. 34–38.

34. For a sampling of the views expressed in the media on television's influence in foreign policy, see Michael Schwelien, "CNN: Television for the Global Village," *World Press Review*, December 1990, p. 34.; William A. Henry III, "History as It Happens," *Time*, January 6, 1992, pp. 24–25; Reese Cleghorn, "Telewars Today, Telepeace Tomorrow," *Washington Journalism Review*, October 1990, p. 4; and Marvin Kalb, "How TV News Has Come to Dominate Public Policy," *Boston Globe*, July 14, 1991, p. 90.

35. See, for example, Robert J. Donovan and Ray Scherer, *Unsilent Revolution: Television News and American Public Life* (New York: Cambridge University Press, 1992); Neuman, Just, and Crigler (see n. 32); Shanto Iyengar, *Is Anyone Responsible? How Television Frames Political Issues* (Chicago: University of Chicago Press, 1991); and Doris A. Graber, ed., *Media Power in Politics* (Washington, D.C.: Congressional Quarterly Press, 1994).

36. Peter Kann, "The Twilight of the Networks," *Wall Street Journal*, September 20, 1991, p. 10.

37. Barbara Matusow, "Changing TV's Golden Age into Lead," *Washington Post National Weekly Edition*, September 2–8, 1991, p. 35.

38. Todd Gitlin, "Zapped!" *New York Times Book Review*, August 25, 1991, p. 3.

39. Ken Auletta, *Three Blind Mice: How the TV Networks Lost Their Way* (New York: Random House, 1991), p. 3.

40. Bill Carter, "TV Networks, in a Crisis, Talk of Sweeping Changes," *New York Times*, July 29, 1991, p. D1.

41. Jon Katz, "Beyond Broadcast Journalism," *Columbia Journalism Review*, March/April 1992, pp. 19–23.

42. Elizabeth Jensen, "Major TV Networks, Dinosaurs No More, Tune in to New Deals," *Wall Street Journal*, March 17, 1994, p. 1.

43. Paul Farhi, "Walt Disney Co. to Buy Capital Cities/ABC," *Washington Post*, August 1, 1995, p. 1; and Paul Farhi, "Westinghouse to Buy CBS," *Washington Post*, August 2, 1995, p. 1.

44. John Lippman, "What Will Jack Welch Do with NBC Now?" *Wall Street Journal*, August 2, 1995, p. B1.

45. Howard Kurtz, "Mousetrap? Disney Stuns ABC News," *Washington Post*, August 1, 1995, p. E1.

46. Bill Kovach, "Big Deals, with Journalism Thrown In," *New York Times*, August 3, 1995, p. 25.

47. David Zurawik and Christina Stoehr, "Eclipsing the Nightly News," *American Journalism Review*, November 1994, p. 36.

48. For a good discussion of the emerging newsmagazine genre of news, see David Zurawik and Christina Stoehr, "Eclipsing the Nightly News," pp. 32–38 (see n. 47).

49. David Zurawik and Christina Stoehr, "Eclipsing the Nightly News," p. 37 (see n. 47).

50. See Michael Massing, "Is the Most Popular Evening Newscast the Best?" *Columbia Journalism Review*, March/April 1991, p. 30.

51. "Call It Courage," remarks by Dan Rather to the Radio and Television News Directors Association Annual Convention, Miami, Fla., September 29, 1993, p. 6.

52. Richard Zoglin, "Assessing the War Damage: ABC Establishes Air Supremacy, But the Future of Network News Is Fuzzier than Ever," *Time*, March 18, 1991, p. 88.

53. Edwin Diamond, *The Media Show: The Changing Face of the News, 1985–1990* (Cambridge, Mass.: MIT Press, 1991), p. 25.

54. See Penn Kimball, *Downsizing the News: Network Cutbacks in the Nation's Capital* (Washington, D.C.: Woodrow Wilson Center Press, 1994).

55. Interview with Jonathan Wald, senior broadcast producer for domestic news, NBC Nightly News, New York, May 17, 1996.

56. Edward Jay Epstein, *News from Nowhere* (New York: Vintage Books, 1973), pp. 42–43.

57. See Herbert J. Gans, *Deciding What's News: A Study of CBS Evening News, NBC Nightly News, Newsweek and Time* (New York: Vintage Books, 1979).

58. The interviews included: Tom Nagorski, senior producer/foreign editor, ABC World News Tonight in New York; Jonathan Wald, senior broadcast producer for domestic news, NBC Nightly News in New York; Mark Brender, Pentagon producer for ABC World News Tonight; Mary Walsh, Pentagon producer, CBS Evening News; Fred Francis, former Pentagon correspondent, NBC Nightly News.

59. See, for example, Robert Goldberg and Gerald Jay Goldberg, *Anchors: Brokaw, Jennings, Rather and the Evening News* (New York: Carol Publishing Group, 1990).

60. See, for example, "How CBS Puts Out Its Evening News," *U.S. News & World Report*, September 5, 1983, p. 56; see also, "New producer for Jennings' News; Paul Friedman replaces William Lord, who reportedly clashed with anchor," *Broadcasting*, January 11, 1988, p. 48.

61. For example, Foote's most recent analysis, covering 1994, put three White House correspondents, one Pentagon correspondent and a Washington correspondent in the top five slots. See Joe Foote, "Mitchell, Braver Head National TV News Corps in '94," University News Service, Southern Illinois University at Carbondale, November 1, 1995.

62. See Joe Foote, "Washington Is *the* Place in TV Correspondent Race," News Release, University News Service, Southern Illinois University at Carbondale, August 22, 1988.

63. See Joe Foote, "Network Women Correspondents Still Lag in Visibility, Study Reveals," University News Service, Southern Illinois University at Carbondale, May 24, 1991.

64. Stephen Hess, *The Washington Reporters* (Washington, D.C.: Brookings Institution, 1981), p. 51.

65. See, for instance, Michael Nelson, "The Press and the President: How the Press Views the President," *Current*, October 1994, p. 21.

66. Dan Goodgame, who covered the White House for *Time* magazine, was quoted in Dan Cogan, " 'More champagne, Ms. Mitchell?' Investigation of White House Travel Office," *Washington Monthly*, July 1993, p. 17.

67. See, for instance, Jennifer Toth, "Judy Woodruff: Trouncing the 'Weather Girl' Image on Her Way Up; Television Journalist Judy Woodruff," *Quill*, July 1992, p. 18.

68. See, for instance, Graeme Browning, "Too Close for Comfort," *National Journal*, October 3, 1992, p. 2243.

69. See, for example, "Speaking Out: Inside the Reagan White House," *Broadcasting*, April 25, 1988, p. 62.

70. Interview with Fred Francis, former NBC Pentagon correspondent, April 30, 1996; and interview with Mark Brender, ABC Pentagon producer, May 3, 1996.

71. David Martin, "Covering the Pentagon for Television: A Reporter's Perspective," in *Defense Beat: The Dilemmas of Defense Coverage*, ed. Loren Thompson (New York: Lexington Books, 1991), p. 87.

72. See David Oliver Relin, "A Day in the Life of the Evening News," *Scholastic Update*, September 8, 1989, p. 7.

73. Susan Dillon, "Network News: Changing as It Remains the Same," *Broadcasting*, September 24, 1990, p. 34.

74. Interview with Jonathan Wald, senior broadcast producer for domestic news, NBC Nightly News in New York, May 17, 1996.

75. See "Fresh Start for Fall in Evening News," *Broadcasting*, September 5, 1983, p. 36.

76. Interview with Fred Francis, former NBC Pentagon correspondent, April 30, 1996; and interview with Mark Brender, ABC Pentagon producer, May 3, 1996.

77. Martin, in *Defense Beat*, p. 87 (see n. 71).

78. Martin, in *Defense Beat*, p. 85 (see n. 71).

79. See Gans, *Deciding What's News*, p. 136, (see n. 57).

80. Hess, *The Washington Reporters*, p. 66 (see n. 64).

81. Martin, in *Defense Beat*, p. 83 (see n. 71).

82. See Larry McGill, András Szántó, et al., *Headlines and Sound Bites: Is That the Way It Is?* (New York: Freedom Forum Media Studies Center, 1995).

83. During the periods analyzed, there were 2,947 items or news reports compiled from 18 months of the three networks evening newscasts. There are about 500 days worth of coverage, averaging about 5 to 6 items per evening. Divided by the three networks, it averages out to 1 to 2 items per newscast.

84. The Society of Professional Journalists' Code of Ethics for 1993 was my benchmark for judging individual reports. The pertinent sections are reprinted in appendix 1.

85. See appendix 1 for a more detailed discussion of my overall approach.

86. See, for instance, Richard A. Stubbing, *The Defense Game* (New York: Harper & Rowe, 1986), p. 89.

87. For a different interpretation of the economic period during the Reagan years, see Robert L. Bartley, *The Seven Fat Years and How to Do It Again* (New York: Free Press, 1992); for a discussion of the driving strategy behind the defense buildup, see Peter Schweizer, *Victory: The Reagan Administration's Secret Strategy That Hastened the Collapse of the Soviet Union* (New York: Atlantic Monthly Press, 1994), p. 283, where he

asserts that "the buildup was designed not only to raise the relative military strength of the United States vis-à-vis the Soviet Union but also to contribute to the absolute decline in Soviet economic power."

88. See Dennis S. Ippolito, "Defense Budgets and Spending Control: The Reagan Era and Beyond," in *Defense Policy in the Reagan Administration*, ed. William P. Snyder and James Brown (Washington, D.C.: National Defense University Press, 1988), p. 176; and *The 1996 Economic Report of the President* (Washington, D.C.: GPO, 1996), tables B-74 and B-75.

89. See S. Robert Lichter, Stanley Rothman, and Linda S. Lichter, *The Media Elite: America's New Powerbrokers* (New York: Hastings House, 1986), p. 62.

90. See Ippolito, in *Defense Policy in the Reagan Administration*, p. 182 (see n. 88).

91. See, for example, David Hoffman, "GOP Senators Say Reagan Must Cut Military Spending," *Washington Post*, January 5, 1983, p. 1; and Julia Malone, "For Reagan, It's Uphill on the Hill," *Christian Science Monitor*, April 11, 1983, p. 4.

92. See, for example, George Wilson, "Planners Say Defense Budget Is Insufficient; Much More Is Needed to Meet U.S. Strategy, Senate Hearing Is Told," *Washington Post*, March 8, 1982, p. 1; Bill Peterson, "Conservative Pitches Muffle Cabinet Members' Bats," *Washington Post*, February 19, 1983, p. 7; "Arms and the Woman," *New York Times*, May 5, 1986, p. B8; and David Hoffman, "Reagan Seized Idea Shelved in '80 Race; Activists Nurtured Shift to 'Star Wars,' " *Washington Post*, March 3, 1985, p. 1.

93. See Ippolito, in *Defense Policy in the Reagan Administration*, p. 184 (see n. 88).

94. See Lee D. Olvey, James R. Golden, and Robert C. Kelly, *Weighing the Costs of Defense: The Economics of National Security* (Wayne, N.J.: Avery Publishing Group, 1984), especially pp. 98–101.

95. See Richard J. Cattani, "On Capitol Hill, a Trend toward Unity on Budget," *Christian Science Monitor*, April 5, 1983, p. 1.

96. After the Republicans took control of the House of Representatives in 1995, the 104th Congress changed the name of the House Armed Services Committee to the House National Security Committee.

97. See, for example, James Fallows, *National Defense* (New York: Random House, 1981), p. 11. He points out that, according to one analysis, in the three decades from 1950 to 1980, defense spending never increased more than three years in a row.

98. See Ippolito, in *Defense Policy in the Reagan Administration*, p. 170 (see n. 88).

99. Interview with former Secretary of Defense Caspar W. Weinberger, chairman of Forbes, Inc., May 4, 1994.

100. See Fred Reed, "Let's Reform the Military Reformers; Pentagon Critics Can't Tell a Laser from a Latrine Fan," *Washington Post*, October 11, 1987, p. H1.

101. Ernest Fitzgerald, *The High Priests of Waste* (New York: W.W. Norton & Company, 1972). See p. 326 for the reference to "The Great Plane Robbery."

102. See Edgar Ulsamer, "How the World's Largest Aircraft Revolutionizes Strategy and Technology," *Air Force Magazine*, April 1968, pp. 64–77.

103. Edgar Ulsamer in *Air Force Magazine, p. 65* (see n. 102).

104. Jay H. Smith, *Anything, Anywhere, Anytime: An Illustrated History of the Military Airlift Command, 1941–1991* (Scott Air Force Base, Ill.: Office of History, Military Airlift Command, May 1991), p. 131.

105. Smith, *Anything, Anywhere, Anytime*, p. 157 (see n. 104).

106. See the C-5 transport entry in the Air Force Almanac, *Air Force Magazine*, May 1996, p. 138.

107. See Bill Siuru and Allan Lockheed, "Lockheed: a Legacy of Speed; Aircraft," *Mechanical Engineering*, May 1990, p. 60.

108. See Christopher Georges, "Confessions of an investigative reporter," *Washington Monthly*, March 1992.

109. See Rick Atkinson and Fred Hiatt, "The Son-of-Jeep's Long Road Winds to an End; Army Started Its Journey Toward Vehicle 45 Years Ago," *Washington Post*, May 2, 1985, p. A1.

110. See "Helicopter Casualties in the Panama Invasion," *Flight International*, January 24, 1990.

111. See "Apache Safety Improves," *Flight International*, April 25, 1990.

112. See "GAO Lashes Apache Record," *Flight International*, October 10, 1990.

113. Bill Turque, "The Apache's Battle Test," *Newsweek*, March 4, 1991, p. 34.

114. See "GAO Lashes Apache Record," *Flight International*, October 10, 1990.

115. See David Bond, "Apache Readiness Problems Emerge as Threat to Longbow Development," *Aviation Week & Space Technology*, October 29, 1990, p. 79.

116. See John Boatman, "Apache '50% Mission Capable,' " *Jane's Defence Weekly*, October 13, 1990, p. 702.

117. See William V. Kennedy, *The Military and the Media* (Westport, Conn.: Praeger Publishers, 1993), p. 36.

118. Mark Hewish, "Apache a True Multi-Role Helicopter," *International Defense Review*, December 1, 1991, p. 1356.

119. See note 118.

120. See Richard Mackenzie, "Apache Attack," *Air Force Magazine*, October 1991, p. 54.

121. See Bruce Smith, "AH-64 Versatility Helps Aircraft Perform Roles in Persian Gulf War," *Aviation Week & Space Technology*, February 18, 1991, p. 54. On the GAO point, see Stephen Mraz, "Killing Tanks in Their Tracks, Apache Helicopter and A-10 Thunderbolt Destroy Iraqi Tanks," *Machine Design*, March 7, 1991, p. 12.

122. See, for example, Patrick Tyler, "Did Patriot Missiles Work? Not So Well, Scientists Say," *New York Times*, April 17, 1991, p. 11; and R. Jeffrey Smith, "Effectiveness of Patriot Missile Questioned," *Washington Post*, April 17, 1991, p. 27.

123. Theodore A. Postol, "Lessons of the Gulf War Experience with Patriot," *International Security*, vol. 16, no. 3, Winter 1991/92, p. 119.

124. Reuven Pedatzur and Theodore Postol, "The Patriot Is No Success Story; It Pays to Know the Truth on Weapon's Performance," *Defense News*, December 2, 1991, p. 24; see also, Reuven Pedatzur and Theodore Postol, "Patriot Article Fails," letters, *Defense News*, January 13, 1992, p. 18.

125. Charles Zraket, "Patriot Gave Stellar Gulf Performance," *Defense News*, December 9, 1991, p. 31; see also Charles Zraket, "Patriot Defense," letters, *Defense News*, January 20, 1992, p. 18.

126. See Daniel Golden, "Missile-blower: How MIT Professor Theodore Postol Punctured the Patriot Myth," *Boston Globe Magazine*, July 19, 1992, p. 21.

127. See Seymour M. Hersh, "Missile Wars," *New Yorker*, September 26, 1994, p. 86.

128. "Evidence Supports 9% Patriot-vs.-Scud Success Rate During War, GAO Says," *Aerospace Daily*, October 1, 1992, p. 6.

129. "Critical Patriot Report Is Withdrawn as Credibility Issues Surface," *Aerospace Daily*, October 5, 1992, p. 23.

130. Michael P. W. Stone, "The Patriot Controversy: Close the Critics' Book," *Christian Science Monitor*, October 16, 1992, p. 19.

131. See Maj. Gen. Jay Garner, USA, assistant deputy chief of staff for operations and plans, force development, "Army Stands by Patriot's Persian Gulf Performance," testimony before the House Government Operations Committee, April 7, 1992, published in *Defense Issues* (Washington, D.C.: Department of Defense), vol. 7, no. 26, 1992.

132. See, for example, John T. Correll, "Scoping the Spares Problem," *Air Force Magazine*, January 1984, pp. 82–84.

133. See, for example, J. Ronald Fox with James L. Field, *The Defense Management Challenge: Weapons Acquisition* (Boston: Harvard Business School Press, 1988), p. 31.

134. See Caspar W. Weinberger, "How the Pentagon Bought 3,500 Pliers at $3.10 Each," *Washington Post*, April 13, 1985, p. A21.

135. Interview with Caspar W. Weinberger, conducted May 4, 1994.

136. See note 133; see also, Jacques S. Gansler, *Affording Defense* (Cambridge, Mass.: MIT Press, 1989), pp. 195–196.

137. Fox with Field, *The Defense Management Challenge*, p. 32 (see n. 133).

138. Gansler, *Affording Defense*, pp. 4, 196–197 (see n. 136).

139. For a brief discussion on the effects of program instability on industry, see Fen Hampson, *Unguided Missiles: How America Buys its Weapons* (New York: W.W. Norton & Co., 1989) pp. 73–77.

140. Loren Thompson, "Buying More B-2 Bombers at Today's Bargain Prices Makes Good Fiscal Sense," *Chicago Tribune*, March 7, 1996, p. 27.

141. See note 140.

142. Secretary of the Air Force Donald Rice and Air Force Chief of Staff Gen. Merrill McPeak, testimony before the Senate Armed Services Committee, June 19, 1991.

143. See Edward Luttwak, "The Great Budget Games and the Lessons of History," chap. 9 in *The Pentagon and the Art of War* (New York: Simon & Schuster, 1985).

144. See, for example, Schuyler Foerster, "The Reagan Administration and Arms Control: Redefining the Agenda," in *Defense Policy in the Reagan Administration*, ed. William P. Snyder and James Brown (Washington, D.C.: National Defense University Press, 1988), pp. 10–15.

145. See, for example, Paul Warnke, "It's Time to Get Serious on Arms Control," *USA Today*, December 28, 1982, p. 10; and Paul Warnke, " 'Zero' May Mean Nothing," *New York Times*, January 26, 1983, p. 23.

146. See Paul Nitze, "Assuring Strategic Stability in an Era of Detente," in *Arms Control and Security: Current Issues*, ed. Wolfram Hanrieder (Boulder, Colo.: Westview Press, 1979), pp. 39–65.

147. See, for example, Charles Corddry, "Nitze May Be Tapped as Top Missile Negotiator," *Baltimore Sun*, August 19, 1981, p. 1; see also Fred Hiatt, "Richard Perle's War Against Arms Control," *Washington Post National Weekly Edition*, January 21, 1985, p. 6.

148. For a good summary of the strategic issues, see Robert W. Tucker, et al., *SDI and U.S. Foreign Policy* (Boulder, Colo.: Westview Press, 1987).

149. A quick review of Marshal V. D. Sokolovskiy's classic work, *Soviet Military Strategy* (New York: Crane, Russak & Company, 1975), will reveal in clear terms the seriousness with which the Soviets treated the idea of fighting a nuclear war. See also A. A. Sidorenko, *The Offensive*, trans. United States Air Force (Washington, D.C.: GPO, 1970).

150. See, for example, Louis Rene Beres, "Reagan Calls It MX; Actually It's M-HEX," *New York Times*, November 26, 1982, p. 27.

151. For example, in 1982 and early 1983, the US ASAT R&D program was linked to ballistic missile defense through the research underway on space-based laser weapons. Secretary of Defense Caspar Weinberger's Annual Report for FY 1984, released in February 1983, stated: "To support an anti-satellite capability beyond this decade, we are currently assessing the feasibility of space-based laser weapons." It went on to discuss the BMD components being explored, noting, "the program is structured, therefore, to sustain our understanding of this technology so that we could field an advanced and highly effective BMD quickly should the need arise." See Secretary of Defense Caspar W. Weinberger, *Annual Report to the Congress Fiscal Year 1984* (Washington, D.C.: GPO, February 1, 1983), p. 227.

152. See McGill, Szántó, et al., *Headlines and Sound Bites*, (see n. 82); see also Andrew Kohut, "A Content Analysis: International News Coverage Fits Public's Ameri-Centric Mood" (Washington, D.C.: Times Mirror Center for the People and the Press, 1995), p. 10.

153. Stephen Hess, *International News & Foreign Correspondents* (Washington, D.C.: Brookings Institution, 1996), p. 4.

154. For a good recap of developments in 1986, see T. W. McGarry, "Challenges to Combat-Zone Use of 'Weekend Warriors' Fail," *Los Angeles Times*, December 18, 1986, p. 8.

155. The Department of Defense Radio-TV Dialog for the few days before and after the Nicaraguan elections included mostly NBC transcripts. In the case of ABC and CBS coverage, the service that compiles these transcripts may have determined that the stories did not have a strong enough national security component. Fortunately, ABC transcripts of this time period were available on the Lexis-Nexis service. CBS, however, was not available on any database service going back to 1990. Nevertheless, its coverage was likely similar to that of ABC or NBC.

156. See Elaine Sciolino, "Turnover in Nicaragua; Americans Laud Result but Differ on the Moral," *New York Times*, February 27, 1990, p. 14.

157. James Fallows, *Breaking the News: How the Media Undermine American Democracy* (New York: Pantheon Books, 1996), p. 260.

158. Jack Fuller, *News Values: Ideas for an Information Age* (Chicago: University of Chicago Press, 1996), p. 30.

159. Fuller, *News Values*, p. 31 (see n. 158).

160. See, for example, Fox with Field, *The Defense Management Challenge*, p. 38 (see n. 133).

161. See, for example, Charles Mohr, "A Tough Road to the Witness Chair," *New York Times*, February 25, 1983, p. 18.

162. See, for example, George Wilson, "Pentagon Expert Warns of Cost Overruns," *Washington Post*, February 26, 1983, p. 5.

163. See, for example, *The People, The Press & Their Leaders* (Washington, D.C.: Times Mirror Center for the People and the Press, 1995), pp. 24–27, which addresses how the public, journalists themselves, and opinion leaders view media practices. While 66 percent of the public thinks journalists focus too much on misdeeds, a mere 29 percent of journalists do. See also, "Armageddon Live at 6!" *MediaCritic*, Summer 1995, pp. 53–57; and Marc Gunther, "Local TV News Diet Is Not Very Nutritious, National Survey Says," *Rocky Mountain News*, February 22, 1995, p. D5; and Fuller, *News Values*, pp. 90–91.

164. In fact, the Times Mirror Center database of Public Attentiveness to Major News Stories (1986–1995) shows that the most followed stories are indeed disasters, from the explosion of the space shuttle Challenger in January 1986 to the October 1989 San Francisco earthquake, the riots after the Rodney King verdict in May 1992, and the floods in the Midwest in July 1993, to name a few. See also note 12.

165. David Field, "Military Aircraft Crashes Down 75% in 21 Years," *Washington Times*, February 6, 1996, p. 3; see also James Kitfield, "Flying Safety: The Real Story," *Air Force Magazine*, June 1996, pp. 56–61.

166. See, for example, Rowan Scarborough, "Leftist Press? Suspicions Right; Reporters Working in Washington Acknowledge Liberal Leanings in Poll," *Washington Times*, April 18, 1996, p. 1; see also, S. Robert Lichter, Stanley Rothman, and Linda S. Lichter, *The Media Elite* (see n. 89).

167. See, for instance, Charles Tyroler II, ed., *Alerting America: The Papers of the Committee on the Present Danger* (McLean, Va.: Pergamon-Brassey's, 1984).

168. See, for example, International Institute for Strategic Studies, *The Military Balance 1983–1984* (London: International Institute for Strategic Studies, 1983). It maintains that the numerical balance had gradually shifted to the East and that the United States and the West had lost its technological superiority.

169. Epstein, *News from Nowhere*, pp. 4–5 (see n. 56).

170. Transcripts of the three major news networks' evening broadcasts were obtained from the Pentagon's Current News Analysis and Research Service. Where necessary for clarity, the network correspondent and the date of the broadcast will be noted.

171. On the CBS Evening News, June 15, 1989, Pentagon correspondent David Martin discussed the B-2 Bomber program mainly in terms of cost. On the NBC Nightly News, June 26, 1989, Mary Alice Williams focused on the charges that Northrop Corp. was overcharging for the B-2 and mismanaging the program.

172. See William B. Scott, et al., "USAF, Northrop Unveil B-2 Next-Generation Bomber," *Aviation Week & Space Technology*, November 28, 1988, pp. 20–22.

173. See John H. Cushman, "Air Force Lifts Curtain, a Bit, on Secret Plane," *New York Times*, November 11, 1988, p. 27.

174. Jay H. Goldberg, "The Technology of Stealth," *Technology Review,* May–June 1989, p. 33.

175. See note 174.

176. See, for instance, Nick Kotz, chap. 14 in *Wild Blue Yonder* (Princeton, N.J.: Princeton University Press, 1988), pp. 180–200.

177. For a detailed account of whether top Pentagon officials had orchestrated the leaks, see "Leaks of Classified National Defense Information—Stealth Aircraft," Hearings before the Investigative Subcommittee of the Committee on Armed Services, US House of Representatives, August 27, September 4, 16, and October 1, 1980 (Washington, D.C.: GPO, 1980).

178. An article by Craig Covault appeared in the January 29, 1979, issue of *Aviation Week & Space Technology* under the title, "Advanced Bomber, Missile in Definition," pp. 113–121.

179. See "Cheney Tours B-2 Plant, Gets 'Nuts and Bolts' Briefing," *Aerospace Daily*, May 30, 1989, p. 340.

180. Don Oliver, NBC Nightly News, November 22, 1988.

181. David Martin, CBS Evening News, November 22, 1988.

182. David Martin, CBS Evening News, June 15, 1989.

183. Henry Champ, NBC Nightly News, June 26, 1989.

184. See, for instance, Ralph Vartabedian, "Northrop: Will It Fly or Falter," *Military Forum*, August 1989.

185. See "Northrop to Challenge Suspension Pending Trial over Parts Fraud," *Aerospace Daily*, July 14, 1989, p. 68.

186. Rick Wartzman and Andy Pasztor, "Northrop Is Suspended from US Work, Seeks Immediate Talks to Resolve Matter," *Wall Street Journal*, July 13, 1989, p. 4.

187. Gregg Easterbrook, "Sticker Shock: The Stealth Is a Bomb," *Newsweek*, January 23, 1989, pp. 20–22.

188. Robert Ropelewski, "Stealth Bomber Schedule and Cost Reflect Risks," *Armed Forces Journal International*, February 1989, p. 28.

189. Barbara Amouyal, "Propulsion Expert Labels B-2 Flying Wing Design a Recycled Mistake," *Defense News*, March 20, 1989, p. 43.

190. Barbara Amouyal, "Top Air Force General Offers Details in Defense of Stealth Bomber," *Defense News*, May 8, 1989, p. 14.

191. Jane Callen, "B-2 Passes Top Review Despite Former USDA Protests; $70 Billion Effort Emerges," *Inside the Pentagon*, June 9, 1989, p. 1.

192. Bob Zelnick, ABC World News Tonight, July 12, 1989.

193. Bob Zelnick, ABC World News Tonight, July 12, 1989.

194. David Martin, CBS Evening News, July 12, 1989.

195. David Martin, CBS Evening News, July 15, 1989.

196. Bob Zelnick, ABC World News Tonight, July 15, 1989.

197. Fred Francis, NBC Nightly News, July 15, 1989.

198. David Martin, CBS Evening News, July 17, 1989.

199. Fred Francis, NBC Nightly News, July 17, 1989.

200. Sandy Gilmore, NBC Nightly News, July 23, 1989.

201. Jacqueline Adams, CBS Evening News, July 23, 1989.

202. Bob Zelnick, ABC World News Tonight, July 25, 1989.

203. Carole Simpson, ABC World News Tonight, August 12, 1989.

204. Bob Schieffer, CBS Evening News, August 16, 1989.

205. Mary Alice Williams, NBC Nightly News, August 25, 1989.

206. Susan Spencer, CBS Evening News, August 26, 1989.

207. The *Tyndall Report* appears monthly out of New York, except over the summer months. The September 1989 issue covered the summer statistics cited. A review of the report between December 1988, which contained November 1988 rankings, and November 1989 showed that the B-2 bomber never made the top 30 stories, except in July 1989.

208. See Bernard Randolph, "The B-2 Bomber: Technology in Transition," *Vital Speeches of the Day*, June 1, 1989, pp. 494–496.

209. George Wilson, "B-2 Becomes Hill Target," *Washington Post*, June 27, 1989, p. 7.

210. Richard Halloran, "Stealth Bomber Suffers from Secrecy, High Cost and an Unclear Purpose," *New York Times*, July 17, 1989, p. 14.

211. Molly Moore, "Air Force Counterattacks in Defense of B-2 'Stealth,' " *Washington Post*, July 13, 1989, p. 18.

212. Adela Gooch, "B-2 Bomber Essential, Cheney Tells House Panel," *Washington Post*, July 14, 1989, p. 4.

213. Richard W. Stevenson, "US Stealth Bomber Makes Test Flight Without Mishap," *New York Times*, July 18, 1989, p. 15.

214. Ralph Vartabedian, "Stealth Bomber Makes 1st Flight: Air Force Pleased by 2-Hour Test, But Cost Doubts Are Not Erased," *Los Angeles Times*, July 18, 1989, p. 1.

215. See, for instance, George Wilson, "Two Pentagon Weapons Experience Setbacks," *Washington Post*, August 17, 1989, p. 22. This piece appeared around the same time that two brief negative stories appeared on the network news programs.

216. Lynton McLain, "How the B-2 Flew Past the Prototype," *Financial Times*, September 15, 1989, p. 31.

217. See, for instance, "B-2 Bomber 'Thinks It Is a Fighter,' " *Flight International*, October 4, 1989, p. 23, and "Test Pilots Describe Performance, Handling Characteristics of B-2," *Aviation Week & Space Technology*, October 9, 1989, p. 40.

218. "B-2's Handling Qualities: Better than Expected," *Defense Daily*, October 2, 1989, p. 5.

219. "B-2 in Fourth Flight at Edwards," *Aerospace Daily*, September 22, 1989, p. 505.

220. George Wilson, "B-2 'Stealth' Bomber Has Shorter Cruising Range than Older, Cheaper B-1," *Washington Post*, October 6, 1989, p. 14.

221. Rowan Scarborough, "Air Force Defends B-2, Disputes Report," *Washington Times*, October 17, 1989, p. 4.

222. ADT Research (New York), *Tyndall Report*, November 1989, p. 6.

223. C. P. Gilmore, "B-2: What Stealth's First Flight Reveals," *Popular Science*, October 1989, p. 45.

224. See Rick Atkinson, "Stealth: From 18-inch Model to $70 Billion Muddle," *Washington Post*, October 8, 1989, p. 1; See also the following articles in the series by Rick Atkinson for the *Washington Post*: "Unraveling Stealth's 'Black World,' " October 9, 1989, p. 1; and "How Stealth's Consensus Crumbled," October 10, 1989, p. 1.

225. "What's the Stealth's Mission?" *Hartford Courant*, July 25, 1989, p. B8.

226. "The Stealth Bomber: A Wing and a Prayer," *Atlanta Constitution*, July 21, 1989, p. 18.

227. "Rethinking the Triad," *Arizona Republic*, July 23, 1989, p. C4.

228. George Will, "B-2: The Question of Soviet Intentions," *Washington Post*, July 23, 1989, p. D7.

229. Paul Walker, "Stealth Soars—in Sky and in Cost," *Boston Globe*, July 23, 1989, p. 71.

230. David Broder, "If the B-2 Is Necessary, Then Let's Pay for It," *Washington Post*, July 26, 1989, p. 25.

231. Benjamin Schemmer, "Nine Is Enough: Let's Bag This $70-Billion Bird," *Armed Forces Journal International*, August 1989, p. 5; and John G. Tower, "Don't Bag the B-2," September 1989, p. 5.

232. Bruce Van Voorst, "The Stealth Takes Wing," *Time*, July 31, 1989, p. 18.

233. Jay Mallin, "Shadow Warrior: How Radar-dodging Stealth Developed from Sawdust, Glue," *Washington Times*, September 29, 1989, p. B7.

234. Tom Squitieri, "Stealth May Not Elude New Radar," *USA Today*, October 13, 1989, p. 1; and Tom Squitieri, "Development Came as Surprise to Australians," *USA Today*, October 13, 1989, p. 10.

235. Mark Thompson, "Foe Will Be Able to Detect Stealth, Air Force Says," *Baltimore Sun*, November 2, 1989, p. 1.

236. Chris Harvey, "Nunn Links B-2 to Arms Control," *Washington Times*, July 24, 1989, p. 1.

237. Charles Krauthammer, "Stealth: The Weapon for Going It Alone," *Washington Post*, July 21, 1989, p. 21.

238. Richard Wolf, "Bomber's Backers Cite Jobs," *USA Today*, July 26, 1989, p. 4.

239. Donald Atwood, "Why Stealth Makes Sense," *New York Times*, July 27, 1989, p. 21.

240. John T. Chain, "The B-2 Stealth Bomber and the Definition of Security," *Christian Science Monitor*, July 26, 1989, p. 20.

241. ADT Research (New York), *Tyndall Report*, January 1990, p. 10.

242. Budapest Television Service, December 17, 1989, in FBIS-EEU-89-241, December 18, 1989, p. 74.

243. "Hungarian Media Report Anti-Ceausescu Protest in Romania," *Reuters* (Budapest), December 17, 1989.

244. Jim Drinkard, "US Protests Romania Crackdown," *Associated Press* (Washington), December 18, 1989.

245. Roland Prinz, "Source Reports Deaths in Romania; Unconfirmed Report of Hundreds Dead," *Associated Press* (Vienna), December 18, 1989.

246. Viorel Urma, "Two Reported Killed in Biggest Romanian Protests in Years," *Associated Press* (Vienna), December 18, 1989.

247. "Dozens Reported Killed in Romanian Protests," *Reuters* (Belgrade), December 18, 1989.

248. The following analysis is based on a review of videotapes of all the ABC, CBS, and NBC evening news reports on Romania from December 18, 1989, until January 25, 1990.

249. Bryan Brumley, "Time May Be Catching Up to Ceausescu," *Associated Press* (Washington), December 19, 1989.

250. Stanko Sajtinac, *Tanjug*, December 19, 1989, in FBIS-EEU-89-244, December 20, 1989, p. 69.

251. Viorel Urma, "More Gunfire Reported, Borders Sealed After Rioting," *Associated Press* (Vienna), December 19, 1989. See also Budapest Domestic Service, December 19, 1989, FBIS-EEU-89-242, December 19, 1989, p. 84.

252. Alison Smale, "Violence Reported Continuing in Romania; Hundreds Feared Dead," *Associated Press* (Vienna), December 19, 1989.

253. *Tanjug*, December 19, 1989, in FBIS-EEU-89-243, December 20, 1989, p. 71.

254. See note 253.

255. "Up to 2,000 Feared Killed in Romania, Bodies Packed in Lorries," *Reuters* (Vienna), December 20, 1989.

256. Alison Smale, "Chanting Protesters Demand Bodies of Dead in Romania," *Associated Press* (Vienna), December 20, 1989.

257. Erika Laszlo, "Troops Leave Timisoara as Thousands March," *UPI*, December 20, 1989.

258. "Up to 4,000 Reported Dead in Romania, Emergency Declared," *Reuters* (East Berlin), December 20, 1989.

259. "Over 30 Children Massacred by Romanian Police, Tanjug Says," *Reuters* (Belgrade), December 20, 1989. Compare to *Tanjug*, December 20, 1989, FBIS-EEU-89-244, December 21, 1989, p. 72.

260. Viorel Urma, "Romanian Security Forces Fire on Crowds in Bucharest," *Associated Press* (Vienna), December 21, 1989.

261. Alison Smale, "Security Forces Reportedly Open Fire in Romanian Capital; Deaths Reported," *Associated Press* (Vienna), December 21, 1989.

262. Erika Laszlo, "Romanian Protesters Defy Bullets as Uprising Spreads," *UPI* (Budapest), December 21, 1989.

263. Neil Fleming, "Romanian Doctor Witnessed Timisoara Killings," *UPI* (London), December 21, 1989.

264. Erika Laszlo, "Ceausescu Ousted in Romania, Fighting in Capital," *UPI* (Budapest), December 22, 1989.

265. Dusan Stojanovic, "Celebrations in Timisoara over Fall of Ceausescu," *Associated Press* (Timisoara), December 22, 1989.

266. "Romanian Television Shows Corpses Found Dumped in Mass Graves," *Reuters* (Vienna), December 22, 1989.

267. Mort Rosenblum, "Romanians Overthrow Ceausescu; Hundreds Dead in Fierce Fighting," *Associated Press* (Bucharest), December 22, 1989.

268. Peter Green, "Romanians Recount Massacre," *UPI* (Nagalyk, Hungary), December 23, 1989.

269. "Soviet Television Reports New Fighting in Timisoara," *Reuters* (Moscow), December 23, 1989.

270. "Ceausescu Loyalist Paratroops Launch Night Attack on Timisoara," *Reuters* (Belgrade), December 23, 1989.

271. Dusan Stojanovic, "Government Calls Cease-Fire, Halt Civilian Vigilantes," *Associated Press* (Bucharest), December 24, 1989.

272. See note 267.

273. See, for instance, Mort Rosenblum, "Government Calls for Cease-Fire, Snipers Paralyze Capital," *Associated Press*, December 24, 1989. Rosenblum writes that "Ceausescu's security forces are elite, heavily armed police who are essentially fighting for their lives."

274. Viorel Urma, "Purged Communist Party Official Holds the Limelight," *Associated Press* (Vienna), December 25, 1989.

275. I outlined this point in much greater detail in a longer study. See Stephen P. Aubin, "Portrait of a Romanian Revolution: Massacres, Monsters, and Media Manipulation," *Media Studies Project Occasional Paper* (Washington, D.C.: Woodrow Wilson International Center for Scholars, 1992).

276. Mary Battiata, "Christmas Dawn Brings New Battles; Army Units, Ceausescu Loyalists Exchange Gunfire in Timisoara," *Washington Post*, December 26, 1989, p. 1.

277. See Michel Castex, "Vous avez dit: 'Genocide'?" chap. 2 in *Un mensonge gros comme le siècle: Roumanie, histoire d'une manipulation* (Paris: Albin Michel, 1990), pp. 57–63.

278. For a discussion of the concept and literature on genocide, see Frank Chalk and Kurt Jonassohn, *The History and Sociology of Genocide* (New Haven, Conn.: Yale University Press, 1990), pp. 3–51.

279. Chalk and Jonassohn, *The History and Sociology of Genocide*, p. 23.

280. Budapest Domestic Service, December 24, 1989, in FBIS-EEU-89-246, December 26, 1989, p. 76.

281. *Agence France-Presse*, December 25, 1989, in FBIS-EEU-89-246, December 26, 1989, p. 76.

282. Nicolas Miletitch, *Agence France-Presse* (Timisoara), December 30, 1989, in FBIS-EEU-90-001, January 2, 1990, p. 60.

283. *Tanjug*, January 27, 1990, in FBIS-EEU-90-230, January 29, 1990, p. 105.

284. Bucharest Domestic Service, February 20, 1990, in FBIS-EEU-90-036, February 22, 1990, p. 75.

285. *Rompres*, March 24, 1990, in FBIS-EEU-90-059, March 27, 1990, p. 57.

286. *Agence France-Presse*, March 2, 1990, in FBIS-EEU-90-043, March 5, 1990, p. 60.

287. *Rompres*, March 13, 1990, in FBIS-EEU-90-051, March 15, 1990, p. 53.

288. See Jean-Claude Guillebaud, "Roumanie: qui a menti," *Le Nouvel Observateur*, April 5–11, 1990, p. 46; and David Funderburk, "Gorbachev nodded approval for ouster of Romanian tyrant Ceausescu," *Freedom Bulletin* (International Freedom Foundation), vol. 4, no. 4, April 1990, p. 6.

289. Patrick Worsnip, "Little Known East European Agencies Scoop Romania Story," *Reuters*, December 23, 1989, BC Cycle.

290. See Michel Castex, *Un mensonge gros comme le siècle: Roumanie, histoire d'une manipulation* (Paris: Albin Michel, 1990).

291. See, for instance, Blaine Hardon, "Anti-Jewish Bias Rising in Poland," *Washington Post*, July 16, 1990, p. 1; Judy Dempsey, "The Past Casts Its Long Shadows," *Financial Times*, September 6, 1990, p. 15; "Pogroms, Skinheads and Empire," *Boston Globe*, February 10, 1990, p. 22; Mark Nelson, "As Shroud of Secrecy Lifts in East Europe, Smog Shroud Emerges," *Wall Street Journal*, March 1, 1990, p. 1; and Celestine Bohlen, "Through a Thick Veil of Soot, Romanian City Faces Future," *New York Times*, March 5, 1990, p. 1.

292. See, for instance, Todd Gitlin, "Conflicting Security Paradigms: A Contest for the Press to Cover," *Deadline*, March/April 1990, pp. 12–16. (*Deadline* is the bulletin of New York University's Center for War, Peace, and the News Media.)

293. Robert Ivie, "A New Cold War Parable in the Post–Cold War Press," *Deadline*, January/February 1990, p. 1.

294. Castex, *Un mensonge gros comme le siècle*, pp. 13–20 (see n. 290).

295. Ignacio Ramonet, "Télévision nécrophile," *Le Monde Diplomatique*, March 1990, p. 3.

296. "Tiananmen: What Did Happen?" *Asiaweek*, December 22–29, 1989, p. 30.

297. See Olivier Weber, "La révolution confisquée," *Le Point*, April 30, 1990, p. 46, and Alain Louyot, "La révolution a été confisquée," *L'Express*, March 23, 1990, p. 10.

298. See Stanculescu's discussion of the former Securitate cadres in *Romania Libera*, February 21, 1990, in FBIS-EEU-90-054, March 20, 1990, p. 67.

299. "Securitate Man Comes to Vienna as Diplomat," *Kurier* (Vienna), January 21, 1990, in FBIS-EEU-90-017, January 25, 1990, p. 79.

300. Vincent Hugeux, "Roumanie: la grande désillusion," *L'Express*, May 18, 1990, p. 51; see also, Gabriel Topliceanu, "Crypto-Communism: Public Enemy No. 1," *Dreptatea*, April 21, 1990, in FBIS-EEU-90-086, May 3, 1990, p. 52.

301. *Agence France-Presse*, January 31, 1990, in FBIS-EEU-90-021, January 31, 1990, p. 58.

302. Christopher Booker, "Iliescu Block on Free Media Investigated," *Daily Telegraph* (London), February 12, 1990, in FBIS-EEU-90-032, February 15, 1990, p. 54.

303. Bernard Estrade, "Iliescu Urges Creation of Antifascist Movement," *Agence France-Presse*, February 23, 1990, in FBIS-EEU-90-038, February 26, 1990, p. 73.

304. Bucharest Domestic Service, March 12, 1990, in FBIS-EEU-90-050, March 14, 1990.

305. Editorial, *Dreptatea*, April 12, 1990, in FBIS-EEU-90-077, April 20, 1990, p. 59.

306. See Olivier Weber, "Roumanie: le passé revient en force," *Le Point*, June 18, 1990, p. 41.

307. Chuck Sudetic, "Freed Romanians Tell of Beatings by Police," *New York Times*, June 22, 1990, p. 8.

308. Jean-Claude Guillebaud in *Le Nouvel Observateur*, p. 48 (see n. 288).

309. Ilie Stefanescu, "A Wise Despot," *Dreptatea*, April 26, 1990, in FBIS-EEU-90-094, May 15, 1990, p. 60.

310. Sylvie Kauffmann, *Le Monde*, May 17, 1990, in FBIS-EEU-90-097, May 18, 1990, p. 48.

311. Chuck Sudetic, "Timisoara Protests Again, but Against New Rulers," *New York Times*, December 17, 1990, p. 10.

312. See, for example, John J. Fialka, *Hotel Warriors: Covering the Gulf War* (Washington, D.C.: Woodrow Wilson Center Press, 1992); see also Hedrick Smith, ed., *The Media and the Gulf War: The Press and Democracy in Wartime* (Washington, D.C.: Seven Locks Press, 1992), especially the section titled, "What We Missed," pp. 194–220.

313. Fred Francis, speech at the National Press Club, Washington, D.C., during a conference titled "Preparing Journalists to Cover the Next War (If There Is One)," sponsored by Boston University's Center for Defense Journalism, September 26, 1991.

314. See note 313.

315. See, for example, John R. MacArthur, *Second Front: Censorship and Propaganda in the Gulf War* (Los Angeles: University of California Press, 1992); see also, Jason DeParle, "After the War; Long Series of Military Decisions Led to Gulf War News Censorship," *New York Times*, May 5, 1991, p. 1, and Jason DeParle, "After the War; Keeping the News in Step: Are the Pentagon's Gulf War Rules Here to Stay?" *New York Times*, May 6, 1991, p. 9.

316. See Fialka, *Hotel Warriors*, chaps. 2–4 (see n. 312).

317. See, for instance, Philip M. Taylor, *The War and the Media: Propaganda and Persuasion in the Gulf War* (New York: Manchester University Press, 1992).

318. See Fred Hoffman, "The Panama Press Pool Deployment: A Critique," in *Newsmen and National Defense: Is Conflict Inevitable?* ed. Lloyd J. Matthews (New York: Brassey's (US), 1991), pp. 91–109.

319. See Perry M. Smith, *How CNN Fought the War: A View from the Inside* (New York: Carol Publishing Group, 1991).

320. See, for example, Daniel Yankelovich and I. M. Destler, eds., *Beyond the Beltway: Engaging the Public in U.S. Foreign Policy* (New York: W.W. Norton & Co., 1994); and Kathleen Hall Jamieson and Karlyn Kohrs Campbell, *The Interplay of Influence: News, Advertising, Politics and the Mass Media* (Belmont, Calif.: Wadsworth Publishing, 1992).

321. Yankelovich and Destler, *Beyond the Beltway*, pp. 48–51 (see n. 320).

322. See, for example, Simon Serfaty, ed., *The Media and Foreign Policy* (New York: St. Martin's Press, 1991); and Patrick O'Heffernan, *Mass Media and American Foreign Policy* (Norwood, N.J.: Ablex Publishing, 1991).

323. Interview with former Assistant Secretary of Defense for Public Affairs Robert Sims, April 18, 1994.

324. Interview with Herbert J. Coleman, chief of Current News Analysis and Research Service, April 14, 1994.

325. Memorandum from Herbert J. Coleman, SAF/AAR, to Robert J. McCormick, SAF/AA, October 6, 1988.

326. In 1998, the "Supplement" was converted to an electronic publication, available to military users from the Internet.

327. Coleman memorandum, October 6, 1988 (see n. 325).

328. Coleman memorandum, October 6, 1988 (see n. 325).

329. Coleman memorandum, October 6, 1988 (see n. 325).

330. For a fuller discussion of the implications of this transfer, see appendix 2.

331. Coleman interview, April 14, 1994 (see n. 324).

332. Coleman interview, April 14, 1994 (see n. 324).

333. Institute for Defense Analyses, "Assessment of Current News Analysis and Research Service (CNARS) Early Bird and Early Bird Supplement," prepared for the Assistant Secretary of Defense for Public Affairs (American Forces Information Service), October 1991, p. S3.

334. Harry Zubkoff, memorandum to Mr. Crittenden, "Subject: Radio-TV Defense Dialog—Background," March 17, 1981. The conclusion in this memo is supported by polling data. In fact, according to the Roper Organization, 1963 was the first year that the number of Americans getting their news only from television ranked higher than those getting their news only from newspapers, by 23 percent to 21 percent. See the Roper Organization, "America's Watching: Public Attitudes Toward Television," for trend data (see n. 19).

335. Zubkoff memorandum, March 17, 1981 (see n. 334).

336. Zubkoff memorandum, March 17, 1981 (see n. 334).

337. Zubkoff memorandum, March 17, 1981 (see n. 334).

338. Interview with Harry Zubkoff, July 15, 1993.

339. William Proxmire, letter to the Honorable Melvin Laird, June 10, 1971.

340. Daniel Z. Henkin, letter to the Honorable William Proxmire, June 22, 1971.

341. Zubkoff interview, July 15, 1993.

342. Jared Stout, "News Taped for Pentagon," *Washington Star*, June 11, 1971.

343. Thomas Collins, "News Monitoring: 'Snooping' or Not?" *Long Island Newsday*, July 14, 1971.

344. See Rearden, *History of the Office of the Secretary of Defense*, pp. 80–81 (see n. 17). See also Office of the Historian, Office of the Secretary of Defense, unpublished background paper titled, "Defense Information Services Activity," January 22, 1987, pp. 1–2.

345. Interview with Capt. Michael Doubleday, USN, director for Defense Information from 1993–1994, Office of the Assistant to the Secretary of Defense for Public Affairs, April 27, 1994.

346. Interview with Miguel Monteverde, former director for Defense Information, May 6, 1994.

347. Interview with David H. Burpee, former director for Defense Information, 1991–1993, April 26, 1994.

348. Doubleday interview, April 27, 1994 (see n. 345).

349. Monteverde interview, May 6, 1994 (see n. 346).

350. Doubleday interview, April 27, 1994 (see n. 345).

351. Monteverde interview, May 6, 1994 (see n. 346).

352. Michael R. Beschloss, *Presidents, Television and Foreign Crises* (Washington, D.C.: Annenberg Washington Program, 1993), p. 6.

353. Hedrick Smith, *The Power Game: How Washington Works* (New York: Ballantine Books, 1988), pp. 160, 162.

354. Interview with Robert B. Sims, former assistant secretary of defense for Public Affairs, April 18, 1994.

355. Interview with former Secretary of Defense Caspar W. Weinberger, May 4, 1994.

356. Remarks of Daniel Z. Henkin, Military-Media Conference, Naval War College, Newport, R.I., November 29, 1978.

357. Weinberger interview, May 4, 1994 (see n. 355).

358. Hedrick Smith, *The Power Game*, p. 163 (see n. 353).

359. Hedrick Smith, *The Power Game*, p. 163 (see n. 353).

360. Weinberger interview, May 4, 1994 (see n. 355).

361. Weinberger interview, May 4, 1994 (see n. 355).

362. Weinberger interview, May 4, 1994 (see n. 355).

363. Robert B. Sims, *The Pentagon Reporters* (Washington, D.C.: National Defense University Press, 1983), pp. 109–110.

364. See Lichter, Rothman, and Lichter, *The Media Elite* (see n. 89).

365. See, for example, Rowan Scarborough, "Leftist Press? Suspicions Right: Reporters Working in Washington Acknowledge Liberal Leanings in Poll," *Washington Times*, April 18, 1996, p. 1.

366. Stephen Hess, *The Washington Reporters*, p. 87 (see n. 64).

367. Lichter, Rothman, and Lichter, *The Media Elite*, pp. 40–42 (see n. 89).

368. See David Weaver and G. Cleveland Wilhoit, *The American Journalist in the 1990s* (Arlington, Va.: Freedom Forum, 1992).

369. See, for example, Hedrick Smith, "The National Mood," *New York Times*, May 29, 1981, p. 13.

370. See Penn Kimball, *Downsizing the News*, p. 122 (see n. 54).

371. Kimball, *Downsizing the News*, p. 123 (see n. 54).

372. The main contractor has been a company called Radio-TV Reports. It is now called RTV and is a subsidiary of Competitive Media. The current Defense Department contract has no specific guidelines other than "defense–related news." However, subjects to be transcribed were determined early on, including Department of Defense-related news, intelligence news, foreign policy news, reports on weapons, military operations, space news with military dimensions, and news related to senior defense officials, among other areas. The same person prepared the "Radio-TV Dialog" for 15 years, including all of the years covered in this study. The preceding was based on an interview with senior account executive Renee Robertson on May 22, 1996. Robertson has been with RTV since the 1970s. An interview was also conducted with Denise Brown of the Pentagon's Current News Analysis and Research Service on the same day. She is currently the liaison to RTV and maintains the contract.

373. For an historical perspective on these standards, see Mitchell Stephens, "The Journalistic Method," chap. 13 in *A History of News* (New York: Penguin Books, 1988), pp. 226–270.

374. Reprinted by permission. The Society of Professional Journalists' "Code of Ethics" appeared in full in the *Quill*, November 1993.

375. Interview with Harry Zubkoff, June 4, 1993.

376. Interview with Harry Zubkoff, June 4, 1993. See also Steven L. Rearden, *History of the Office of the Secretary of Defense*, pp. 410–422 (see n. 17).

377. Memorandum from Research and Analysis Division, SAFAA, June 23, 1958, titled "History of 'Current News' (1949–58)."

378. Memorandum from Research and Analysis Division, June 23, 1958 (see n. 377).

379. Interview with Harry Zubkoff, June 4, 1993.

380. Memorandum from Research and Analysis Division, June 23, 1958 (see n. 377).

381. Memorandum from Research and Analysis Division, June 23, 1958 (see n. 377).

382. Memorandum from Research and Analysis Division, June 23, 1958 (see n. 377).

383. Richard Scheinin, "Harry Zubkoff and His Pentagon Papers," *Washington Journalism Review*, March 1985, p. 1.

384. Interview with Harry Zubkoff, June 4, 1993.

385. Interview with Harry Zubkoff, June 4, 1993.

386. Interview with Harry Zubkoff, June 4, 1993.

387. Memorandum from Deputy Secretary of Defense Roswell Gilpatric, "Department of Defense News Analysis and Clipping Service in the Washington Area," December 12, 1963.

388. Department of Defense Directive, Number 5160.52, March 18, 1965, states that "the Secretary of the Air Force, or his designee, shall manage, conduct, and exercise supervisory control over the DoD News Clipping and Analysis Service (N/CAS), including certain research and reference services."

389. Two memoranda serve as examples of these efforts to defend his operation. See Harry Zubkoff, Memorandum for the Administrative Assistant to the Secretary of the Air Force, "Subject: SAFAAR Staffing," undated but references indicate year is 1979; and Harry Zubkoff, Memorandum for Mr. Nelson, "Subject: Impact of Projected Reductions," July 28, 1977.

390. While the public affairs aspect of the Department of Defense is beyond the scope of this project, the author has reviewed hundreds of news clips from the Pentagon dating back to 1949. There is ample evidence of the struggle between the military services public affairs and the attempts to centralize contact with the media by the Office of the Secretary of Defense. These struggles crossed Republican and Democratic administrations alike. For example, both the Eisenhower administration and the Kennedy administration were plagued by charges of "news management." Rep. John Moss (D-CA), chairman of the House Subcommittee on Government Information, continually spoke out against the information policies of both administrations. Another example of the controversy surrounding Pentagon public relations and information policies is the famous CBS documentary of 1971, "The Selling of the Pentagon."

391. See Molly Moore, "Pentagon News Digest Under New Management," *Washington Post*, October 21, 1988, p. 21, and Richard Halloran and David Binder, "Controlling the News," *New York Times*, October 5, 1988, p. 6.

392. See Peggy Roth, "Pentagon's Early Bird Goes On-Line, *Defense News*, November 22, 1993, p. 40.

393. Interview with Herbert Coleman, April 14, 1994.

394. Kathleen deLaski was one of the few occupants of this position not to have the rank of assistant secretary. She was actually titled assistant to the secretary of defense for Public Affairs. When then Secretary of Defense Les Aspin entered office and reorganized his policy-making operation, he downgraded Public Affairs in order to comply with the fixed number of assistant secretaries of defense specified by law. While such a change may seem insignificant, in the hierarchical world of the Pentagon, there is a significant difference in terms of rank and status between an "Assistant to the Secretary" and an "Assistant Secretary of Defense."

395. Interview with Harry Zubkoff, April 25, 1994.

396. Warren S. Lacy, Colonel, USA, Assistant Director, AFIS, AFPPS, Memorandum for Chief, Current News Analysis and Research Branch, "Subject: Early Bird Support of Office of Secretary of Defense," April 14, 1994.

397. See Tony Capaccio, "Pentagon's 'Early Bird' to 'Fine Tune' News Content, *Defense Week*, April 25, 1994, p. 1.

398. See Rod Dreher, "Pentagon Scurries to Disavow Memo on News Clips," *Washington Times*, April 26, 1994, p. 3.

References

Adatto, Kiku. "Sound Bite Democracy: Network Evening News Presidential Campaign Coverage, 1968 and 1988," Research Paper R-2, Joan Shorenstein Barone Center on the Press, Politics and Public Policy, June 1990.

Allen, Thomas B., F. Clifton Berry, and Norman Polmar. *CNN: War in the Gulf*. Atlanta, Ga.: Turner Publishing, 1991.

Altschull, J. Herbert. *Agents of Power: The Media and Public Policy*. White Plains, N.Y.: Longman Publishers, 1995.

Ang, Ien. *Desperately Seeking the Audience*. New York: Routledge, 1991.

Arnett, Peter. *Live from the Battlefield*. New York: Simon & Schuster, 1994.

Auletta, Ken. *Three Blind Mice: How the Networks Lost Their Way*. New York: Random House, 1991.

Aylesworth, Thomas G. *Great Moments in Television*. New York: Bison Books, 1987.

Barrett, Marvin, ed. *Broadcast Journalism: The Eighth Alfred I. Dupont/Columbia University Survey*. New York: Everest House, 1982.

Bartley, Robert L. *The Seven Fat Years and How to Do It Again*. New York: Free Press, 1992.

Berger, Arthur Asa. *Media Analysis Techniques*. Newbury Park, Calif.: Sage Publications, 1991.

Bernardo, C. Joseph, and Eugene H. Bacon. *American Military Policy: Its Development Since 1775*. Harrisburg, Pa.: Stackpole Co., 1961.

Binnendijk, Hans, ed. *Strategic Defense in the 21st Century*, Center for the Study of Foreign Affairs, Foreign Service Institute, U.S. Department of State. Washington, D.C.: GPO, 1986.

Blechman, Barry M., and Victor A. Utgoff. *Fiscal and Economic Implications of Strategic Defenses*. Washington, D.C.: Johns Hopkins Foreign Policy Institute, 1986.

Bliss, Edward Jr. *Now the News: The History of Broadcast Journalism*. New York: Columbia University Press, 1991.

Block, Alex Ben. *Outfoxed: The Inside Story of America's Fourth Television Network*. New York: St. Martin's Press, 1990.

Bogart, Leo. *The Age of Television*. New York: Frederick Unger Publishing, 1972.

Bozell, L. Brent III, and Brent H. Baker. *And That's the Way It Is(n't): A Reference Guide to Media Bias*. Alexandria, Va.: Media Research Center, 1990.

Braestrup, Peter. *Battle Lines: Report of the Twentieth Century Fund Task Force on the Military and the Media*. New York: Priority Press Publications, 1985.

Braun, Aurel. *Romanian Foreign Policy Since 1965*. New York: Praeger Publishers, 1978, p. 88.

Broad, William J. *Star Warriors: A Penetrating Look into the Lives of the Young Scientists Behind Our Space Age Weaponry*. New York: Simon & Schuster, 1985.

————. *Teller's War*. New York: Simon & Schuster, 1992.

Brown, Harold, ed. *The Strategic Defense Initiative: Shield or Snare?* Washington, D.C.: Johns Hopkins Foreign Policy Institute, 1987.

Brzezinski, Zbigniew, ed. *Promise or Peril: The Strategic Defense Initiative*. Washington, D.C.: Ethics and Public Policy Center, 1986.

Buhl, Dieter. "Window to the West: How Television from the Federal Republic Influenced Events in East Germany," Discussion Paper D-5, Joan Shorenstein Barone Center on the Press, Politics and Public Policy, 1991.

Bulkeley, Rip, and Graham Spinardi. *Space Weapons: Deterrence or Delusion?* Totowa, N.J.: Barnes & Noble Books, 1986.

Burns, Eric. *Broadcast Blues*. New York: HarperCollins Publishers, 1993.

Burns, James MacGregor. *The Vineyard of Liberty*. New York: Vintage Books, 1982.

Campbell, Richard. *60 Minutes and the News: A Mythology for Middle America*. Urbana, Ill.: University of Illinois Press, 1991.

Carlucci, Secretary of Defense Frank C. *Annual Report to the Congress Fiscal Year 1989*. Washington, D.C.: GPO, February 18, 1988.

Cary, James W., ed. *Media, Myths, and Narratives: Television and the Press*. Newbury Park, Calif.: Sage Publications, 1988.

Castex, Michel. *Un mensonge gros comme le siècle: Roumanie, histoire d'une manipulation*. Paris: Albin Michel, 1990.

Chalk, Frank, and Kurt Jonassohn. *The History and Sociology of Genocide*. New Haven, Conn.: Yale University Press, 1990.

Charlton, Michael. *From Deterrence to Defense: The Inside Story of Strategic Policy*. Cambridge, Mass.: Harvard University Press, 1987.

Clurman, Richard M. *Beyond Malice: The Media's Years of Reckoning*. Markham, Ontario: Penguin Books Canada Limited, 1990.

Cook, Philip S., Douglas Gomery, and Lawrence W. Lichty. *The Future of News: Television, Newspapers, Wire Services, Newsmagazines*. Washington, D.C.: Woodrow Wilson Center Press, 1992.

Daalder, Ivo H. *The SDI Challenge to Europe*. Cambridge, Mass.: Ballinger Publishing, 1987.

Dallmeyer, Dorinda G., ed. *The Strategic Defense Initiative: New Perspectives on Deterrence*. Boulder, Colo.: Westview Press, 1986.

Davis, Vincent. "Presidential Politics and the Policy Process: The President's Key Players," in *Presidential Leadership and National Security: Style, Institutions and Politics*, ed. Sam C. Sarkesian. Boulder, Colo.: Westview Press, Inc., 1984.

Dennis, Everette, et al. *The Media at War: The Press and the Persian Gulf Conflict*. New York: Gannett Foundation, 1991.

Desmond, Robert W. *Crisis and Conflict: World News Reporting between Two World Wars*

1920–1940. Iowa City: University of Iowa Press, 1982.

———. *The Information Process: World News Reporting to the Twentieth Century.* Iowa City: University of Iowa Press, 1978.

———. *Tides of War: World News Reporting 1931–1945.* Iowa City: University of Iowa Press, 1984.

———. *Windows on the World: The Information Process in a Changing Society 1900–1920.* Iowa City: University of Iowa Press, 1980.

Destler, I. M. "The National Security System: Structure and Process," in *U.S. National Security: A Framework for Analysis.* Eds. Daniel J. Kaufman, Jeffrey S. McKitrick and Thomas J. Leney. Lexington, Mass.: Lexington Books, 1985.

Diamond, Edwin. *The Media Show: The Changing Face of the News, 1985–1990.* Cambridge: The MIT Press, 1991.

Donaldson, Sam. *Hold On, Mr. President!* New York: Random House, 1987.

Donovan, Robert J., and Ray Scherer. *Unsilent Revolution: Television News and American Public Life.* New York: Cambridge University Press, 1992.

Emery, Michael, and Edwin Emery. *The Press and America: An Interpretive History of the Mass Media.* Englewood Cliffs, N.J.: Prentice Hall, 1992.

Epstein, Edward Jay. *News from Nowhere.* New York: Vintage Books, 1973.

Fallows, James. *Breaking the News: How the Media Undermine American Democracy.* New York: Pantheon Books, 1996.

———. *National Defense.* New York: Random House, 1981.

Fialka, John J. *Hotel Warriors: Covering the Gulf War.* Washington, D.C.: Woodrow Wilson Center Press, 1992.

Filoreto, Carl, with Lynn Setzer. *Working in TV News: The Insider's Guide.* Memphis, Tenn: Memphis Publishing, 1993.

Fink, Conrad C. *Inside the Media.* New York: Longman, 1990.

Fitzgerald, Ernest. *The High Priests of Waste.* New York: W.W. Norton & Company, 1972.

———. *The Pentagonists: An Insider's View of Waste, Mismanagement, and Fraud in Defense Spending.* Boston: Houghton Mifflin, 1989.

Fitzwater, Marlin. *Call the Briefing! Reagan and Bush, Sam and Helen: A Decade with Presidents and the Press.* New York: Times Books, 1995.

Fowles, Jib. *Why Viewers Watch: A Reappraisal of Television's Effects.* Newbury Park, Calif.: Sage Publications, 1992.

Fox, Ronald J., with James L. Field. *The Defense Management Challenge: Weapons Acquisition.* Boston: Harvard Business School Press, 1988.

Frank, Reuven. *Out of Thin Air: The Brief Wonderful Life of Network News.* New York: Simon & Schuster, 1991.

Fuller, Jack. *News Values: Ideas for an Information Age.* Chicago: University of Chicago Press, 1996.

Gans, Herbert J. *Deciding What's News: A Study of CBS Evening News, NBC Nightly News, Newsweek and Time.* New York: Vintage Books, 1979.

Gansler, Jacques S. *Affording Defense.* Cambridge, Mass.: MIT Press, 1989.

———. *The Defense Industry.* Cambridge, Mass.: MIT Press, 1980.

Garthoff, Raymond. *Policy versus the Law: The Reinterpretation of the ABM Treaty.* Washington, D.C.: Brookings Institution, 1987.

Gilder, George. *Life after Television.* Knoxville, Tenn.: Whittle Direct Books, 1990.

Godson, Dean. *SDI: Has America Told Her Story to the World?* Washington, D.C.: Pergamon-Brassey's for the Institute for Foreign Policy Analysis, 1987.

Goldberg, Robert, and Gerald Jay Goldberg. *Anchors: Brokaw, Jennings, Rather and the Evening News*. New York: Birch Lane Press, 1990.

Goldstein, Norm. *The History of Television*. Surrey, England: Portland House, 1991.

Graber, Doris A. *Mass Media and American Politics*. Washington, D.C.: Congressional Quarterly Press, 1989.

———, ed. *Media Power in Politics*. Washington, D.C.: Congressional Quarterly Press, 1994.

Graham, Daniel O. *Case for Space Defense*. Louisville, Ky.: Publishers Press, 1986.

———. *Confessions of a Cold Warrior*. Fairfax, Va.: Preview Press, 1995.

Gray, Colin S. *American Military Space Policy: Information Systems, Weapon Systems and Arms Control*. Cambridge, Mass.: Abt Books, 1982.

Grossman, Michael, and Martha Kumar. *Portraying the President: The White House and the News Media*. Baltimore, Md.: Johns Hopkins University Press, 1981.

Gunther, Marc. *The House that Roone Built: The Inside Story of ABC News*. Boston: Little, Brown, and Company, 1994.

Hale, Julian. *Ceausescu's Romania: A Political Documentary*. London: George G. Harrap & Co., 1971.

Hallin, Daniel. "Sound Bite News: Television Coverage of Elections, 1968–1988," Occasional Paper, Media Studies Project, Woodrow Wilson International Center for Scholars, 1991.

Hampson, Fen. *Unguided Missiles: How America Buys Its Weapons*. New York: W.W. Norton & Co., 1989.

Hanrieder, Wolfram, ed. *Arms Control and Security: Current Issues*. Boulder, Colo.: Westview Press, 1979.

Hess, Stephen. *International News & Foreign Correspondents*. Washington, D.C.: Brookings Institution, 1996.

———. *The Washington Reporters*. Washington, D.C.: Brookings Institution, 1981.

Hirsch, Alan. *Talking Heads: Political Talk Shows and Their Star Pundits*. New York: St. Martin's Press, 1991.

Hoeber, Francis P., and William Schneider Jr., eds. *Arms, Men, and Military Budgets*. New York: Crane, Russak & Company, 1977.

Iorga, Nicolae. *A History of Roumania: Land, People, Civilisation*. Trans. Joseph McCabe. London: T. Fisher Unwin, Adelphi Terrace, 1925.

Iyengar, Shanto. *Is Anyone Responsible? How Television Frames Political Issues*. Chicago: University of Chicago Press, 1991.

Iyengar, Shanto, and Donald R. Kinder. *News That Matters: Television and American Opinion*. Chicago: University of Chicago Press, 1987.

Jamieson, Kathleen Hall, and Karlyn Kohrs Campbell. *The Interplay of Influence: News, Advertising, Politics and the Mass Media*. Belmont, Calif.: Wadsworth Publishing, 1988.

Kalb, Marvin. *A Conversation with Dan Rather*. Cambridge, Mass.: Joan Shorenstein Barone Center on the Press, Politics and Public Policy, 1990.

Keane, John. *The Media and Democracy*. Cambridge, Mass.: Policy Press, 1991.

Kellner, Douglas. *Television and the Crisis of Democracy*. Boulder, Colo.: Westview Press, 1990.

Kelly, Orr. *King of the Killing Zone: The Story of the M1, America's Super Tank*. New York: Berkley Books, 1989.

Kennedy, William V. *The Military and the Media: Why the Press Cannot Be Trusted to*

Cover a War. Westport, Conn.: Praeger Publishers, 1993.

Kimball, Penn. *Downsizing the News: Network Cutbacks in the Nation's Capital.* Washington, D.C.: Woodrow Wilson Center Press, 1994.

Krulak, Victor H. *Organization for National Security: A Study.* Washington, D.C.: United States Strategic Institute, 1983.

Kurtz, Howard. *The Media Circus.* New York: Random House, 1993.

Leonard, Bill. *In the Storm of the Eye: A Lifetime at CBS.* New York: G.P. Putnam's Sons, 1987.

Lichter, S. Robert, Stanley Rothman, and Linda S. Lichter. *The Media Elite: America's New Powerbrokers.* New York: Hastings House, 1986.

———. *Watching America.* New York: Prentice Hall Press, 1991.

Logsdon, John M. *The Decision to Go to the Moon: Project Apollo and the National Interest.* Cambridge, Mass.: MIT Press, 1970.

Luttwak, Edward. *The Pentagon and the Art of War.* New York: Simon & Schuster, 1985.

MacArthur, John R. *Second Front: Censorship and Propaganda in the Gulf War.* Los Angeles, Calif.: University of California Press, 1992.

Marc, David, and Robert J. Thompson. *Prime Time Prime Movers.* Boston: Little, Brown and Co., 1992.

Matthews, Lloyd J., ed. *Newsmen and National Defense: Is Conflict Inevitable?* New York: Brassey's (U.S.), 1991.

Mazzocco, Dennis W. *Networks of Power: Corporate TV's Threat to Democracy.* Boston: South End Press, 1994.

McGill, Larry, András Szántó, et al. *Headlines and Sound Bites: Is That the Way It Is?* New York: Freedom Forum Media Studies Center, 1995.

McGinniss, Joe. *Selling of the President.* New York: Penguin Books, 1988.

McLuhan, Marshall. *Understanding Media: The Extensions of Man.* New York: Penguin Books, 1964.

McLuhan, Marshall, and Quenten Fiore. *The Medium is the Massage.* New York: Bantam Books, 1967.

———. *War and Peace in the Global Village.* New York: Touchstone, 1968.

McLuhan, Marshall, and Eric McLuhan. *Laws of Media: The New Science.* Toronto: University of Toronto Press, 1988.

Meyrowitz, Joshua. *No Sense of Place: The Impact of Electronic Media on Social Behavior.* New York: Oxford University Press, 1985.

Miller, Jonathan. *McLuhan.* London: Wm. Collins & Co. Ltd, 1971.

Miller, Steven E., and Stephen Van Evera, eds. *The Star Wars Controversy.* Princeton, N.J.: Princeton University Press, 1986.

Minow, Newton N. *How Vast the Wasteland Now?* New York: Gannett Foundation Media Center, 1991.

Mullins, James P. *The Defense Matrix: National Preparedness and the Military-Industrial Complex.* San Diego, Calif.: Avant Books, 1986.

Neuman, Johanna. *Lights, Camera, War: Is Media Technology Driving International Politics?* New York: St. Martin's Press, 1996.

Neuman, W. Russell, Marion R. Just, and Ann N. Crigler. *Common Knowledge: News and the Construction of Political Meaning.* Chicago: University of Chicago Press, 1992.

O'Heffernan, Patrick. *Mass Media and American Foreign Policy.* Norwood, N.J.: Ablex Publishing, 1991.

Olvey, Lee D., James R. Golden, and Robert C. Kelly. *Weighing the Costs of Defense: The*

Economics of National Security. Wayne, N.J.: Avery Publishing Group, 1984.

Pacepa, Ion Mihai. *Red Horizons: Chronicles of a Communist Spy Chief*. Washington, D.C.: Regnery Gateway, 1987.

Parrott, Bruce. *The Soviet Union and Ballistic Missile Defense*. Boulder, Colo.: Westview Press for the Foreign Policy Institute, Johns Hopkins University, 1987.

Payne, Keith. *Strategic Defense: "Star Wars" in Perspective*. Lanham, Md.: Hamilton Press, 1986.

Postman, Neil and Steve Powers. *How to Watch TV News*. New York: Penguin Books, 1992.

Powell, Jody. *The Other Side of the Story*. New York: William Morrow and Company, 1984.

Powers, Ron. *The Beast, the Eunuch, and the Glass-Eyed Child: Television in the '80s and Beyond*. New York: Anchor Books, 1991.

Quester, George. *The International Politics of Television*. Lexington, Mass.: Lexington Books, 1990.

Ramo, Simon. *The Business of Science: Winning and Losing in the High-Tech Age*. New York: Hill and Wang, 1988.

Rasor, Dina, ed. *More Bucks, Less Bang: How the Pentagon Buys Ineffective Weapons*. Washington, D.C.: Fund for Constitutional Government, 1983.

Rathjens, G. W., Abram Chayes, and J. P. Ruina. *Nuclear Arms Control Agreements: Process and Impact*. Washington, D.C.: Carnegie Endowment for International Peace, 1974.

Revel, Jean-Francois. *Flight from Truth: The Reign of Deceit in the Age of Information*. Trans. Curtis Cate. New York: Random House, 1991.

Ritchie, David. *Space War*. New York: Atheneum, 1982.

Rosenblum, Mort. *Who Stole the News? Why We Can't Keep Up with What Happens in the World*. New York: John Wiley & Sons, 1993.

Rosenstiel, Tom. *Strange Bedfellows: How Television and the Presidential Candidates Changed American Politics, 1992*. New York: Hyperion, 1993.

Sabato, Larry J. *Feeding Frenzy: How Attack Journalism Has Transformed American Politics*. New York: Free Press, 1991.

Schramm, Wilbur. *The Science of Human Communication*. New York: Basic Books, 1963.

Schudson, Michael. *The Power of News*. Cambridge, Mass.: Harvard University Press, 1995.

Schweizer, Peter. *Victory: The Reagan Administration's Secret Strategy That Hastened the Collapse of the Soviet Union*. New York: Atlantic Monthly Press, 1994.

Serfaty, Simon, ed. *The Media and Foreign Policy*. New York: St. Martin's Press, 1991.

Sherr, Alan B. *Legal Issues of the "Star Wars" Defense Program*. Boston, Mass.: Lawyers Alliance for Nuclear Arms Control, 1984.

Sims, Robert B. *The Pentagon Reporters*. Washington, D.C.: National Defense University Press, 1983.

Smith, Hedrick. *The Power Game: How Washington Works*. New York: Ballantine Books, 1988.

———, ed. *The Media and the Gulf War: The Press and Democracy in Wartime*. Washington, D.C.: Seven Locks Press, 1992.

Smith, Perry M. *How CNN Fought the War: A View from the Inside*. New York: Birch Lane Press, 1991.

Snyder, William P., and James Brown, eds. *Defense Policy in the Reagan Administration*.

Washington, D.C.: National Defense University Press, 1988.

Star Wars: Delusions and Dangers. Moscow: Military Publishing House, 1985.

Star Wars Quotes. Washington, D.C.: Arms Control Association, 1986.

Stein, Jonathan B. *From H-Bomb to Star Wars*. Lexington, Mass.: Lexington Books, 1984.

Stephens, Mitchell. *A History of News*. New York: Penguin Books, 1988.

Strategic Defense Initiative: The First Five Years, A Conference Report. Cambridge, Mass.: Institute for Foreign Policy Analysis, 1988.

Stubbing, Richard A. *The Defense Game*. New York: Harper & Rowe, 1986.

Taylor, Philip M. *War and Media: Propaganda and Persuasion in the Gulf War*. New York: Manchester University Press, 1992.

Thompson, Loren, ed. *Defense Beat: The Dilemmas of Defense Coverage*. New York: Lexington Books, 1991.

Trask, Roger R. *The Secretaries of Defense: A Brief History 1947–1985*. Washington, D.C.: Historical Office, Office of the Secretary of Defense, 1985.

Trotta, Liz. *Fighting for Air: In the Trenches with Television News*. New York: Simon & Schuster, 1991.

Tucker, Robert W., et al. *SDI and U.S. Foreign Policy*. Boulder, Colo.: Westview Press, 1987.

Tyroler, Charles, II. *Alerting America: The Papers of the Committee on the Present Danger*. McLean, Va.: Pergamon-Brassey's, 1984.

U.S. Congress, Office of Technology Assessment. *SDI: Technology, Survivability, and Software*. Princeton, N.J.: Princeton University Press, 1988.

U.S. Congress, Office of Technology Assessment. *Strategic Defenses: Ballistic Missile Defense Technologies/Anti-Satellite Weapons, Countermeasures, and Arms Control*. Princeton, N.J.: Princeton University Press, 1986.

Vlahos, Michael. *Strategic Defense and the American Ethos: Can the Nuclear World Be Changed?* Boulder, Colo.: Westview Press for the Foreign Policy Institute, Johns Hopkins University, 1986.

"War and the Press," *Nieman Reports*, Summer, 1991.

Weaver, David and G. Cleveland Wilhoit. *The American Journalist in the 1990s*. Arlington, Va.: Freedom Forum, 1992.

Weigley, Russell F. *The American Way of War: A History of United States Military Strategy and Policy*. Bloomington: Indiana University Press, 1973.

Weinberger, Secretary of Defense Caspar W. *Annual Report to the Congress Fiscal Year 1984*. Washington, D.C.: GPO, February 1, 1983.

Weinberger, Caspar W. *Fighting for Peace: Seven Critical Years in the Pentagon*. New York: Warner Books, 1990.

Wiener, Robert. *Live from Baghdad: Gathering News from Ground Zero*. New York: Doubleday, 1992.

White, Ray. *TV News: Building a Career in Broadcast Journalism*. Boston: Focal Press, 1990.

Wolfson, Lewis. "Through the Revolving Door: Blurring the Line Between the Press and Government," Research Paper R-4, Joan Shorenstein Barone Center on the Press, Politics and Public Policy, June 1991.

Yankelovich, Daniel, and I. M. Destler, eds. *Beyond the Beltway: Engaging the Public in U.S. Foreign Policy*. New York: W.W. Norton & Co., 1994.

Index

About the Author

STEPHEN P. AUBIN has specialized in national security affairs for nearly two decades and is currently director of communications for the Air Force Association. He has written widely on defense policy and media issues and has held editorial positions at a number of publications, including *Military Intelligence Magazine*, *Defense Media Review*, *Air Power History*, and *Strategic Review*. He holds a Ph.D. in National Security Studies and Communications from Boston University's University Professors Program.

ISBN 0-275-96303-9

9 780275 963033

90000>

EAN

HARDCOVER BAR CODE

DATE DUE

			Printed In USA

HIGHSMITH #45230